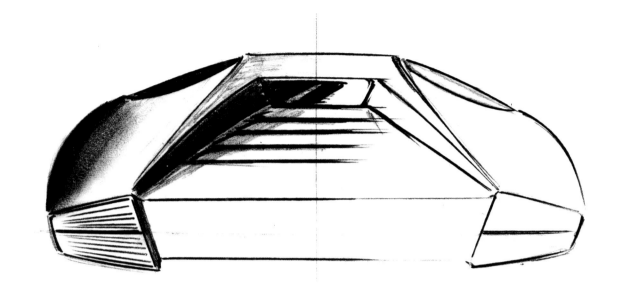

MASTERS OF
CAR DESIGN

Larry Edsall

WHITE STAR PUBLISHERS

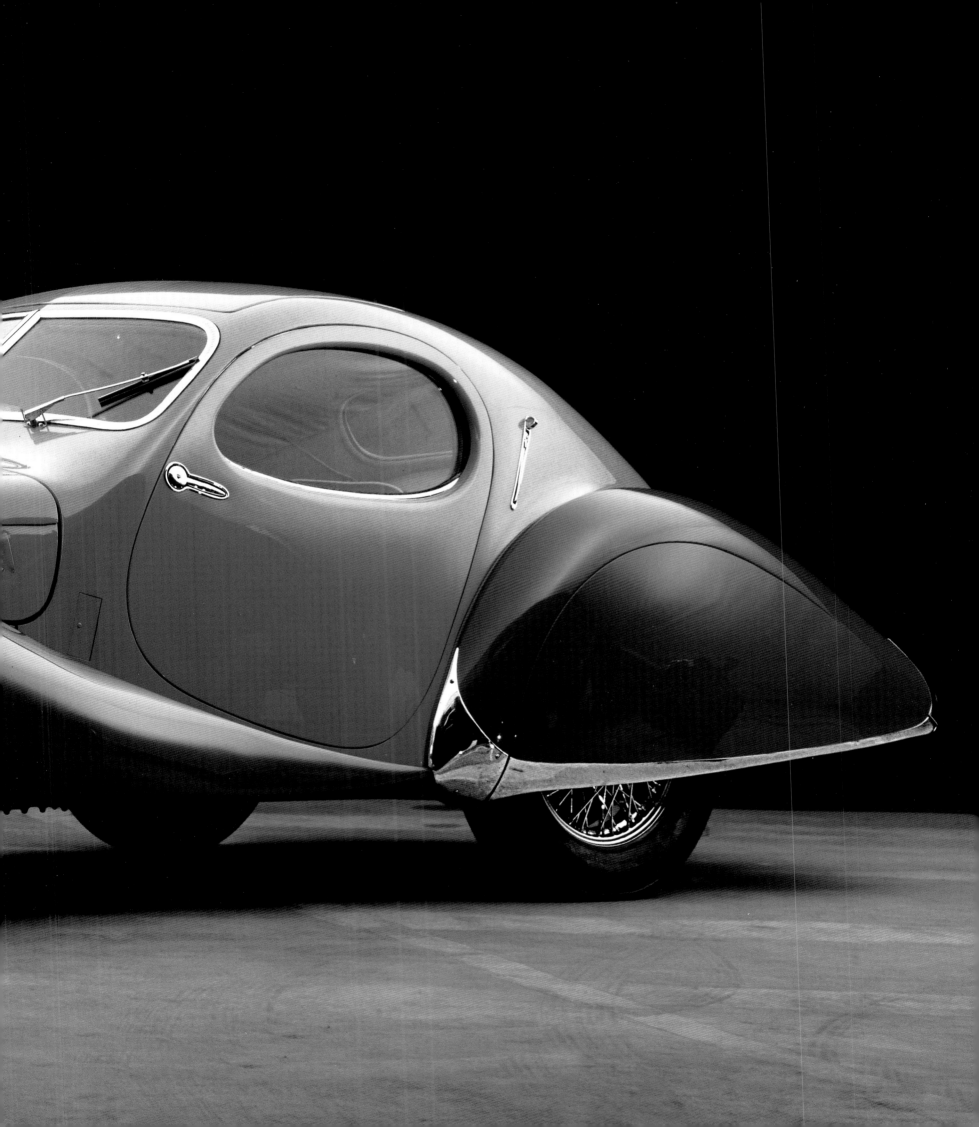

TEXTS
LARRY EDSALL

EDITORIAL DIRECTOR
VALERIA MANFERTO DE FABIANIS

EDITORIAL COORDINATION
LAURA ACCOMAZZO
GIORGIA RAINERI

GRAPHIC DESIGN
MARIA CUCCHI

2-3 MANY CONSIDER THE GOUTTE D'EAU BODYWORK, ESPECIALLY WHEN DONE IN TWO-TONE AS ON THIS 1937 TALBOT LAGO, TO BE THE EPITOME OF THE WORK PRODUCED BY FRENCH COACHBUILDERS FIGONI ET FALASCHI.

4-5 THE FERRARI "ROSSA" CONCEPT, DESIGNED TO CELEBRATE PININFARINA'S 70TH ANNIVERSARY, FEATURES A RACING-STYLE SAIL FIN THAT FRAMES THE FRONT TIRE.

6-7 WHEN MOST AMERICAN CARS WERE BURDENED WITH HEAVY CHROME AND BIG FINS, DEEP-DISH COVES GAVE THE 1957 CHEVROLET CORVETTE A LIGHT AND SPORTY LOOK.

EVERY ART FORM HAS ITS MASTERPIECES, AND ITS MASTERS

Monet, Pisarro, Renoir and Degas were masters of Impressionism. Dalí, Chagall and Miró were Surrealistic superstars. Frank Capra, John Ford and Elia Kazan won multiple Academy Awards for their artistry in directing motion pictures. Frank Lloyd Wright, Antonio Gaudí and Frank Gehry have created architectural masterworks. Coco Chanel, Giorgio Armani and Vera Wang set trends in how we dress.

8-9 ITALDESIGN GIUGIARO CELEBRATED THE 50TH ANNIVERSARY OF THE CHEVROLET CORVETTE IN 2003 BY CREATING THE CORVETTE MORAY CONCEPT CAR.

10-11 WITH A 1.6-LITER ENGINE PUMPING OUT 115 HORSEPOWER, THE 1970 STRATOS BY BERTONE MAY BE THE WORLD'S MOST EXOTICALLY DESIGNED ECONOMY CAR.

12-13 AUTOMOTIVE DESIGN HAS GONE TRULY INTERNATIONAL. THE CAR NAMED FOR ITALY'S REVERED ENZO FERRARI WAS STYLED BY A JAPANESE-BORN DESIGNER KEN OKUYAMA, WHO WAS EDUCATED IN THE UNITED STATES.

14-15 FORM FOLLOWS FUNCTION ON THE 2000 PORSCHE CARRERA GT, WHICH HAS SCULPTURALLY INDUSTRIAL AND EVEN AIRCRAFT-INSPIRED DESIGN CUES MADE NOT FROM HAMMERED STEEL BUT FORMED FROM ULTRA STRONG BUT LIGHTWEIGHT CARBON FIBER.

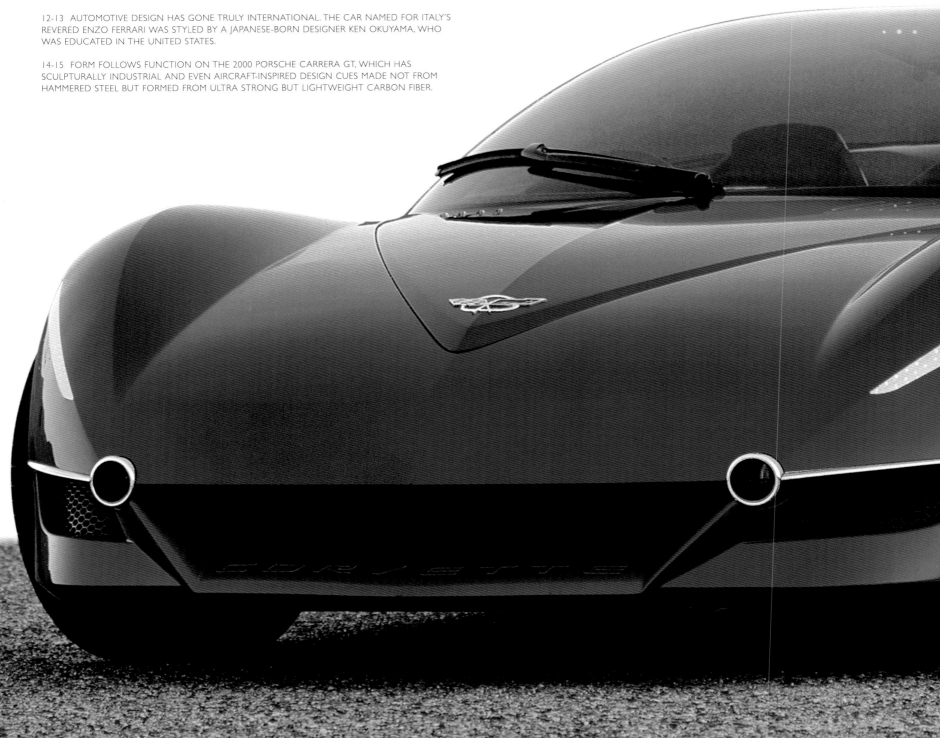

Too often overlooked in such listings of artistic masters are those whose art we might see on any day, not only when we visit a museum or movie house, a gallery or grand city, or while watching celebrities walk a red carpet. These are the masters who design automobiles, rolling metal sculptures that can transcend their role as devices for transportation, for the delivery of people and their goods, to become vehicles that carry us not only to work and to play but that inspire our passions and our dreams.

When the motorcar was created, it was a modern marvel, in many ways a miracle that would change the world, even though it was little more than a traditional wagon or buggy, except for the fact that it had a petroleum-burning engine instead of a hay-eating horse to provide its propulsion.

Tinkerers, inventors and engineers gave us the automobile, but it was designers and artistic craftsmen working in metal and wood and other materials who gave us sleek and exciting and sculptural shapes that cocoon a comfortable place in which we can enjoy the drive.

Engineers may produce the mechanical machines that take us down the road, but it is the designers who imbue the gears and glass, the rubber and radiators with a personality, a face, a soul.

So who are the masters of automotive design? What challenges have they faced – and overcome? What provides their inspiration and their motivation?

This book visits the masters of automotive design, starting with the French coachbuilders of the 1920s and 1930s. The Germans may have created the motorcar and the Americans may have produced them in mass quantities, but it was the French – or at least automotive artisans living in and around Paris – who perfected the package and made it exciting to see and fun to drive.

From France, we travel southeast, to visit the famed Italian styling houses, the carrozzeria founded by Bertone, Ghia, the family Farina, Giugiaro and the rest. While found in – or very close to – the city of Turin, their designs would influence the automobile on a global scale.

Italy's automotive style may have reached around the world, but it wasn't the only nation with a distinct automotive aptitude, attitude and style, and nowhere was this more important than in the United States, and so we work our way through the design departments of the major American marques – General Motors, Chrysler and Ford.

Then, the book looks farther west, so far west it's actually the Far East, and the coming of age of Asian automotive design.

Finally, as befitting a look at sculpture that moves on wheels, we come full circle, to the new coachbuilders, the contemporary counterparts to those who first gave us cars with French – and other – curves.

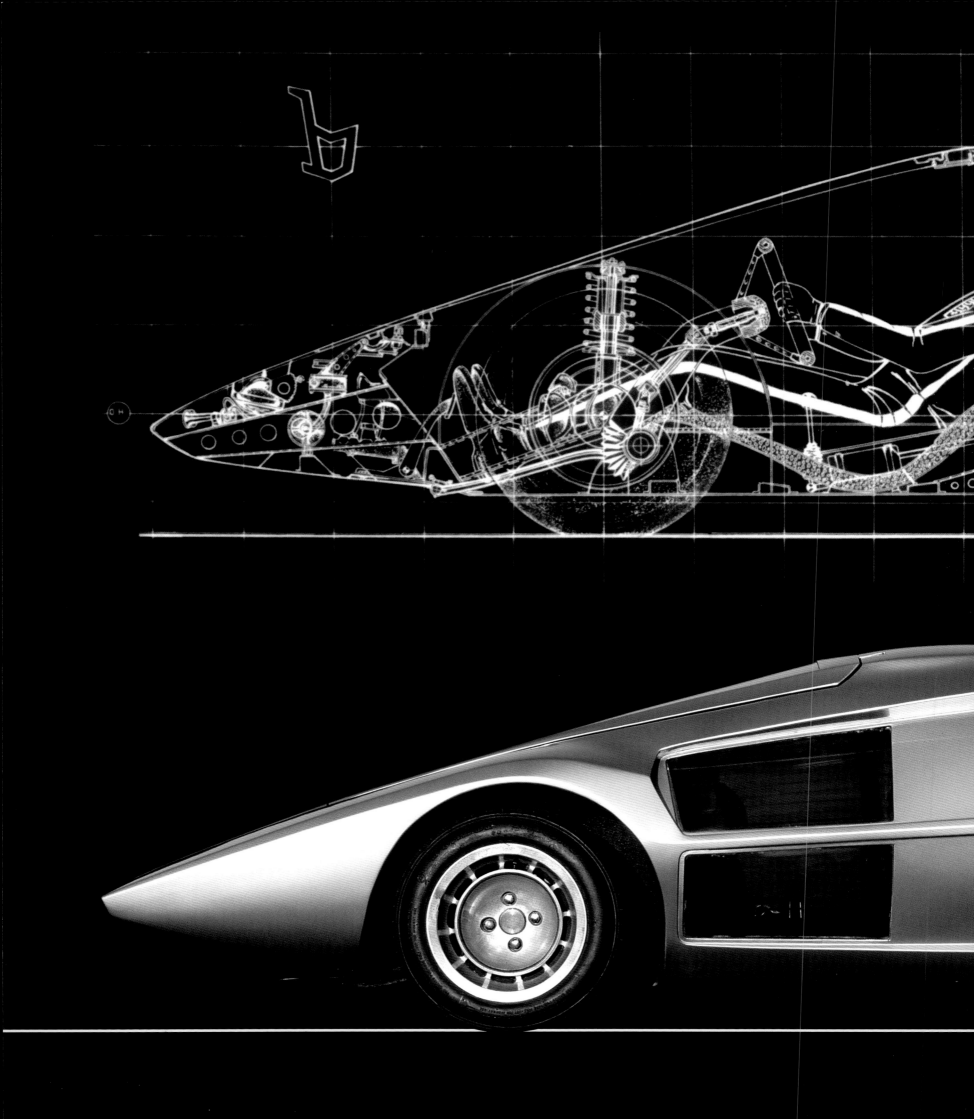

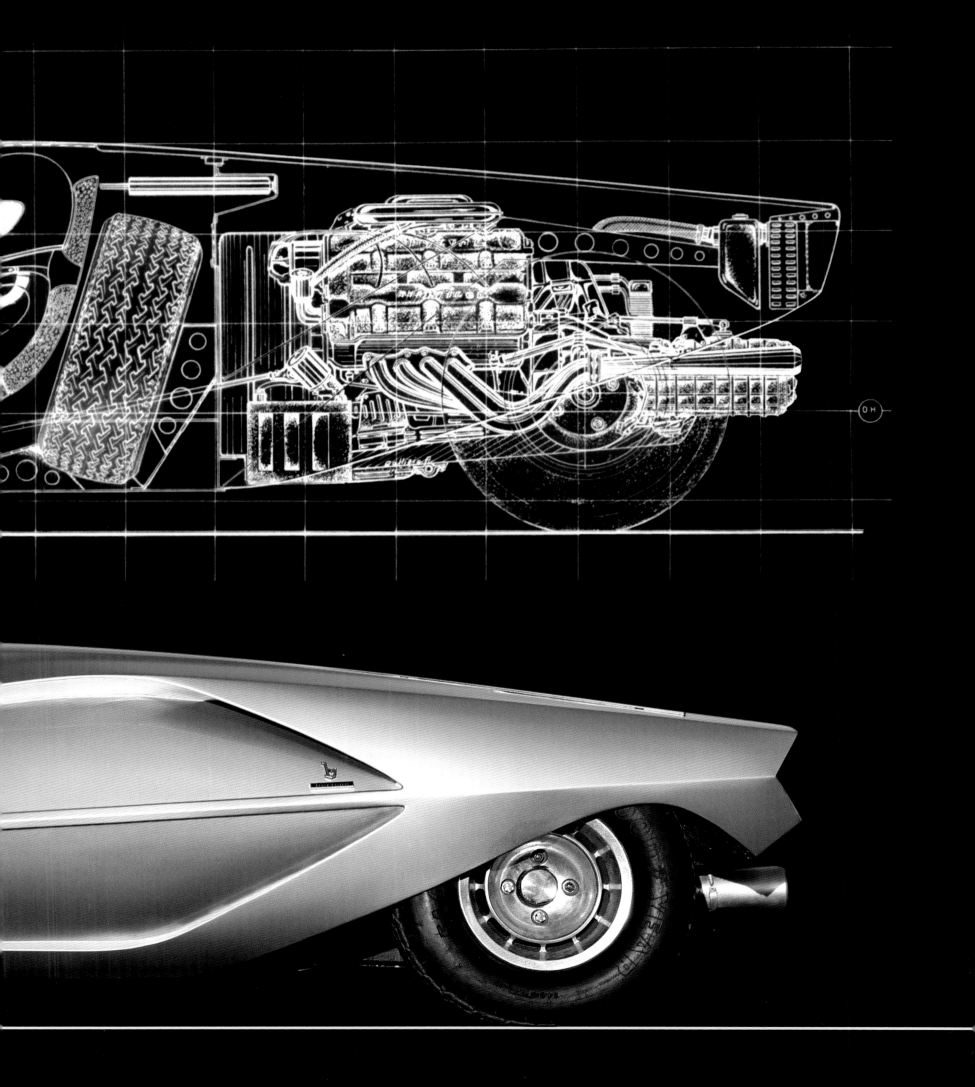

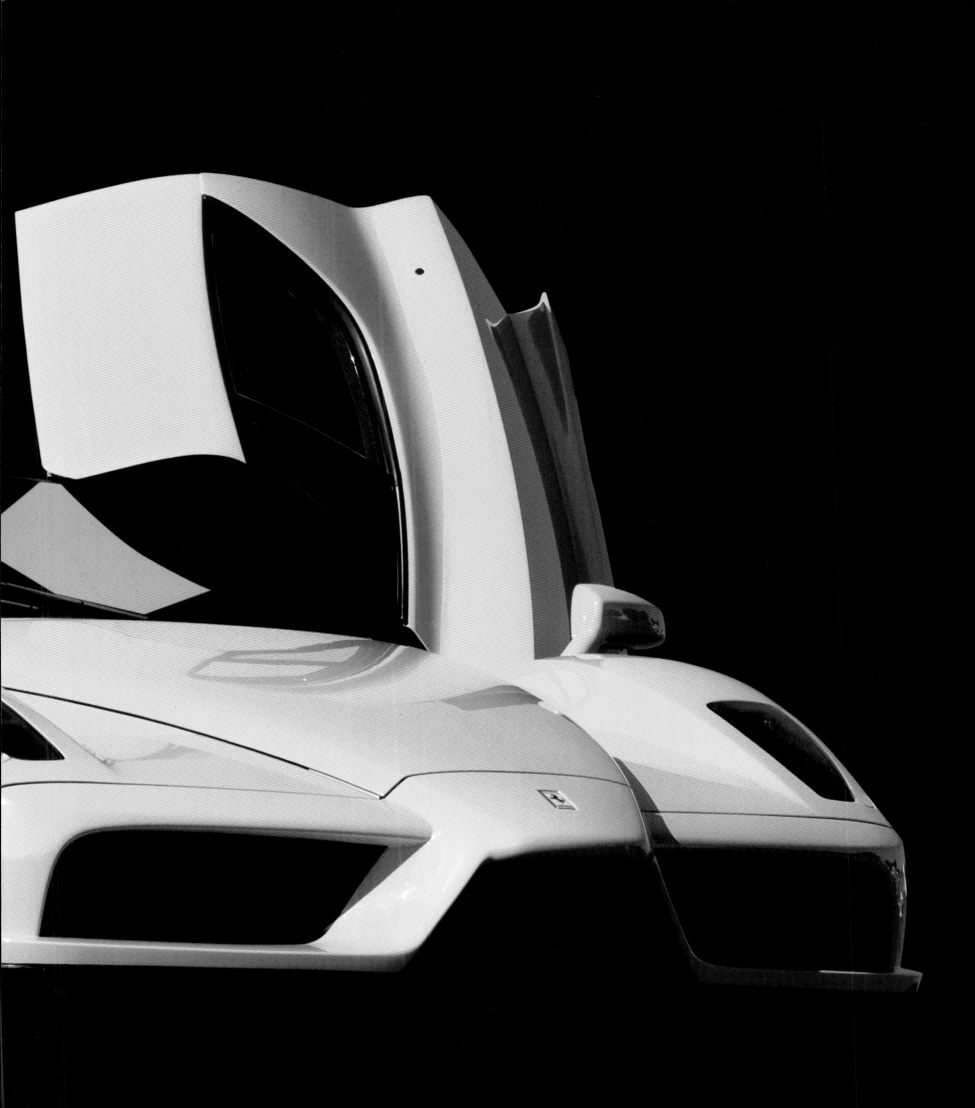

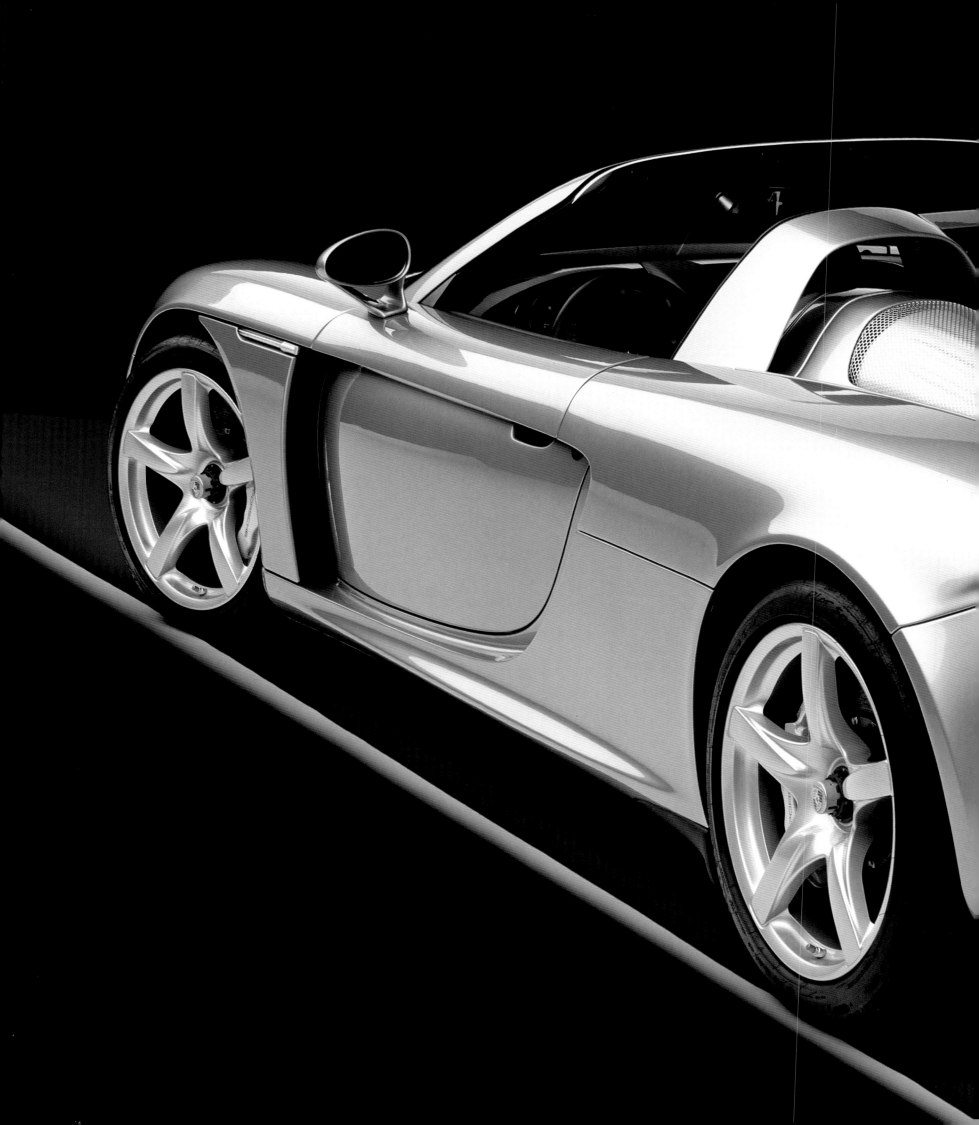

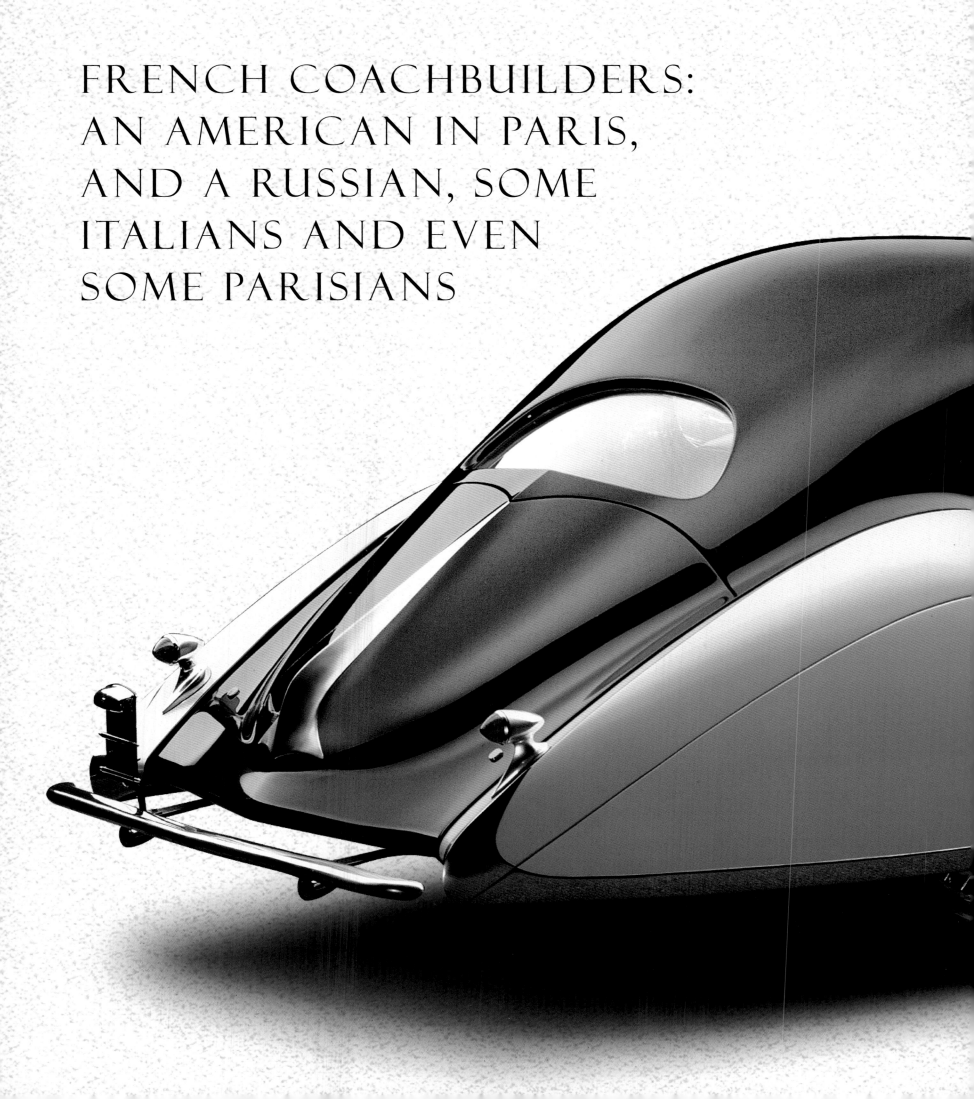

FRENCH COACHBUILDERS: AN AMERICAN IN PARIS, AND A RUSSIAN, SOME ITALIANS AND EVEN SOME PARISIANS

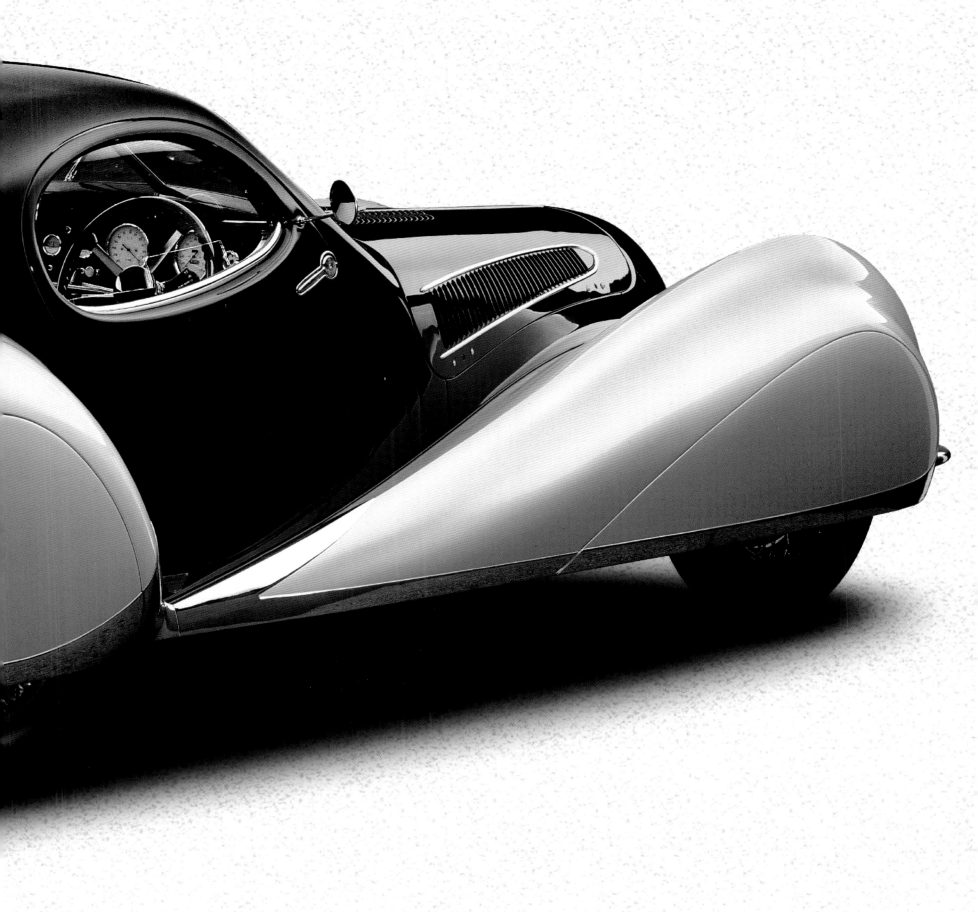

IT'S OBVIOUS WHY THEY CALL THEM "FRENCH CURVES"

16-17 PERHAPS NO VEHICLE ILLUSTRATES THE WONDERFUL BEAUTY OF FRENCH CURVES MORE THAN THE TALBOT LAGO. SHOWN HERE IS A 1937 MODEL WITH COACHWORK BY FIGONI ET FALASCHI.

18 TOP AN ADVERTISEMENT FOR PEUGEOT IS A WORK OF ARTISTIC DESIGN IN ITS OWN RIGHT. THIS ADVERTISEMENT IS FROM 1926.

*I*n the 1920s and 1930s, the most beautiful cars in the world were being built in and around Paris – some of them by Frenchmen. Jean-Baptiste Franay, Henri Chapron, Marcel Pourtout, Jean-Henri Labourdette, Jean-Marie Letourner and Jean-Arthur Marchand were constructing beautiful bespoke bodies around various motorcar chassis. At the time, of course, Paris was the center of the universe – and not just for custom carbuilders. The French capital had emerged unscathed from the world war, and afterward it had a magnetic attraction for the most artistic people on the planet – Ernest Hemingway, F. Scott Fitzgerald, Gertrude Stein, Ezra Pound, Igor Stravinsky, Pablo Picasso, Salvador Dali, with Gabrielle "Coco" Chanel reigning over French fashion. Also drawn to Paris were Americans Howard "Dutch" Darrin and Tom Hibbard. In the City of Light, they would join some other ex-patriots – one from Russia and a couple of Italians – in creating some of the most spectacular car bodies ever seen. While they were not French by birth, Hibbard and Darrin, "Jacques" Saoutchik, and "Joseph" Figoni and Ovidio Falaschi, together with their French craftsmen and with the strong influence of French culture, would produce vehicles that would become the essence of French design, and would themselves influence automotive design for many years to come.

Before the age of computers, detailed design drawing was aided by the use of what was known as the French curve, a template full of smooth and flowing curves to connect point A to point B, to add grace and beauty to straight lines and harsh angles. Vehicles produced by Hibbard and Darrin, Saoutchik and Figoni et Falaschi offer strong evidence of why those curves were "French."

18 BOTTOM IN THE 1930S, RENAULT BUILT ITS FACTORY ON ILE SEGUIN, A KILOMETER-LONG ISLAND IN THE SEINE RIVER AT BILLANCOURT, A SUBURB OF PARIS. THE FACTORY WAS HERALDED AS "THE MOST POWERFUL" IN ALL OF EUROPE.

19 THIS PERIOD ILLUSTRATION SHOWS A HUGE 40CV RENAULT MAKING ITS WAY AROUND THE ARCH DE TRIUMPH. NOTE THAT NOT ONLY DOES THE CAR HAVE A CHAUFFEUR, BUT ALSO AN EXTRA MANSERVANT TO OPEN THE LEFT-SIDE DOOR FOR THOSE RIDING INSIDE.

JACQUES SAOUTCHIK

Though known in France as Jacques Saoutchik, Jacques was born Iakov Saoutchik in Minsk in 1880, a time of political ferment and of worker revolt against Russian czars who were particularly oppressive to minority groups, and one-third of Minsk's population – including the Saoutchik family – was Jewish.

As a teenager, Iakov worked as an apprentice cabinetmaker.

When he was 19 years old, his mother and her children left Russia for Paris, where "Jacques" became a partner in a cabinetmaking business. Within five years, Saoutchik had married and soon opened his own business, to do custom coachwork for expensive automobiles.

Saoutchik was a skilled woodworker, and, it seems, a good businessman who hired people with similarly fine skills in working with metal, upholstery and the other crafts required for doing high-quality motorcar coachwork.

His first commission was to design a body for an Isotta-Fraschini, an Italian luxury car. Soon, well-to-do Parisians were paying tens of thousands of dollars for Saoutchik bodywork on a Rolls-Royce or Hispano-Suiza chassis. *Automobile Quarterly* magazine noted that for many years, Saoutchik's work "represented the essence of Parisian chic."

But Saoutchik's customers were not just Parisians. He created a special Delage for Hollywood actress Mary Pickford, and did very well building custom Mercedes-Benzes for Americans in the Roaring '20s.

Saoutchik's style evolved over the years. Rather than forcing certain cues, his designs were done to fit each vehicle's particular characteristics.

At the same time, however, each of Saoutchik's designs offered something that would attract the attention of all who saw the vehicle traveling down the boulevard. Among his most attention-grabbing designs were a torpedo-

bodied 1928 Mercedes-Benz with polished aluminum trim and a lizard-skin interior, as well as the famed Minerva 32CV "Empire," a car with a gold-plated interior for the Duchesse de Talleyrand. Many of Saoutchik's cars were designed for heads of state, and in such diverse geographic locations as Siam, Egypt, Norway and, of course, France.

In addition to styling, Saoutchik was an innovator who patented the "Transformable" body – with a convertible top designed to weather all seasons.

He also patented a two-piece, V-shaped windshield with each glass section individually adjusted to provide varying amounts of ventilation for the driver and front-seat passenger, as well as a sliding door that operated much like those that would be used decades later on the modern minivan.

Like other coachbuilders, Saoutchik struggled back into business after World War II. Notably, he gave Paul Bracq his first design job. Bracq later went to Mercedes-Benz and then became chief designer at BMW.

20-21 AND 21 TOP RUSSIAN-BORN IAKOV SAOUTCHIK WAS ONE OF SEVERAL FOREIGN-BORN COACHBUILDERS WHO OPERATED IN PARIS IN THE 1930S. SAOUTCHIK'S STYLE WAS TO EMPHASIZE EACH VEHICLE'S INHERENT CHARACTER. HE CREATED THE CUSTOM COACHWORK FOR THIS MERCEDES-BENZ 710 SS IN 1931.

22 TOP INSIDE AND OUT: SAOUTCHIK ENHANCED THIS 1929 MERCEDES-BENZ 680 S WITH A LUXURIOUS AND CUSTOMIZED INTERIOR AS WELL AS ITS SPECIAL EXTERIOR BODYWORK.

22-23 THIS 1928 MERCEDES-BENZ 680 S CARRIES A "TORPEDO" STYLE BODY CREATED BY FRENCH COACHBUILDER JACQUES SAOUTCHIK, WHO EMPHASIZED THE LONG AND LOW BODY FORM BY PARING THE TRADITIONAL RUNNING BOARDS.

23 TOP LEFT COACHBUILDERS SUCH AS SAOUTCHIK OFTEN STARTED WITH A "ROLLING CHASSIS," A FRAME AND POWERTRAIN A CLIENT PURCHASED FROM AN AUTOMAKER. SOMETIMES THE CARS CAME WITH BODIES AND INTERIORS THAT THE COACHBUILDERS MODIFIED OR REPLACED.

23 TOP RIGHT THE 1928 MERCEDES-BENZ S WAS POWERED BY A SUPERCHARGED SIX-CYLINDER ENGINE DEVELOPED BY MERCEDES' CHIEF ENGINEER FERDINAND PORSCHE.

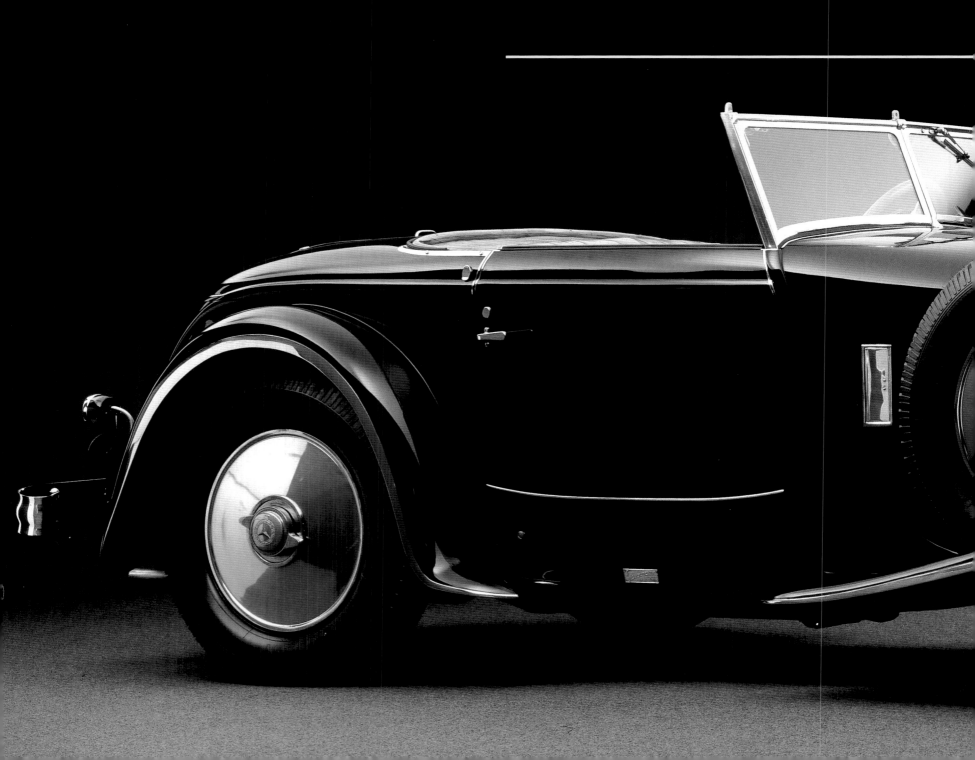

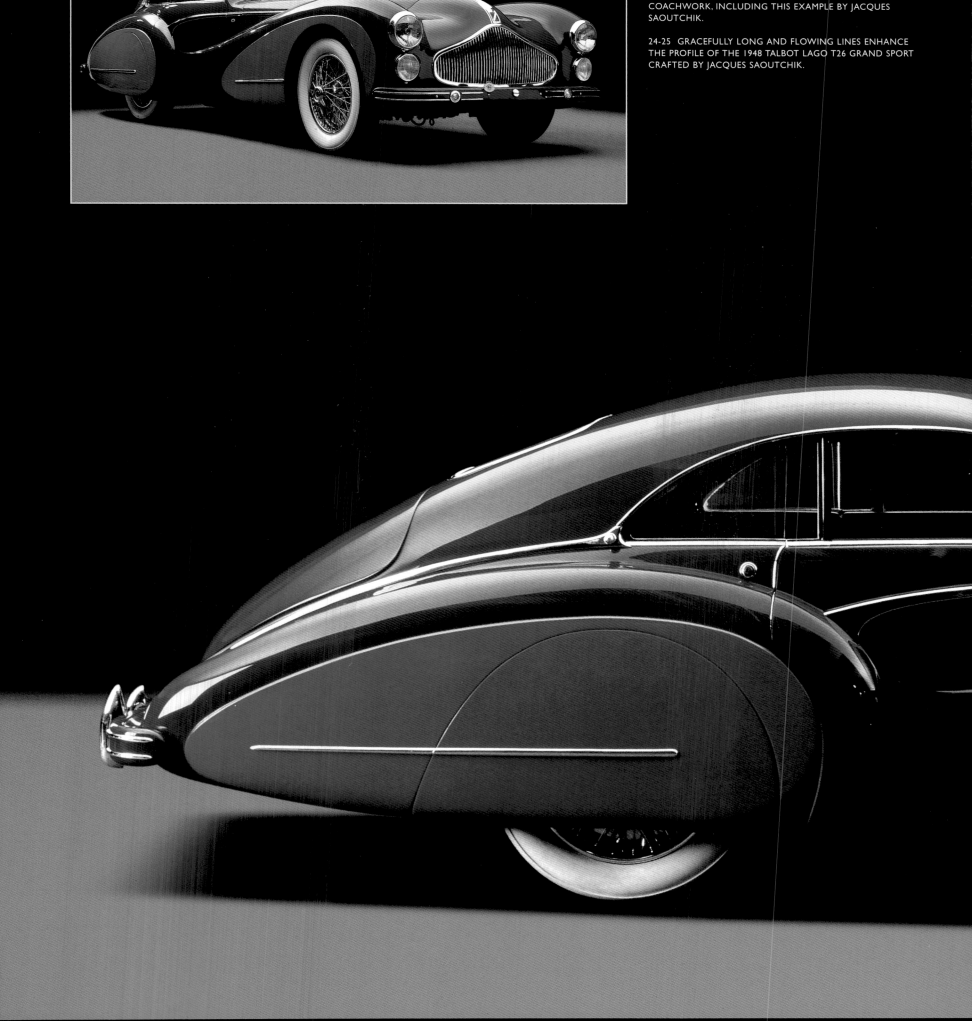

COACHWORK, INCLUDING THIS EXAMPLE BY JACQUES SAOUTCHIK.

24-25 GRACEFULLY LONG AND FLOWING LINES ENHANCE THE PROFILE OF THE 1948 TALBOT LAGO T26 GRAND SPORT CRAFTED BY JACQUES SAOUTCHIK.

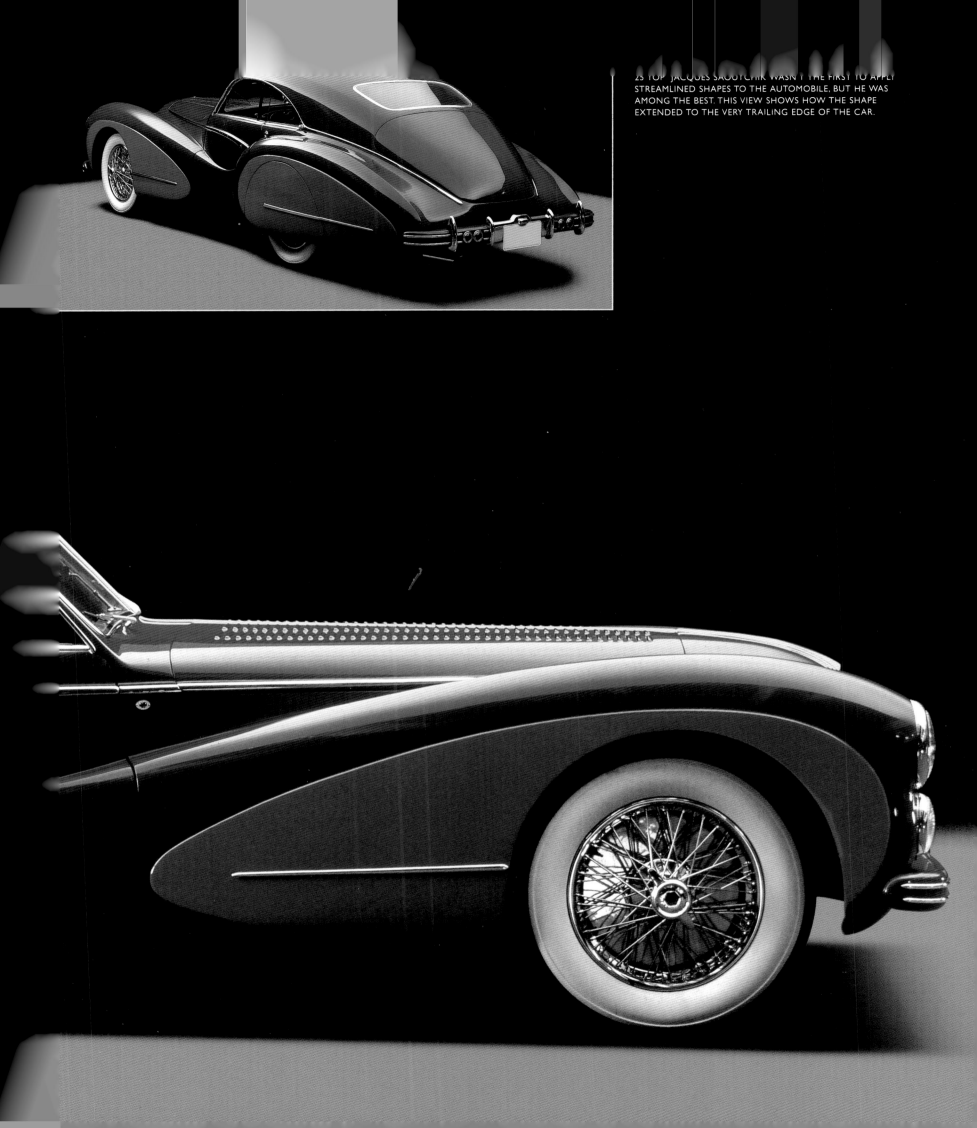

JACQUES SAOUTCHIK WASN'T THE FIRST TO APPLY STREAMLINED SHAPES TO THE AUTOMOBILE, BUT HE WAS AMONG THE BEST. THIS VIEW SHOWS HOW THE SHAPE EXTENDED TO THE VERY TRAILING EDGE OF THE CAR.

FIGONI & FALASCHI

Giuseppe Figoni, like so many great car designers, was born in Italy, in 1894, in the city of Piacenza, between Milan and Parma. Forty years later, Piacenza would beget another master stylist, fashion designer Giorgio Armani. When Figoni was three years old, his family moved to Paris, where, at age 14, Joseph, as he was called in his adopted country, apprenticed to a wagon builder. Figoni became a French citizen, and when France entered the Great War, Figoni spent several years in military service.

He mustered out in 1921; within two years he had opened an automotive body repair business – Carrozzeria Figoni – near the Longchamp horseracing track.

Soon, Figoni was not just repairing cars, but was creating custom bodies for customers, including the financially well-off sporting crowd that liked horsepower, whether on the racetrack or on the roadway.

Though an outstanding artist, Figoni was both innovative and yet a perfectionist. His sketches may not have been extremely detailed, but he was among the first European auto designers to use modeling clay. Once he had the shape he wanted, others in his shop would do detailed drawings from which wooden forms would be built for shaping the steel and aluminum body panels.

Figoni was particularly known for his organically voluptuous, teardrop-shaped and compound-curved fenders, which Figoni called *enveloppantes*, or curved envelopes. He also was a master at the use of chrome to underscore a vehicle's flowing lines.

But his was not the heavy use of chrome that characterized American cars in the 1950s. Figoni's "sweepspear" was a curving, sometimes even swirling chromed accent that ran from radiator ornament to the rear of the car.

When the Museum of Modern Art in New York City held the first exhibit of automobiles as art in 1951, the curator included only eight vehicles. He praised the Figoni et Falaschi-bodied 1939 Talbot for its "sculptural modeling," its "witty juxtaposition of highly stylized curves" and for its "smooth exuberance."

While automotive historian Griffith Borgeson noted that Figoni did much to move car

La 135 Sport
DELAHAYE

1ère au Rallye de Monte-Carlo.
1ère au Rallye féminin Paris Saint-Raphaël.
1ère des voitures sans compresseur dans l'épreuve des 1.000 Miles d'Italie.

voiture idéale de grand tourisme
vous donnera "sûrement" toutes les joies attendues dans vos déplacements de week-end et de vacances!

DELAHAYE

26 TOP CARS FROM DELAHAYE BECAME FAVORITES FOR CUSTOMIZATION BY FRENCH COACHBUILDERS. THIS ADVERTISEMENT SHOWS THE 135 SPORT MODEL.

26-27 "JOSEPH" FIGONI, CRAFTED LONG, TAPERED FENDERS AND A BOAT TAIL BODY FOR THIS 1933 DUESENBERG MODEL SJ SPEEDSTER.

27 TOP FIGONI GAINED FAME WHEN HE CREATED THE LONG-TAILED BODYWORK FOR THE ALFA ROMEOS THAT WON THE 24 HOURS OF LE MANS RACE IN 1932 (SHOWN HERE) AND 1933.

27 BOTTOM RIGHT RENAULT PRODUCED THIS ADVERTISEMENT FOR THE VIVASTELLA IN THE MID-1930S.

design from architecture to sculpture, the Italian-born Frenchman was something of an engineer as well as an artist, taking patents on his convertible top and sunroof designs and on a retracting windshield that cranked down into the car's cowl.

Figoni's fame spread in 1932 and 1933 when he designed the bodywork for the Alfa Romeos that won the 24 Hours of Le Mans race. In 1934 he designed coachwork for a Delahaye 18CV Superluxe that set not only 24-hour but also 48-hour speed and endurance records on the Montlhéry track.

Before Figoni started doing custom bodies, much of Delahaye's business had been industrial chassis and fire engines.

But there were stunning Figoni-bodied Delahayes at the Paris Salon (auto show) in 1934 and 1935.

In the spring of 1935, the artist went into partnership with businessman Ovidio Falaschi, who also had been born in Italy and who had a sincere appreciation for and attraction to sleek and luxurious automobiles. Falaschi brought financial stability that allowed Figoni to explore his imagination. For the Paris Salon in 1936, Figoni et Falaschi, with some help from motorsports artist George Ham, created a stunning, two-tone, two-seat Delahaye cabriolet. The Aly Khan was so impressed he bought the car off the auto show stand for a reported 150,000 French francs.

Figoni et Falaschi also designed exotic bodies for Talbot-Darracq, Bugatti, Duesenberg, Delage, Hotchkiss and other chassis. They did a Talbot for Tasmanian-born Frederick McEvoy, who not only

28 TOP DESIGNER JOSEPH FIGONI WENT INTO PARTNERSHIP WITH BUSINESSMAN OVIDIO FALASCHI IN 1935 AND FREED FROM PRESSING ECONOMIC DEMANDS DID SOME OF HIS BEST WORK, INCLUDING THE OUTRAGEOUS BODYWORK FOR THIS 1935 DELAHAYE FOR THE PARIS AUTO SHOW.

28-29 THE CHASSIS OF DELAHAYE'S 135 MODEL PROVIDED A SHOWCASE FOR A COACHBUILDER'S DESIGNS. FIGONI ET FALASCHI CREATED THIS COUPE DESIGN FOR A 1936 DELAHAYE 135 COMPETITION COURT. THE DESIGN INCLUDES A SUNROOF, BUT SEEMINGLY NO STRAIGHT LINES.

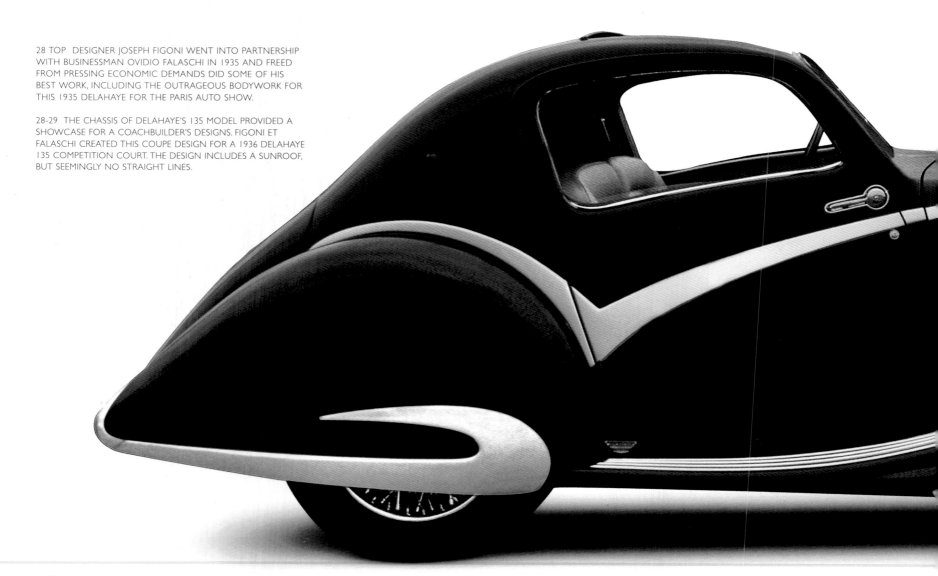

competed in top-level European auto races, but was a member of Britain's medal-winning bobsled team in the 1936 Winter Olympics. McEvoy was a friend of actor Errol Flynn and became the subject of the book *The Last Playboy*.

He commissioned several copies of his car built for sale in the United States, where the fame of Figoni et Falaschi was enhanced when they displayed a Delahaye V12 that incorporated their stunning bodywork and patented convertible top and retracting windshield at the 1939 New York auto show.

In 1938, Figoni's *Goutte d'Or* ("golden drop") body for the Talbot T-150 chassis was considered an outstanding example of streamlining. With the outbreak of World War II, the Figoni et Falaschi workshop shifted to production of aircraft equipment.

When France fell, Figoni moved away from Paris and established a successful company that made household electrical appliances.

29 TOP JOSEPH FIGONI CREATED SCALE MODELS OF HIS DESIGNS AND HIRED DRAFTSMEN WHO CONVERT THEM INTO DETAILED DRAWINGS THAT SKILLED CRAFTSMEN USED TO HAMMER OUT THE GORGEOUS METAL SHAPES THAT ADORN THE COACHBUILDER'S CREATIONS.

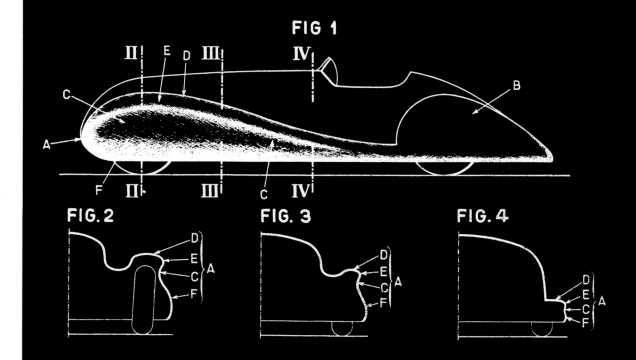

Société à responsabilité limitée dite :
Établissements **Figoni** et **Falaschi**

FIG 1

FIG. 2   FIG. 3   FIG. 4

30-31 AND 31 TOP FIGONI ET FALASCHI, INSPIRED BY THE WORK OF AUTOMOTIVE ARTIST GEORGE HAM, STYLED THE BODYWORK FOR A DELAHAYE THEY DEBUTED AT THE PARIS AUTO SHOW IN 1936. SHOWN HERE IS A STUNNING 1937 DELAHAYE 135 TORPEDO-BODIED CABRIOLET BASED ON THAT CONCEPT. EVEN THE HEADLAMPS ON THIS FIGONI ET FALASCHI-DESIGNED 1937 DELAHAYE 135 COMPETITION COURT CONVERTIBLE HAVE STREAMLINED STYLING.

FLOWING AND STREAMLINED SHAPES THAT FIGONI ET FALASCHI USED FOR THE
ENVELOPE AROUND THE 1937 TALBOT LAGO.

33 TOP IN 1938, FIGONI AND FALASCHI TOOK DELIVERY OF A TALBOT LAGO T-150
CABRIOLET CHASSIS. FOR A PRIVATE CLIENT, THEY SKETCHED THIS VERSION WITH A
FOLDING WINDSHIELD AND WITH THEIR TYPICAL SWEEPING STYLING CUES ACROSS
THE DOOR PANELS.

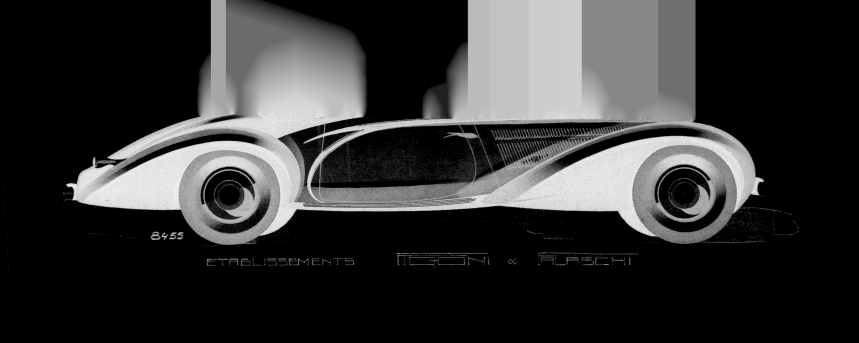

ETABLISSEMENTS ITGONI & ALASCHI

8455

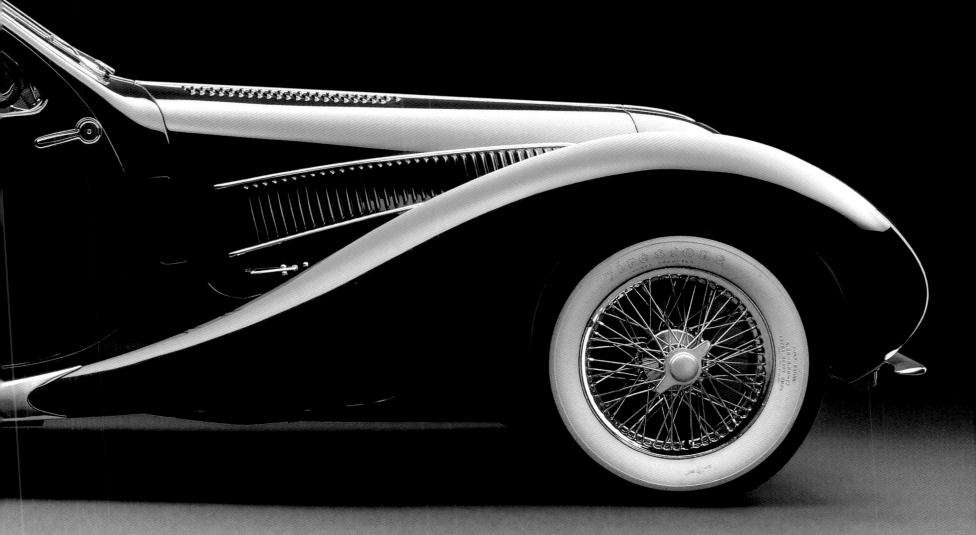

After the war, Figoni et Falaschi resumed operation in Paris, building custom bodies for Simca Arondes that had been built before the war. But after doing more than 400 such vehicles, Simca, which also was building its own sporty cars, quit selling its chassis to Figoni et Falaschi. Apparently seeing the handwriting on the wall, and with France levying heavy taxes on powerful and luxurious cars, Falaschi left the company in 1949. Figoni and his son, Claude, continued to build custom bodywork; their *La Squale,* a Citroën 15CV-based and snark-nosed car, won a design award at the Paris show in 1952. But with Delahaye ending production and Simca refusing to sell them cars, the Figonis found themselves back in the body shop business.

Figoni et Falaschi had produced some 1150 cars, most of them before the outbreak of World War II. But by the mid 1950s, not only a business, but an era, had come to an end.

"This team conferred upon mere cold sheet metal an organic form the flowing, luxurious grace

and harmony of which had never been seen before," automotive historian Griffith Borgeson wrote in *Automobile Quarterly.* Figoni, says the massive, four-volume Beaulieu automotive encyclopedia, "might have laid claim to being France's most innovative stylist as well as a high-quality custom coachbuilder over a period spanning the years 1923 to 1956."

Today, cars bodied by Figoni et Falaschi are among the most sought after by collectors.

35 WITH BUSINESS WANING AFTER THE WAR, OVIDIO FALASCHI LEFT THE COMPANY IN 1949, LEAVING FALASCHI AND HIS SON, CLAUDE, TO CARRY ON. THEY SHOWED A FEW CARS AT THE 1950 PARIS AUTO SHOW, INCLUDING THEIR CUSTOM BODYWORK FOR SIMCA (FAR LOWER LEFT).

HOWARD "DUTCH" DARRIN & TOM HIBBARD

Howard "Dutch" Darrin not only was a late arrival in Paris, he was a late convert to custom car creation. He was an electrical engineer working at Westinghouse in 1916 when he took on the challenge of trying to design an electronically activated automatic transmission for John North Willys' car company. The gearbox didn't work, and with World War I interrupting development, an automatic gearshift wouldn't go into series auto production until Oldsmobile introduced the General Motors Hydramatic in 1937.

Darrin was a man of many interests and talents and friends, among them polo player and fellow flier, Howard Hughes. In 1920 Darrin started an airline based in Miami, Florida, but it closed after four of his pilots died when their plane plunged into the ocean. His work on the Willys transmission had whetted his interest in things automotive and Darrin moved from Miami to New York, where he bought two Delage chassis and created new bodywork for them, bodywork so attractive that entertainer Al Jolson bought one of the cars.

In New York, Darrin met Tom Hibbard, a designer for American coachbuilder Brewster. Hibbard and fellow Brewster designer Ray Dietrich had started doing their own car body designs that they offered for sale – and subsequently were dismissed for competing with their employer. They started their own company, which they named LeBaron because of the prestige inherent in a coachbuilding company with a French-sounding name. After they took on a third partner, Hibbard headed for Paris; since LeBaron sounded French, and since the top coachbuilders in the world were in France, it made sense that LeBaron should open a facility there.

36 TOP HOWARD "DUTCH" DARRIN AND TOM HIBBARD WERE AMERICAN DESIGNERS WHO TEAMED IN PARIS, WHERE THEIR WORK INCLUDES THIS 1930 CADILLAC 353 BERLINE WHICH FEATURES A TRANSFORMABLE OR ALL-WEATHER CONVERTIBLE TOP.

36-37 "DUTCH" DARRIN CONSIDERED THIS 1933 ROLLS-ROYCE PHANTOM TOWN CAR TO HAVE BEEN AMONG HIS BEST WORK AS A CAR DESIGNER AND COACHBUILDER.

37 TOP THIS ILLUSTRATION SHOWS DARRIN AND HIBBARD'S IDEAS FOR CUSTOM COACHWORK THAT IS BOTH ELEGANT AND SPORTING FOR A 1929 RENAULT REINASTELLA, THE FRENCH AUTOMAKER'S LUXURY MODEL AND ITS FIRST CAR POWERED BY AN EIGHT-CYLINDER ENGINE.

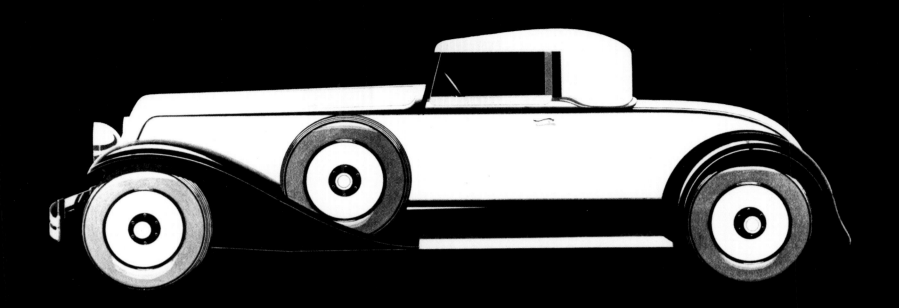

HIBBARD & DARRIN
PARIS

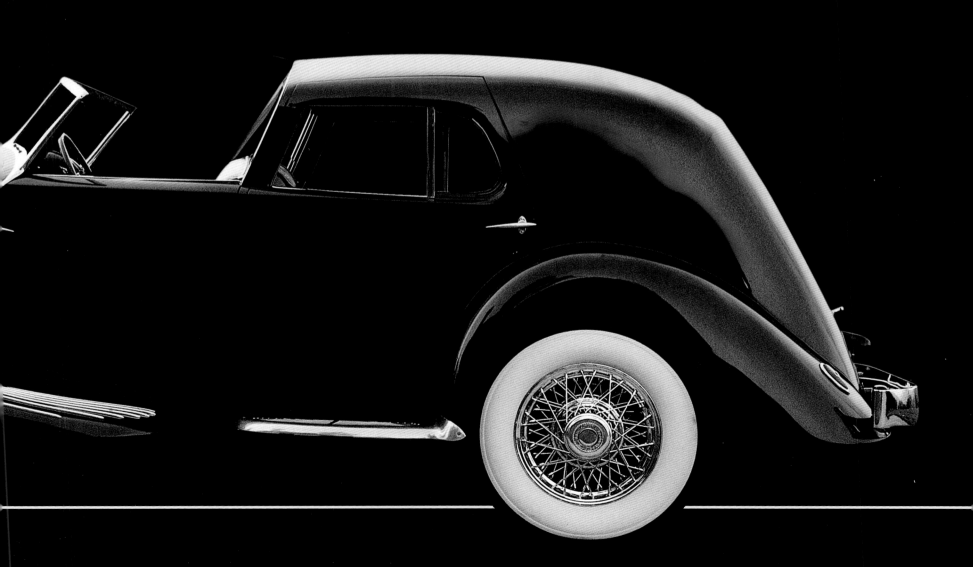

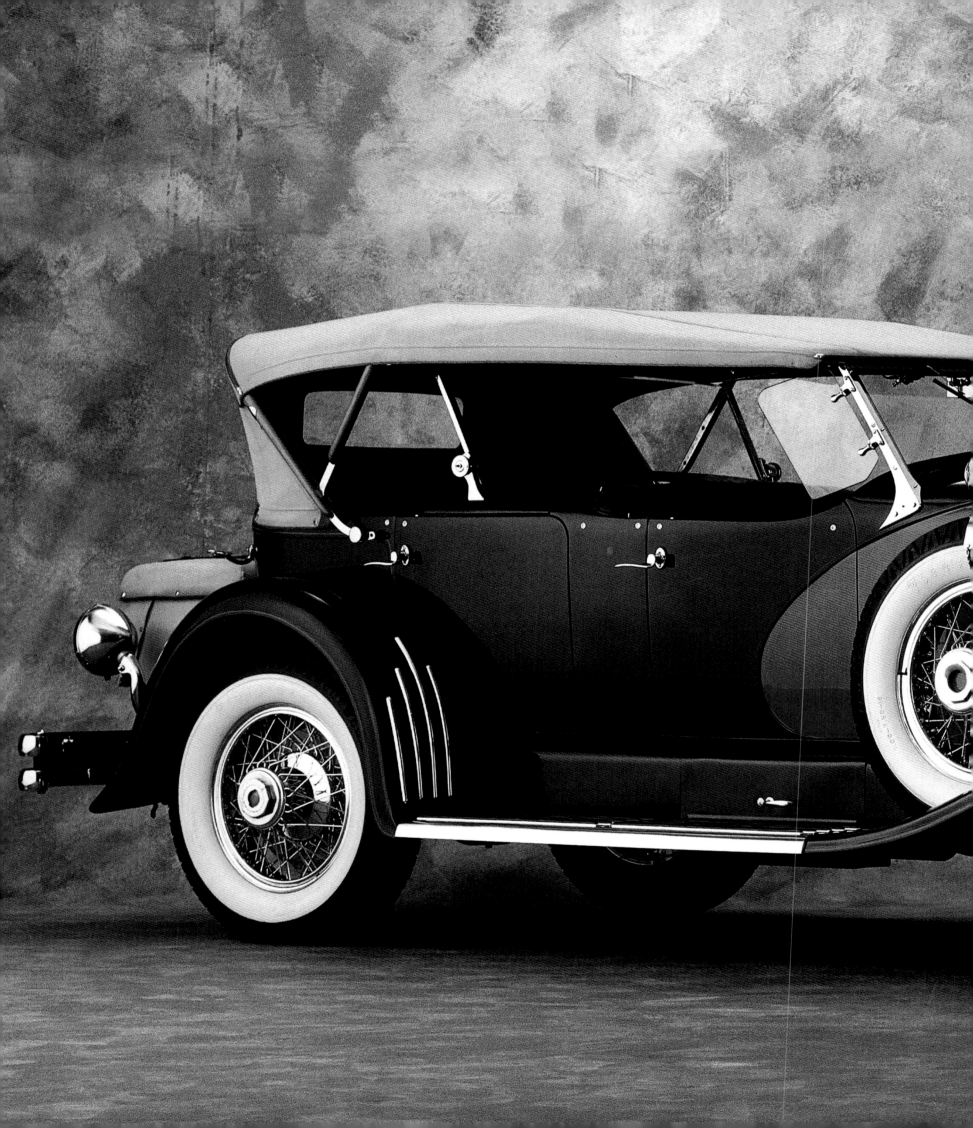

Darrin also was headed for France, a country he came to appreciate during military service in World War I. Darrin was going to France because New York auto dealer Brooks Ostruck wanted custom European-built bodywork created for the Minervas he was importing from the Belgium automaker. But instead of launching a French branch of LeBaron, Hibbard sold his share in that company and joined Darrin to launch a company to build custom bodies for Ostruck as well as for other cars they hoped to sell to the many Americans living in Paris. Not only American ex-pats but the French and numerous customers from several other countries liked their work, as did automakers on both sides of the At-

lantic. Hibbard and Darrin seemed to be doing design consulting with almost every automaker in the world. The duo championed the use of aluminum rather than wood for the structure beneath the car's steel body. Wood could warp — especially in the North American climate — and that led to squeaks and rattles and unhappy customers. Hibbard left the partnership in 1931 to return to the United States and join the design staff at General Motors, and later to become the chief designer at Ford. Darrin took on a new partner, South American banker J. Fernandez, but Fernandez and Darrin were only in business for a few years. With war looming, Darrin returned to the United States in

1937, setting up shop on Sunset Strip in Los Angeles and designing custom bodies for clientele that included many Hollywood stars — Dick Powell, Clark Gable and Errol Flynn among them. His "proudest achievement," Darrin wrote in a series of articles for *Automobile Quarterly* magazine, was the aluminum-bodied Rolls-Royce Phantom town car he created for Countess Dorothy di Frasso. While the design was Darrin's, he eagerly credited his metalworkers, Rudy Stoessel and Paul Erdos, for their incredible craftsmanship on a car that was featured in the movie *Midnight* staring Claudette Colbert as well as in several product advertisements. Darrin was commissioned to design the Packard Clipper — and in

only 10 days – though he was disappointed when the automaker changed the sweeping front fender lines when the car went into production. With the United States entering the war, Darrin recruited polo players into a coastal horse patrol – Ronald Reagan was his first lieutenant – and soon Darrin was running a flight school to train pilots for the military. After the war, following a stint as a crop-duster, Darrin returned to automobile design, doing custom bodies for luxury cars as well as the 1951 Kaiser and a car designed to compete with the new Chevrolet Corvette – the Kaiser-Darrin, also a fiberglass-bodied sports car but with doors that slid forward into the hollow section of the front quarter panels.

38-39 TOM HIBBARD AND RAY DIETRICH FOUNDED LEBARON IN 1920 IN NEW YORK, GIVING IT A FRENCH-SOUNDING NAME TO TAKE ADVANTAGE OF THE REPUTATION OF FRENCH COACHBUILDERS. THIS IS A 1930 DUESENBERG MODEL J PHAETON WITH LEBARON CUSTOM COACHWORK. LEBARON EVENTUALLY MOVED FROM NEW YORK TO DETROIT AND IN 1953 BECAME PART OF CHRYSLER.

40-41 RALPH ROBERTS WAS THE THIRD PARTNER WITH HIBBARD AND DIETRICH IN LEBARON AND CREATED THE STUNNING DUAL-COWL NEWPORT AS A CHRYSLER SHOW CAR IN 1941. THE ALUMINUM-BODIED CAR WAS USED IN PARADES AND ALSO WAS THE PACE CAR FOR THE INDIANAPOLIS 500-MILE RACE.

ITALIAN JOBS: BERTONE'S EYE FOR TALENT PROVIDES A PLACE FOR YOUNG MASTERS TO EXCEL

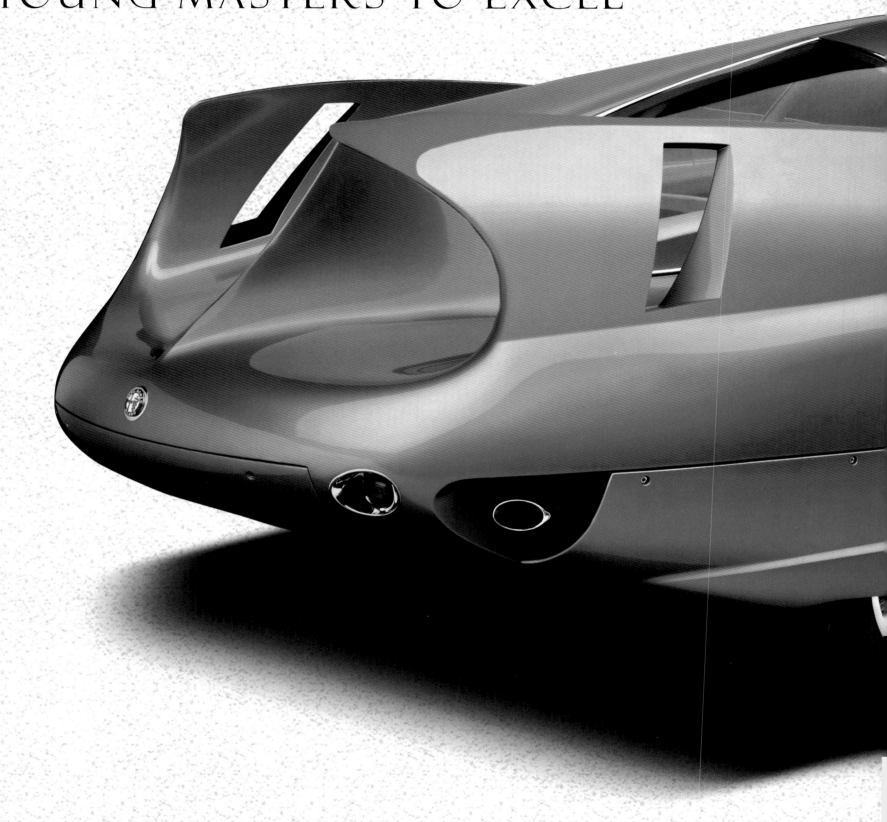

BERTONE b

THE COUNT, THE B.A.T. MAN
AND THE ORCHESTRA LEADER'S SON

Though his name would become synonymous with some of the most gorgeous automotive designs ever created, Nuccio Bertone was not one of the world's greatest automotive designers. However, perhaps no one was more adept than Bertone at identifying those who could – and indeed would – create many of the world's most aesthetically pleasing motor vehicles. It was Nuccio's father, Giovanni Bertone, who founded the family *carrozzeria*. He was born in 1884 at Mondovi, an agricultural community some 60 miles south of Turin, that a few decades earlier had spawned Giovanni Giolitti, the first prime minister of a united Italy.

Young Giovanni Bertone worked for carriage and farm-wagon repair shops until 1907, when he left rural Italy to join his older sister in Turin, working first as a handyman at the school where she was a governess. Bertone soon took his carriage-making skills to a company that made and repaired streetcars. Then, in 1912, he opened his own business and quickly became known for his precise workmanship and his careful selection of materials – he would seek out the finest logs and mark them with a special hammer bearing his initials. Soon, local automakers were ordering from him and in 1921 he did his first complete car bodies, a torpedo-bodied SPA and a Fiat sportster. His reputation grew to the point that by 1927 he built a new garage near Lancia, an automaker for whom he was doing special bodywork.

In 1914, Bertone and his wife had a son. Though given the name Giuseppe, the boy would be known even throughout his adult life by his nickname, Nuccio. In 1934, Nuccio was one of two people who joined Carrozzeria Bertone. The other was Count Mario Revelli de Beaumont, a 29-year-old freelance styling consultant who would work at several leading studios during a career that spanned many decades. Revelli designed a jazzy body for the Fiat 527S Ardita 2500 and a special version of Fiat's 508 Balilla, "the Balilla della Signora," designed with a woman driver in mind. Soon there also were several stunning Bertone convertibles based on the Fiat 1500 chassis.

42-43 THE 1954 B.A.T. 7, A CONCEPT CAR DESIGNED BY BERTONE'S FRANCO SCAGLIONE FOR ALFA ROMEO AND BUILT ON THE CHASSIS OF AN ALFA ROMEO 1900 SPRINT, TOOK ITS NAME NOT FROM ITS BAT-LIKE SHAPE BUT THE INITIALS FOR BERLINETTA AERODINAMICA TECNICA BECAUSE IT WAS A STUDY BOTH IN DESIGN AND AERODYNAMICS.

44 TOP GIOVANNI BERTONE'S FIRST CUSTOM COACHBUILDING DESIGN WAS COMPLETED IN 1921 WITH THIS TORPEDO BODY FOR THE SPA 23S CHASSIS.

44 BOTTOM EVEN MORE DRAMATIC WAS THE TORPEDO BODY BERTONE CREATED IN 1932 FOR THE FIAT 501 S.

45 BERTONE BECAME KNOWN FOR BUILDING ENCLOSED PASSENGER COMPARTMENTS ON VEHICLES CREATED AS OPEN TOURING CARS. SOON, HOWEVER, HE WAS OPENING UP THOSE CLOSED CARS WITH GLASS AND CLOTH ROOF SYSTEMS SUCH AS THE ONE ON THIS 1933 FIAT 518 C ARDITA.

GIOVANNI MICHELOTTI

Giovanni Bertone converted Lancias and Fiats into ambulances during the Second World War, then retired from the business in 1945, leaving Nuccio and his brother-in-law Tiberio Gracco de Lay in charge of the coachbuilding business. Though educated in business and accounting, Nuccio Bertone handcrafted and raced his own Fiat 500-based Barchetta in 1947. Nuccio also collaborated with Vittorio Stanguellini and designer Luigi Rapi on several projects.

In 1950, Giovanni Michelotti, who had worked for coachbuilder Vignale, joined Bertone, which scored a commission from Stanley Howard "Wacky" Arnolt, American marine engine manufacturer and British car importer, to create new bodies on MG mechanicals.

46 TOP GIUSEPPE "NUCCIO" BERTONE AND HIS BROTHER-IN-LAW TOOK OVER THE FAMILY BUSINESS IN 1945. HERE BERTONE AND HIS MECHANIC GET READY FOR A RACE IN HIS FIAT-BASED CORSA.

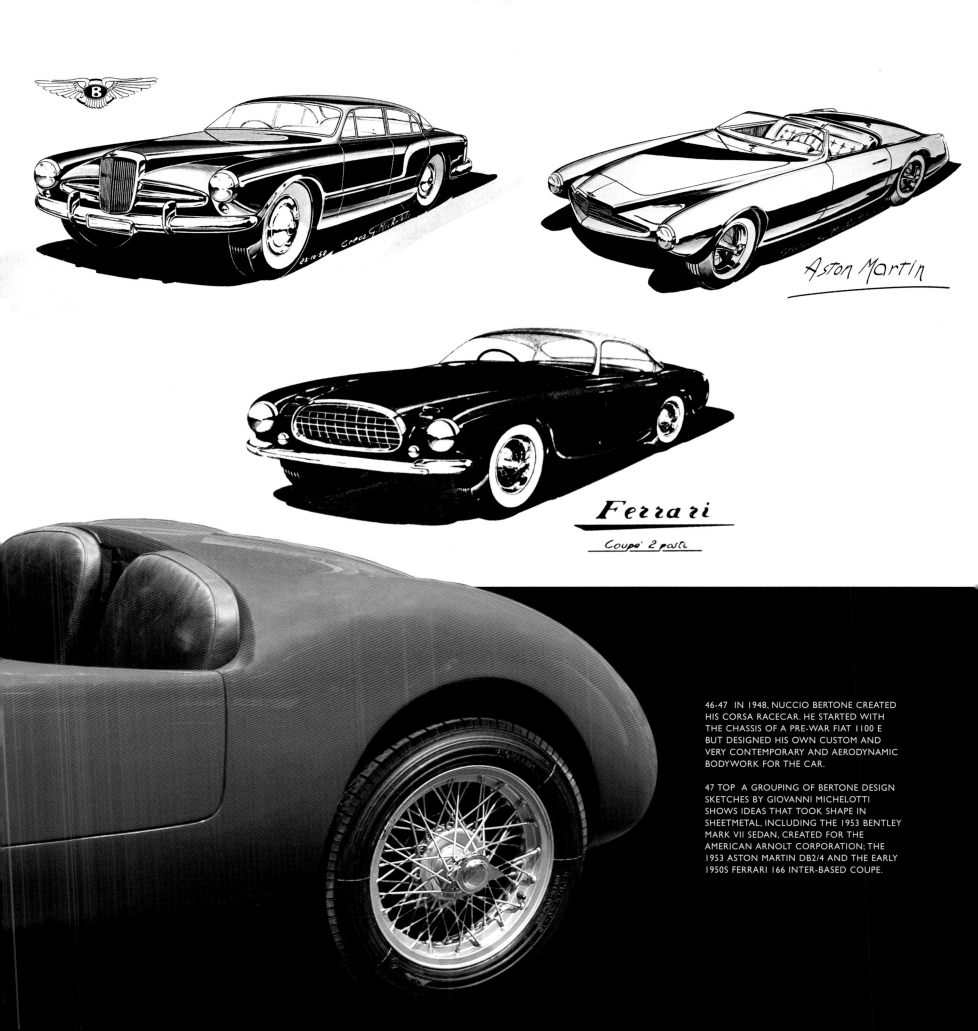

Aston Martin

Ferrari

Coupè 2 posti

46-47 IN 1948, NUCCIO BERTONE CREATED HIS CORSA RACECAR. HE STARTED WITH THE CHASSIS OF A PRE-WAR FIAT 1100 E BUT DESIGNED HIS OWN CUSTOM AND VERY CONTEMPORARY AND AERODYNAMIC BODYWORK FOR THE CAR.

47 TOP A GROUPING OF BERTONE DESIGN SKETCHES BY GIOVANNI MICHELOTTI SHOWS IDEAS THAT TOOK SHAPE IN SHEETMETAL, INCLUDING THE 1953 BENTLEY MARK VII SEDAN, CREATED FOR THE AMERICAN ARNOLT CORPORATION; THE 1953 ASTON MARTIN DB2/4 AND THE EARLY 1950S FERRARI 166 INTER-BASED COUPE.

FRANCO SCAGLIONE

In 1952, Nuccio hired Franco Scaglione. He was born near Florence in 1916. Though the son of a doctor who worked in a military hospital, young Franco was fascinated by aircraft. He was studying to be an aerodynamics engineer when he was drafted into military service during World War II. His service would include five years in a prisoner-of-war camp. Afterward, he finished his degree, but since Italy had no aircraft industry, he was designing women's fashions when he was hired as a freelance designer at Pinin Farina. Three months later, Bertone offered him a full-time job and he eagerly accepted.

Scaglione, at age 36, immediately provided verification of Nuccio's eye for identifying design talent by creating the stunning if Fiat-based Abarth 1500 coupe. The car had dramatic curves, a third headlamp in the center of the grille, a wraparound windshield, deeply sculpted wheel wells and the rear fenders swept back into fins. The car was displayed at the 1952 Turin Motor Show, was purchased on the spot by American luxury car builder Packard and was shipped to the United States.

The Abarth 1500 may have been stunning, but it was overshadowed the following year by Scaglione's B.A.T. 5. Built around mechanical components from the Alfa Romeo 1900 Sprint, the car took its initials from Berlinetta Aerodinamica Tecnica, though its organic curves – including curved rear wings on either side of a fin-like extension of the rear roofline – no doubt reminded many of the flying mammal that its initials spelled.

A year later, Bertone and Scaglione offered B.A.T. 7 with even longer, larger and more pronounced fins. Then, in 1955, came B.A.T. 9, a more conservative if perhaps more practical finale on this three-car study in design and aerodynamics.

48 AND 49 BETWEEN 1953 AND 1955, FRANCO SCAGLIONE DESIGNED FOR BERTONE THREE OF THE MOST STUNNING CONCEPT CARS EVER CREATED, THE ALFA ROMEO 1500-BASED BERLINETTA AERODINAMICA TECNICA OR B.A.T. CARS, STARTING WITH B.A.T. 5 (BOTTOM LEFT) IN 1953, B.A.T. 7 (RIGHT) IN 1954 AND B.A.T. 9 (ABOVE LEFT) IN 1955. EACH CAR WAS UNVEILED AT THE THEN ANNUAL TURIN MOTOR SHOW.

50 AND 50-51 THE LAST OF THE B.A.T. SERIES WAS THE B.A.T. 9 IN 1955. ITS WINGS WERE LESS CURVED, BUT THAT MADE ITS LINES MORE PRACTICAL AND THUS IT FATHERED SUCH VEHICLES AS THE FIAT 1200 SPIDER AMERICA AND ALFA ROMEO GIULIETTA SPRINT SPECIALE, CONCEPTS UNVEILED AT THE TURIN SHOW IN 1957, WITH THE ALFA ENTERING SERIES PRODUCTION TWO YEARS LATER.

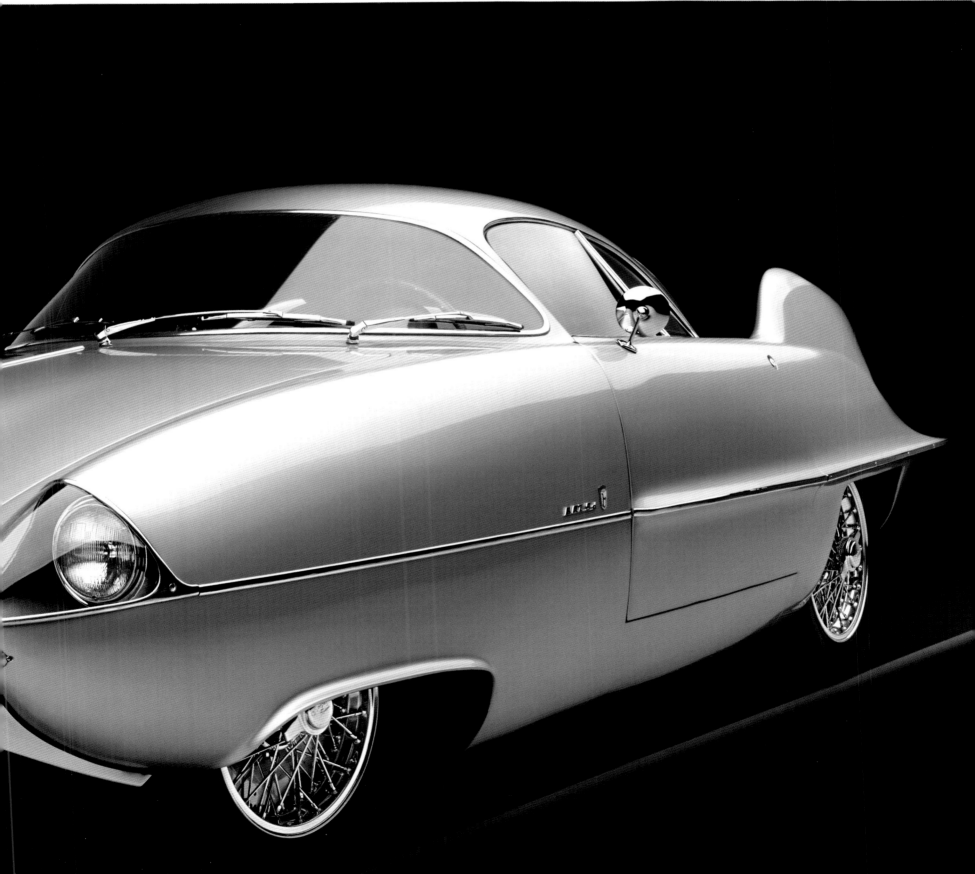

B.A.T. 9d

The Abarth and B.A.T. cars were spectacular, but they comprised only a small portion of Scaglione's portfolio, which would include some 40 cars between 1952 and 1973.

Scaglione signed his sketches "FraSca" and at Bertone they included the Aston Martin DB2/4, the Arnolt Bristol, Alfa Romeo Giulietta Sprint, Spyder Speciale and 2000 Sportiva, the speed record-setting Abarth 750 and others.

Scaglione stayed at Bertone until 1959, then worked as a design consultant to Carlo Abarth and others; he also was the first Italian automotive designer to do work for a Japanese automaker. In 1963 he designed four cars, including the first Lamborghini, the 350 GTV.

In 1967, at age 51, he created the body for the Alfa Romeo Type 33 Stradale.

"When a project was assigned to him, he carefully studied the chassis and structure of the vehicle; secondly, the mechanical portions," his daughter, Giovanna, told *Automobile Quarterly* when discussing her father's work. "In a few days, he would have in his mind the possibilities. Usually he would do three or four preliminary sketches. These were for presentation to the interested parties in order to select the definitive version."

Once the final version was approved, Scaglione "would immediately start drawing full size, taking a certain amount of time," his daughter noted.

"He would then construct a 1:10 scale model in plaster of Paris.

The full-size wooden "former" would now be made up from his drawings."

54-55 AND 55 TOP STANLEY HOWARD 'WACKY' ARNOLT DISTRIBUTED BRITISH CARS IN MIDDLE AMERICA AND COMMISSIONED BERTONE TO CREATE A NEW BODY OVER MG TD MECHANICALS. FRANCO SCAGLIONE THUS DESIGNED THE ARNOLT BRISTOL, WHICH TOOK THEIR SECOND NAME FROM THEIR BRISTOL ENGINES. ONE OF THE CARS WON THE 12-HOUR RACE AT SEBRING, FLORIDA IN 1955 AND THE CARS – THREE COUPES AND MORE THAN 250 ROADSTERS – WERE PRODUCED UNTIL 1960.

" ARNOLT - BRISTOL "
Spyder Sport 2 S.

Type n° 5801

56 TOP AMERICAN IMPORTER MAX HOFFMAN THOUGHT HE COULD SELL A SPORTS CAR BASED ON THE ALFA ROMEO SPRINT BUT WITH A SHORTER WHEELBASE AND BERTONE SET FRANCO SCAGLIONE TO WORK ON THE GIULIETTA SPIDER, WHICH FEATURED SHARPLY CREASED REAR WINGS AND A WRAPAROUND WINDSHIELD.

56-57 THE ALFA ROMEO GIULITTA SPRINT, WHICH ENJOYED AN 11-YEAR PRODUCTION RUN, WAS INSPIRED BY A 1954 PROTOTYPE BY SCAGLIONE AND BERTONE. THE ALFA ROMEO 2000 SPORTIVA WAS A RACY TWO-SEAT COUPE WITH STYLING THAT MADE IT LOOK LONGER THAN IT WAS. THE SPORTIVA'S WHEELBASE WAS SEVEN INCHES (180 MM) SHORTER THAN THE COMPACT SPRINT'S.

GIORGETTO GIUGIARO

Losing a designer of Scaglione's talent might have devastated many studios, but Nuccio simply went out and found another young talent, Giorgetto Giugiaro, who was only 21 years old when tapped by Bertone.

"Bertone had a special insight into people's potential, he shaped and fostered their talents," Giugiaro says in the Bertone corporate history published to celebrate the coachbuilding company's 90th anniversary.

"He combined a flair for business with respect for the creative freedom of the people he worked with, which is rare enough. I never felt so free as in those years of grueling work."

In another interview, Giugiaro admitted that he was overwhelmed in his new job: "I didn't sleep nights. I had failed to realize that every curve I was drawing, every dimension I set, was to become a chalk model, a wooden template, hammered sheetmetal in the space of a few hours. I remember having drawn a side window so tall that it could not be totally housed in the door panel when rolled down. If my indications were incorrect, the whole thing, time, and money, had to be thrown away."

While the young designer still had some things to learn, Bertone knew talent when he saw it and was rewarded with the Alfa Romeo 2000 Sprint in time for the 1960 Turin show.

Even after he was called up into military service, Giugiaro found time to design and gave Bertone the Ferrari 250 GT 2+2 (which would become Bertone's personal car), the Aston Martin DB4 GT "Jet," the BMW 3200 CS coupe, the Maserati 5000 GT and the ASA 1000 GT 2+2, or "la Ferrarina" (Little Ferrari) as it was known.

His military commitment fulfilled, Giugiaro be-

gan sketching early in 1963 on a one-off prototype that Bertone wanted to build around the mechanical components of the Chevrolet Corvair.

The result was the Testudo, Spanish for tortoise, not because the car lacked dynamic capability — Bertone himself drove the car to the Geneva show and Giugiaro drove it back to Turin — but because of the shell-like roof that was hinged at the base of the windshield to ease entry into the low-slung prototype.

There were many more as well, both production vehicles such as the Fiat 850 Spider and prototypes such as the Alfa Romeo Canguro.

58-59 GIORGETTO GIUGIARO WAS 21 YEARS OLD WHEN HE JOINED BERTONE. FOR THE 1963 GENEVA MOTOR SHOW, GIUGIARO (RIGHT) AND NUCCIO BERTONE (LEFT) CREATED TESTUDO, A CAR BASED ON THE CHASSIS OF THE REAR-ENGINE AND FAIRLY CHUBBY CHEVROLET CORVAIR, BUT WITH GIUGIARO STYLING IT BECAME A VERY SLEEK BODY THAT WOULD LATER INSPIRE SUCH VEHICLES AS THE PORSCHE 928.

59 BOTTOM TESTUDO DID NOT HAVE CONVENTIONAL DOORS. INSTEAD, ITS ROOF PANEL WAS HINGED AT THE BASE OF THE WINDSHIELD AND OPENED LIKE A CLAM SHELL TO PROVIDE ACCESS TO THE PASSENGER COMPARTMENT.

60-61 AND 61 IN 1964, BERTONE AND GIUGIARO CREATED CANGURO. THIS CONCEPT WAS BUILT ON THE TUBULAR STEEL CHASSIS OF THE ALFA ROMEO GIULIA TZ RACECAR. THE ENTIRE FRONT END SHEETMETAL OF CANGURO, INCLUDING THE HOOD AND FENDERS, WAS A SINGLE PIECE WITH A FRONT HINGE AND OPENED LIKE A CLAM SHELL TO REVEAL THE ENGINE. CANGURO HAD A VERY LONG REAR BUT STUBBED TAIL SECTION, AS DID SEVERAL RACECARS OF THE ERA.

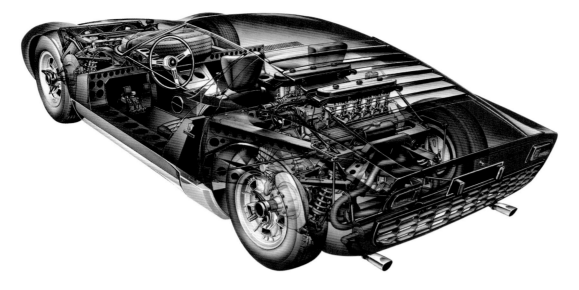

MARCELLO GANDINI

Bertone and Giugiaro had produced an amazing succession of vehicles, but the partnership ended when Ghia hired Giugiaro away. Once again, Bertone would demonstrate his eye for talent by hiring Marcello Gandini, who at 27 was the same age as Giugiaro.

Gandini, son of an orchestra leader, loved auto racing and had been working as a freelancer, at first converting sports cars for racing but then designing sleek bodies that would take advantage of the mechanical changes he had made. Bertone and Gandini met and talked frequently at racing events.

Gandini's first major project for Bertone was an automotive breakthrough, the Lamborghini Miura P400, the first so-called supercar, a road-going racecar with a 12-cylinder engine mounted across the chassis just behind the driver and passenger and with a roofline that reached only 39 inches above the ground. Wearing Gandini's snug-fitting metal suit, the Miura was the fastest car on the world's roads.

Gandini also completed work that Giugiaro had begun on what became the Fiat Dino Coupe, a car powered by the V6 engine that traced its creation to Enzo Ferrari's late son, Alfredino.

"Bertone's hallmark was to astound, to explore totally original morphologies and create a new graphic syntax to project the forms of the automobile into the future," wrote automotive design reviewer Daniele Cornil, who noted that Gandini's Miura represented the ultimate expression of its era. "Beyond the Miura there was nowhere to go. What was needed now was a breakthrough, the creation of a new equilibrium."

Bertone and Gandini rounded out the Miura-inspired era with the Lamborghini Marzal, the Alfa Romeo Montreal (designed to relaunch Alfa Romeo in North America in conjunction with the 1967 Montreal World's Fair), the Jaguar Pirana and the Lamborghini Espada.

Then, at Paris in 1968, they presented the future in the form of the Carabo, showed a more practical form of the language in the Runabout, Stratos and Lamborghini Countach.

62 TOP MARCELLO GANDINI IMMEDIATELY CREATED FOR BERTONE THE LAMBORGHINI MIURA P400, SHOWN HERE IN A CUTAWAY ILLUSTRATION.

62-63 AND 63 TOP THE MIURA WAS UNVEILED AT THE 1965 GENEVA MOTOR SHOW AND WAS ACCLAIMED AS THE FIRST OF A NEW BREED OF "SUPERCAR." TOP RIGHT NUCCIO BERTONE STANDS NEXT TO A 1966 MIURA.

The Runabout was designed as a mini-Miura and evolved into the Fiat X1/9, a compact, mid-engine two-seater with a removable roof panel held up by a built-in rollover bar.

Fiat would produce the car for nearly two decades. The Stratos evolved from its otherworld sculptural design to enter production as the netherworldly Lancia Stratos rally and road car.

The Countach, well, this one had so much sex appeal that many adolescent (and older) men took down pinup photos of Farah Fawcett and replaced them with posters showing the Countach, the first car in production with scissors-hinged doors like those introduced on the Carabo concept.

Gandini's work for Bertone ended in the late 1970s with two more significant concepts, the Alfa Romeo Navajo with its angular double rear wing and the first a fully digital instrument panel, and Sibilo, with its vacuum-formed body panels that made the car look as though it was one solid piece.

64-65 BERTONE AND LANCIA COOPERATED ON THE CREATION OF THE STRATOS, A MID-ENGINE SPORTS COUPE DESIGNED FOR RALLY RACING. THE CAR, WITH A MID-MOUNTED V6 ENGINE, MADE ITS COMPETITIVE DEBUT IN 1973 AND WON THREE CONSECUTIVE WORLD RALLY CHAMPIONSHIPS AND SCORED VICTORIES OVER A SIX-YEAR PERIOD. BERTONE PRODUCED NEARLY 500 STRATOS BODIES.

65 TOP LEFT THE ALFA ROMEO MONTREAL WAS A CONCEPT CAR DESIGNED FOR THE 1967 WORLD'S FAIR IN THE CANADIAN CITY THAT GAVE THE CAR ITS NAME. THE PRODUCTION VERSION SHOWN HERE WAS LAUNCHED IN 1970 BUT WITH A BODY DESIGNED TO FIT A V8 ENGINE UNDER ITS HOOD.

65 TOP RIGHT NUCCIO BERTONE IS SURROUNDED BY BERTONE-DESIGNED VEHICLES, INCLUDING THE LAMBORGHINI MIURA (ORANGE), LAMBORGHINI MARZAL CONCEPT (WHITE WITH EXPOSED INTERIOR), STRATOS CONCEPT (SILVER), LANCIA STRATOS (YELLOW) AND LAMBORGHINI ATHON (BLACK).

66-67 TOP Z.E.R. STANDS FOR ZERO EMISSION RECORD AND WAS THE BERTONE-DESIGNED ELECTRIC VEHICLE CREATED TO SHOWCASE THE POTENTIAL FOR BATTERY-POWERED VEHICLES. THE CAR REACHED A SPEED OF MORE THAN 188 MILES PER HOUR AND TRAVELED NEARLY 290 MILES WHILE AVERAGING MORE THAN 75 MPH ON A SINGLE CHARGER.

66-67 BOTTOM BLITZ WAS AN ELECTRIC-POWERED BERTONE CONCEPT CAR IN 1992. MORE THAN ONE THIRD OF THE CAR'S 1741 POUNDS CAME FROM THE BATTERY PACK THAT PROVIDED POWER TO A PAIR OF DIRECT-CURRENT MOTORS.

67 NUCCIO BERTONE WORKS WITH DESIGNERS.

MARC DESCHAMPS

Bertone separated his design staff from the auto production facility in 1971, establishing Stile Bertone well east of the city at Caprie, a village tucked into the Piedmont hills and the Valle di Susa.

Since the early 1970s, Marc Deschamps had worked alongside Gandini and now the Frenchman was promoted to head Bertone's design staff, which he did through the decade of the 1980s. Deschamps was credited with the Lamborghini Athon concept. His Bertone studio also did the Citroën BX, a car in production for a dozen years, as well as the Citroën XM, a car in production for more than a dozen years, as well as the Volvo 780, the Chevrolet Corvette-based Ramarro, and Genesis, a minivan with a Lamborghini engine and a driver's seat built around the contours of the left front wheel well and accessible by lifting half of the gulling that comprised the hood and front doors, and another Corvette-based concept, the Nivola.

BERTONE TODAY

When Deschamps left in 1990 to head the Italian studio of French coachbuilder Heuliez, Bertone hired Luciano d'Ambrosio from Giugiaro's studio, Italdesign, as chief exterior designer and Eugenio Pogliano to lead interior design work. In addition to production vehicles for Citroën and others, concepts from this era included the electric-powered Blitz and Z.E.R., which established several speed records, as well as the Porsche-based Karisma, small trucksters based on Citroën and BMW platforms and the innovative and Opel-based Slalom wagon.

Nuccio Bertone died in 1997, leaving his majority interest in the family-owned company to his wife and daughters. The company celebrated its 90th anniversary in 2002 with the Novanta, a drive-by-wire concept car. Subsequently it showed Jet 2, homage to the Aston Martin Jet it created in 1961, and Villa, based on a Cadillac SRX crossover utility vehicle but built with a new style of automotive architecture and an emphasis on interior rather than external design.

In 2003, David Wilkie, a native of Scotland who worked at Peugeot and then for 15 years at Ghia and Ford, joined the staff at Caprie. Early in 2006 he was appointed design director for Stile Bertone.

68 TOP THE PORSCHE KARISMA WAS A BERTONE CONCEPT CAR IN 1994 THAT CELEBRATED THE 25TH ANNIVERSARY OF THE BERTONE-DESIGNED PORSCHE 911 SPIDER/ROADSTER CONCEPT. KARISMA WAS A PORSCHE-POWERED FOUR-PASSENGER SEDAN WITH A TRANSPARENT ROOF AND LARGE GULLWING-STYLE DOORS TO PROVIDE EASY ENTRANCE TO THE PASSENGER COMPARTMENT.

68 BOTTOM BERTONE CREATED THE OPEL SLALOM FOR THE GENEVA MOTOR SHOW IN 1996. THE PROSPECTUS WAS FOR AN APPEALING AND SPORTY 2+2 WITH ALL-WHEEL DRIVE. THE CAR'S BOLD PROPORTIONS WERE EMPHASIZED WITH LARGE GLAZED AREAS CREATED TO LOOK LIKE AN ARTIST'S BOLD BRUSHSTROKES.

69 VILLA WAS A BERTONE CONCEPT IN 2005 THAT PUT A VERY DIFFERENT LOOK ON THE CHASSIS OF THE CADILLAC SRX CROSSOVER WAGON. BERTONE'S INTERPRETATION EMPHASIZED THE SPACE INSIDE THE VEHICLE WITH THE EXTERIOR DESIGN FOCUSED NOT AS MUCH ON THE FRONT OR REAR OF THE VEHICLE AS ON ITS SIDES, WHERE BERTONE CREATED UNUSUAL DOORS TO PROVIDE VERY OPEN ACCESS TO THE VEHICLE'S INTERIOR LIVING SPACE. THE IDEA WAS NOT OF SPEED BUT OF WELL-BEING, COMFORT AND BEING CONNECTED.

70-71 AND 71 THE BARCHETTA WAS UNVEILED AT THE 2007 GENEVA MOTOR SHOW TO CELEBRATE BERTONE'S 95TH ANNIVERSARY. THE CONCEPT WAS INSPIRED BY THE FIAT 500 BARCHETTA CREATED IN 1947 BY A YOUNG NUCCIO BERTONE FOR HIS PERSONAL USE. THE BARCHETTA BORROWS MECHANICAL COMPONENTS SUCH AS ITS 100-HORSEPOWER, 1.4-LITER FOUR-CYLINDER ENGINE FROM THE FIAT PANDA AND WRAPS THEM INSIDE AN ALUMINUM BODY. INSTEAD OF TRADITIONAL DOORS, THE ENTIRE REAR QUARTERPANEL HINGES UPWARD TO PROVIDE ENTRY FOR THE DRIVER AND PASSENGER.

ITALIAN JOBS:
GHIA TURNS CREATIVE
CONCEPTS INTO GORGEOUS
ROLLING SCULPTURE

GHIA PROVIDES THE ITALIAN CONNECTION FOR CHRYSLER AND FORD

iacinto Ghia was born in Turin, Italy, in 1887 and learned car-building skills as an apprentice to several of that city's early automakers. Then, with a partner (Gariglio), Ghia opened his own shop in 1915 to create custom coachwork for wealthy clients. Unlike French coachbuilders, however, Ghia didn't limit his work to the most expensive of cars or just to wealthy clients. By 1921 Ghia's workshop outgrew its garage and moved to larger facilities. Gariglio left the partnership in the middle of the decade and with Giacinto running the shop, Carrozzeria Ghia blossomed with a well-received spider body on a 1929 Alfa Romeo 6C 1500 Sport and streamlined Lancia Augustas and Fiat Balillas among a series of projects in the early 1930s.

Ghia's building was destroyed during World War II and Giacinto himself died before the war ended. His family sold the business to Mario Boano, who had worked for both of the Farina brothers — Giovanni at Stablimenti Farina and Battista at Pinin Farina. Boano built a new workshop, focused at first on creating bodies for French and British chassis — and later for Italy's own Fiats. He hired as design consultant Mario Revelli de Beaumont, an artist and freelance stylist who had worked before the war at

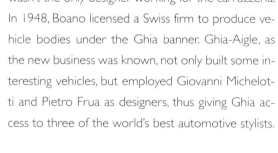

Bertone and Stablimenti Farina. Revelli would provide Ghia with designs from 1946 to 1950, but he wasn't the only designer working for the carrozzeria. In 1948, Boano licensed a Swiss firm to produce vehicle bodies under the Ghia banner. Ghia-Aigle, as the new business was known, not only built some interesting vehicles, but employed Giovanni Michelotti and Pietro Frua as designers, thus giving Ghia access to three of the world's best automotive stylists.

72-73 THE VALLELUNGA WAS DE TOMASO'S FIRST PRODUCTION VEHICLE. IT WAS POWERED BY A MID-MOUNTED FOUR-CYLINDER ENGINE FROM FORD OF BRITAIN. THE BODY'S SLEEK DESIGN WAS CREATED IN THE GHIA STUDIO. THE CAR WAS UNVEILED IN 1962 WITH PRODUCTION BEGINNING IN 1965 AND RUNNING THROUGH TO THE 1968 MODEL (SHOWN HERE).

74-75 GIACINTO GHIA (OPPOSITE PAGE) OPENED A COACHBUILDING BUSINESS WITH A PARTNER IN 1915. A DECADE LATER GHIA LEFT THE PARTNERSHIP TO OPEN CARROZZERIA GHIA, WHICH PRODUCED STREAMLINED BODIES FOR ALFA ROMEO, LANCIA AND FIAT CUSTOMERS.

75 AUTO RACING HELPED DRAW ATTENTION TO THE MOTORCAR IN THE 1920S AND 1930S, WITH LARGE CROWDS GATHERING FOR GRAND PRIX RACES HELD ON PUBLIC ROADS BETWEEN MAJOR CITIES.

LUIGI SEGRE

Business was good, and in 1950 Boano hired Luigi Segre from Siata to be Ghia's sales manager. Now business would become very good indeed. Segre created considerable new opportunities for Ghia's designers and especially for its car-building craftsman, signing a deal with Virgil Exner, chief designer at Chrysler, for Ghia to build Chrysler's show cars – a string of 26 sensational concepts over the course of a decade. Segre also secured an agreement with German coachbuilder Karmann to take one of those Chrysler designs, shrink it down in scale and turn it into the Volkswagen Karmann-Ghia, which in coupe and convertible form would remain in production for two decades, from the mid-1950s into the mid-1970s.

By the mid-1950s, Segre also had Ghia building concept vehicles for Ford – including the Lincoln Futura, a show car that would evolve into the original Batmobile for a popular American television series *Batman*. Ghia designed the Dual Ghia, a four-seat convertible built on a Dodge chassis that proved popular among Hollywood celebrities and American politicians.

Segre eventually bought out Boano, who left to establish the new design department at Fiat. Segre built yet another new Ghia factory, and brought in Giovanni Savonuzzi as Ghia's chief engineer. Although an engineer, Savonuzzi contributed to design as well, especially in the area of aerodynamics. He had helped create the Cisitalia streamliners in the late 1940s and showed the aerodynamic benefit of the tall and fin-like rear fenders that were becoming popular on American cars. Savonuzzi left Ghia in 1957 and moved to the United States to work at Chrysler.

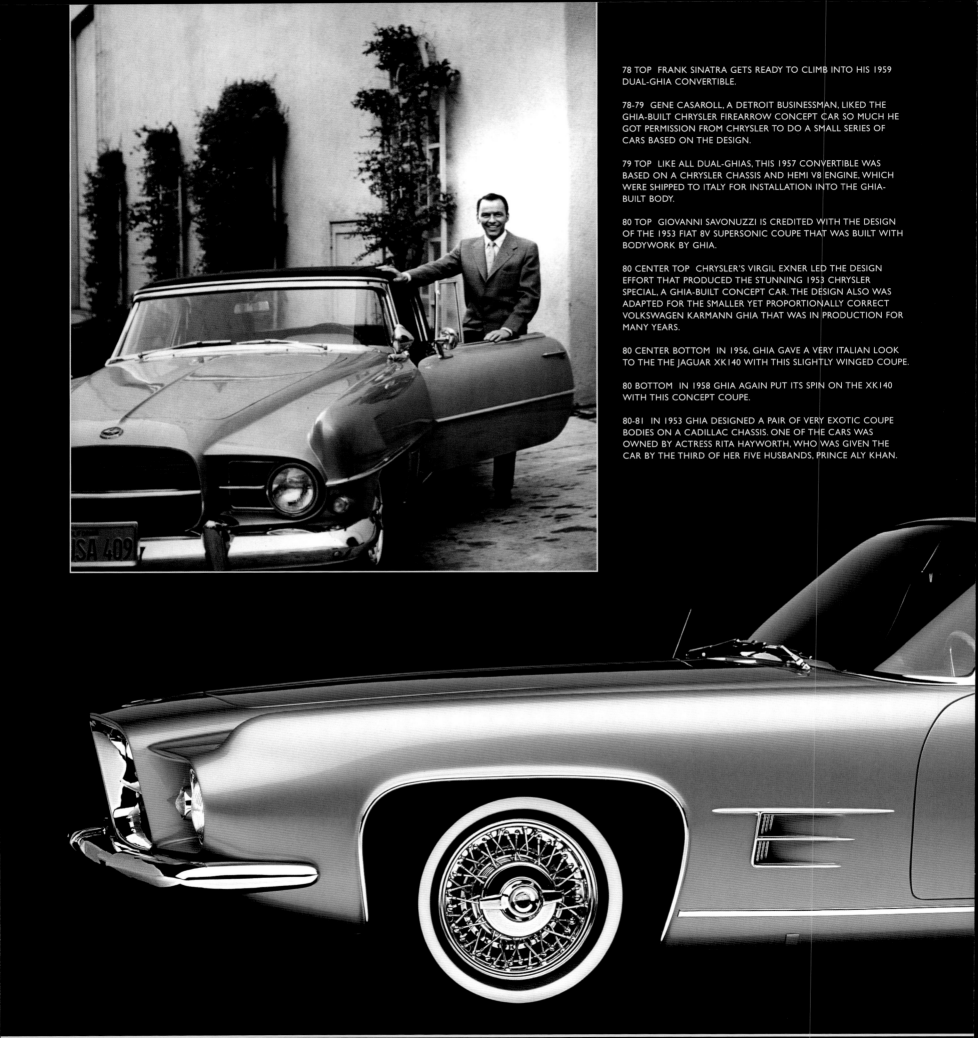

78 TOP FRANK SINATRA GETS READY TO CLIMB INTO HIS 1959 DUAL-GHIA CONVERTIBLE.

78-79 GENE CASAROLL, A DETROIT BUSINESSMAN, LIKED THE GHIA-BUILT CHRYSLER FIREARROW CONCEPT CAR SO MUCH HE GOT PERMISSION FROM CHRYSLER TO DO A SMALL SERIES OF CARS BASED ON THE DESIGN.

79 TOP LIKE ALL DUAL-GHIAS, THIS 1957 CONVERTIBLE WAS BASED ON A CHRYSLER CHASSIS AND HEMI V8 ENGINE, WHICH WERE SHIPPED TO ITALY FOR INSTALLATION INTO THE GHIA-BUILT BODY.

80 TOP GIOVANNI SAVONUZZI IS CREDITED WITH THE DESIGN OF THE 1953 FIAT 8V SUPERSONIC COUPE THAT WAS BUILT WITH BODYWORK BY GHIA.

80 CENTER TOP CHRYSLER'S VIRGIL EXNER LED THE DESIGN EFFORT THAT PRODUCED THE STUNNING 1953 CHRYSLER SPECIAL, A GHIA-BUILT CONCEPT CAR. THE DESIGN ALSO WAS ADAPTED FOR THE SMALLER YET PROPORTIONALLY CORRECT VOLKSWAGEN KARMANN GHIA THAT WAS IN PRODUCTION FOR MANY YEARS.

80 CENTER BOTTOM IN 1956, GHIA GAVE A VERY ITALIAN LOOK TO THE THE JAGUAR XK140 WITH THIS SLIGHTLY WINGED COUPE.

80 BOTTOM IN 1958 GHIA AGAIN PUT ITS SPIN ON THE XK140 WITH THIS CONCEPT COUPE.

80-81 IN 1953 GHIA DESIGNED A PAIR OF VERY EXOTIC COUPE BODIES ON A CADILLAC CHASSIS. ONE OF THE CARS WAS OWNED BY ACTRESS RITA HAYWORTH, WHO WAS GIVEN THE CAR BY THE THIRD OF HER FIVE HUSBANDS, PRINCE ALY KHAN.

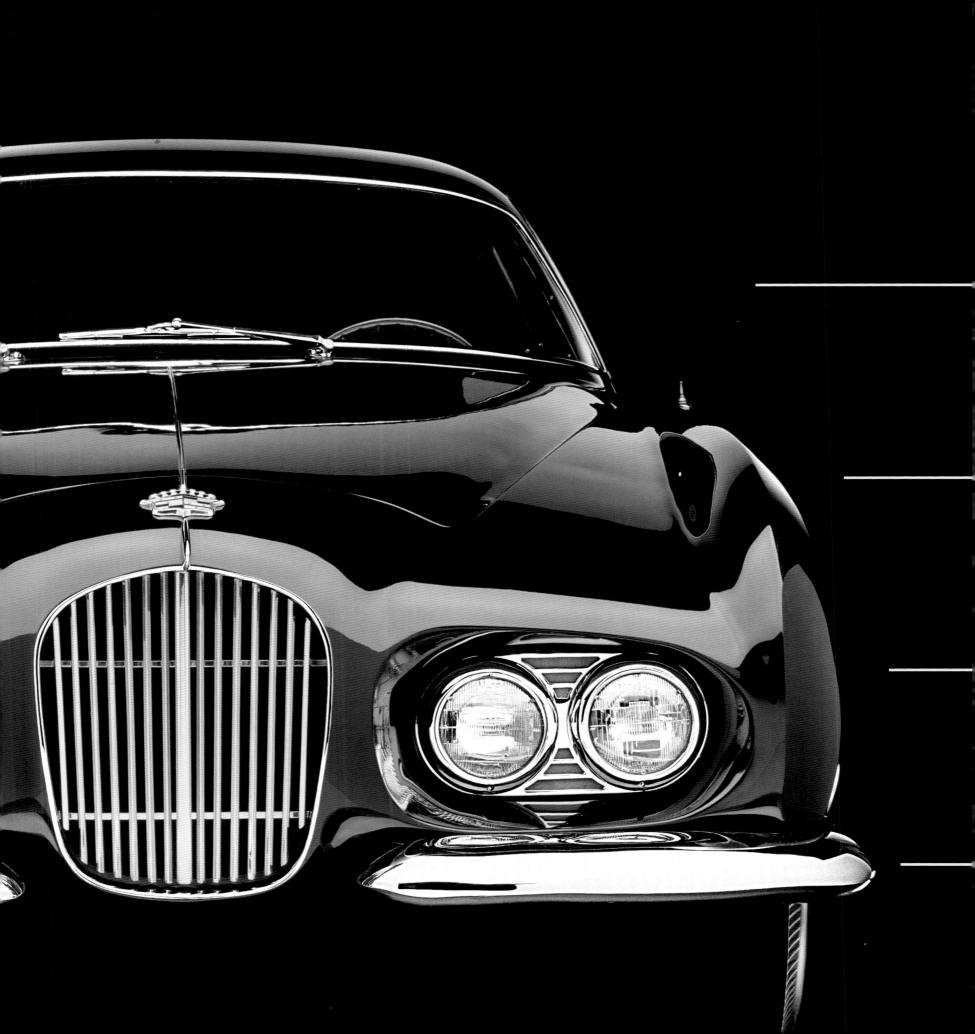

ALEJANDRO DE TOMASO

Sergio Sartorelli served as Ghia's design director from 1958 until 1963, when he became director of advanced design at Fiat. Among the notable vehicles built during Sartoelli's reign was the Selene II, a concept created by Virgil Exner Jr., son of the famed Chrysler design chief. The young Exner's work at Ghia also included the Volvo P1800 and work on the Karmann-Ghia.

In Ghia's history, 1963 was a hugely significant year – and not because Sartoelli left the company. It was the year that Segre died, and after his death his widow sold a 75 percent interest in the company to Leonidas Ramadeas Trujillo, a car enthusiast and son of the former dictator of the Dominican Republic. But the younger Trujillo ended up in jail and in need of money and in 1967 sold Ghia to an American electronics company, Roland Controllers. The sale was brokered by Alejandro De Tomaso, an Argentine-born racecar driver who was married to the former Isabel Haskell, whose brother was the head of Roland and whose grandfather, William Durant, had been one of the founders of General Motors.

Like De Tomaso himself, Isabel raced cars; they met in Italy in the mid-1950s while she was shopping for a new Maserati sports car. De Tomaso was racing an OSCA owned by the Maserati brothers. De Tomaso was a charismatic if controversial figure. His grandfather had emigrated from Italy to Argentina, where Alejandro's father would become minister of agriculture. After his father's death, Alejandro became part of a group that tried to depose Argentine president Juan Perón. He spent time in jail, then fled to Italy, raced and founded a company that built racing and sports cars. De Tomaso established ties to the Ford Motor Company. When his brother-in-law died in a plane crash, he again brokered the sale of Ghia, this time to Ford, with De Tomaso running the Italian company.

From 1965 to1969, Ghia design was led by a budding young superstar of styling, Giorgetto Giugiaro, who while still in his early 20s had been named chief designer at Bertone. Within his first year at Ghia, Giugiaro created five concept vehicles for international auto shows, including two that would become sports car classics – the Maserati Ghibli and the De Tomaso Mangusta. However, Giugiaro and De Tomaso had a stormy relationship and Giugiaro left Ghia to establish his own studio.

82-83 AND 83 TOP
GIORGETTO GIUGIARO WAS
GHIA'S HEAD DESIGNER IN
THE LATE 1960S. THOUGH
STILL IN HIS 20S, HE
CREATED FOUR CARS IN HIS
FIRST YEAR IN THE STUDIO,
INCLUDING THE MASERATI
GHIBLI (BELOW) AND THE
DE TOMASO MANGUSTA
(RIGHT), SHOWN IN FRONT
OF THE FORD WORLD
HEADQUARTERS WITH
ALEJANDRO DE TOMASO,
WHO POWERED HIS CARS
WITH FORD ENGINES.

World Headquarters

T. TJAARDA & F. SAPINO

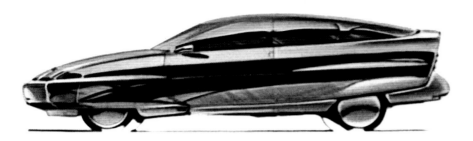

After Giugiaro left, Tom Tjaarda returned to Ghia. Tjaarda's father, John, was born in The Netherlands and was educated as an engineer but had been one of the early stars of automotive design, creating cars such as the Lincoln Zephyr and Packard Clipper.

Tom was born in the United States and was educated as an architect, but accepted a job at Ghia under Luigi Segre and instead of designing buildings, he created vehicles such as the Innocenti Spyder and beyond-exotic concepts including the Selene and IXG. Tjaarda left Ghia after Segre's death and worked at Pininfarina.

Back at Ghia, Tjaarda designed the De Tomaso Pantera, Lancia 1600 Competizione and several concept vehicles, including the Ford Fiesta-based Project Wolf, a car created as a potential challenger to the popular Volkswagen Golf. Tjaarda suffered jealousy from Ford staff designers and left in the late 1970s as Ghia was being enfolded into the Ford studio system.

Filippo Sapino, who was at Ghia from 1960-1967, returned from Pininfarina and led the team that created an impressive portfolio of concepts. Ghia continued to flourish when Don Kopka, who had worked under Virgil Exner when Ghia was building Chrysler concepts in the 1950s, became Ford's Dearborn-based design director.

But Kopka retired in 1987 and while Ghia continued to do stunning futuristic vehicles, the studio's role was severely reduced in the ensuing years.

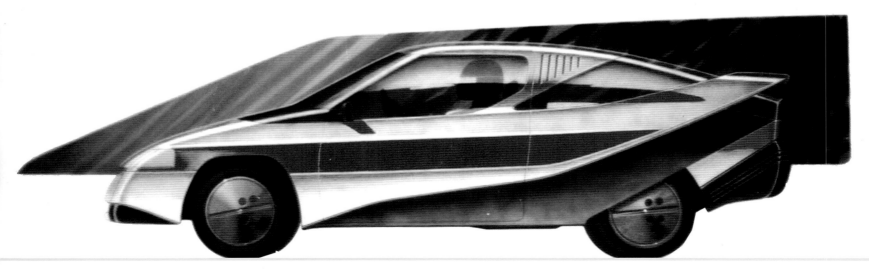

84 LEFT THE PRELIMINARY PROPOSAL FOR A CAR TAKES SHAPE IN A SERIES OF SKETCHES AT GHIA.

84 BOTTOM THE PROPOSAL IS WORKED AND REWORKED INTO LARGER, SOMETIMES EVEN FULL-SCALE, DRAWINGS COMPLETED NOT ONLY IN PROFILE BUT FROM OTHER ANGLES AS WELL.

84 TOP RIGHT THE FULL-SCALE MODEL IS READY FOR AUTO COMPANY EXECUTIVES TO EVALUATE FOR POSSIBLE PRODUCTION.

85 TOP WHAT APPEARS TO BE A FULL-SIZE AUTOMOBILE IS ACTUALLY A CLAY MODEL THAT HAS BEEN PAINTED AND PLACED ON WHEELS AND TIRES FOR EVALUATION.

85 CENTER NOT ONLY IS THE PROTOTYPE OR CONCEPT CAR'S EXTERIOR CREATED, BUT ITS COMPLETE INTERIOR MAY BE HAND-BUILT AS WELL.

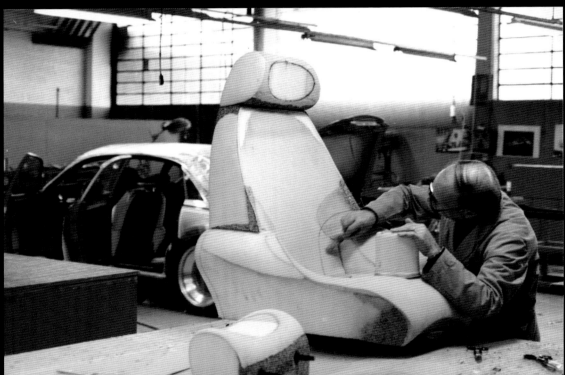

85 BOTTOM USING SUCH DRAWINGS, A FOAM SUB-STRUCTURE IS CREATED AND COVERED WITH CLAY THAT IS SCULPTED BY HAND AND BY MACHINE UNTIL A THREE-DIMENSIONAL SCALE MODEL IS CREATED.

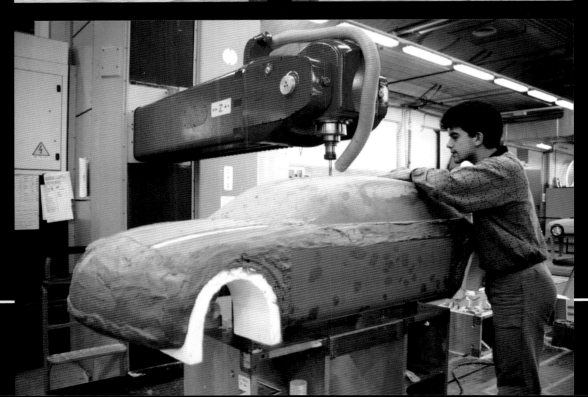

ITALIAN JOBS: FARINA, THE FIRST FAMILY OF DESIGN

THE BABY BROTHER BECOMES SO FAMOUS
HE GETS A NEW FAMILY NAME

At the turn of the 20th century, poverty was a way of life for families such as the Farinas, doing agricultural labor in the fields and vineyards in the Asti region of northern Italy. Years later, Battista Farina would say that his family's story was the story of "a hundred thousand, a million families like ours": a husband, wife and their 11 children comprising "a ship that was taking on water on all sides. But," he added, "we stayed afloat."

Though the sailing wasn't necessarily smooth, the time would come when Battista's family would receive very special recognition from the president of Italy. Battista credited his mother's steady hand at the helm for keeping the family ship on course. Giacinta Vigna Farina believed family was a team event and every member was expected to do his or her part. "I was the baby of the family," Battista recalled, "but I too soon learnt that lesson: my hands were early hardened to work." One of Battista's early memories was learning to polish his mother's metal pans and skillets, their shine "lent an air of peasant nobility" he remembers proudly. Rather than a task to be avoided, the youngster was eager at the work and discovered that he liked the way the metal and its curving surfaces felt beneath his hands.

Battista Farina was the 10th of the family's 11 children. Born in 1893, he was just 5 years old – though still called, as he would be throughout his life – by the Piedmontese nickname "Pinin" (meaning "baby" or "youngest") when the family left the countryside near the village Cortanze to seek better economic fortunes in the industrial city of Turin. In Turin, the oldest of the Farina sons, Giovanni, though only 12 years of age, went to work as an apprentice to coachbuilder Marcello Alessio. Young Pinin loved to hear about his brother's work, and spent whatever free time he had drawing pictures of the motorcars that were being built in Turin.

When Giovanni was 22, he opened his own business, building bodies for carriages and electric cars. With one of the first of the new stamping presses, he became a supplier of metal pressings for Fiat and Turin's other automakers. Giovanni's younger brother Carlo worked for him, and so did a teen-aged Pinin. The boy was just 18 years old when Stablimenti Farina (Establishment Farina) was given the opportunity to compete on the design of a radiator for Fiat's Zero model. Pinin not only designed a radiator, but built – and polished – it by hand.

Giovanni Agnelli, godfather of Turin's auto industry, and his engineers examined the dozen or so radiators that had been submitted – and selected, over all the others, including those done by Fiat's own engineers, Pinin's for production! Agnelli was impressed by the young brothers and their work and asked the Farinas to submit a proposal for bodywork for the new car. They did, and their torpedo-shaped coachwork was selected for series production. As a reward, Agnelli would present Pinin with his own Zero.

Soon after World War I, Stablimenti Farina was building as many as 1500 car bodies a year, and Pinin was becoming known for design that made cars appear longer and lower. In 1924 he traveled to the United States to see Henry Ford's vast automotive operation. After looking at the young Italian's sketches, Ford noted that Pinin was the same age as his son, Edsel, and he offered the young designer a job, which Pinin politely refused, returning instead to Italy to be married. In 1928 Pinin left his brother's company to start his own business, Carrozzeria Pinin Farina. The parting was amicable. Giovanni was becoming increasingly interested in developing new technologies – devising a hydraulic braking system, hydraulic shock absorbers and a hydraulic-powered convertible top, and in manufacturing airplane engines as well as producing car bodies.

86-87 TO CELEBRATE THE 40TH ANNIVERSARY OF THE FERRARI BRAND, THE PININFARINA STUDIOS DESIGNED THE FERRARI F40, WHICH WAS UNVEILED AT THE 1987 FRANKFURT MOTOR SHOW.

88 WITH THIS DOCUMENT, DATED MAY 22, 1930, THE SOCIETÀ ANONIMA CARROZZERIA PININ FARINA WAS FOUNDED.

89 TOP THIS PHOTOGRAPH, SHOT IN BOGOTA, COLOMBIA IN 1920 SHOWS A GROUP OF MEN STANDING WITH A HARLEY-DAVIDSON MOTORCYCLE AND A FIAT MODEL ZERO. HARLEY-DAVIDSON WOULD BECOME THE ICONIC AMERICAN MOTORCYCLE MANUFACTURER. THE FIAT FEATURED BODYWORK DESIGNED BY "PININ" FARINA, WHO WAS WORKING FOR HIS BROTHER'S COACHBUILDING COMPANY IN NORTHERN ITALY.

89 BOTTOM THIS FIAT TIPO ZERO CARRIES A BODY BUILT BY STABLIMENTI FARINA, A COMPANY STARTED BY GIOVANNI FARINA, WHOSE KEY EMPLOYEES INCLUDED HIS YOUNGER BROTHERS CARLO AND BATTISTA, BETTER KNOWN AS "PININ." IT WAS PININ'S DESIGN FOR THE ZERO'S RADIATOR THAT HELPED WIN FARINA A CONTRACT WITH FIAT FOR BODY DESIGN AND CONSTRUCTION.

For his coachbuilding designs, Giovanni hired people such as Francesco Martinengo, Pietro Frua, Mario Boano and Mario Revelli de Beaumont, as well as Alfredo Vignale, the son of Stablimenti Farina's paint shop manager. Alfredo worked at Farina from 1928 to 1940, then after World War II he and his brothers Guglielmo and Giuseppe opened the garage that would grow into the famous coachbuilding business that would bear their family's name.

Later, Giovanni hired Giovanni Michelotti, and Michelotti and Farina did several concept proposals for automakers. But like many coachbuilders who struggled in the aftermath of the war, Farina would close his car body business in 1953. Michelotti went on to work for Ghia, Bertone and Vignale, designed the Cunningham C3 for American racer Briggs Cunningham and did designs for British automakers, including several Triumph sports cars, and for BMW.

Giovanni Farina retired in 1956 and turned over his industrial interests to his sons, Allilio and Giuseppe. While other Farinas were known for their abilities at shaping metal, Giuseppe had become famous for another sort of artistic talent; widely known by his nickname, "Nino," Giuseppe Farina drove for the Alfa Romeo and Ferrari sports car and grand prix teams and was the inaugural champion when the World Driving Champion launched in 1950.

While his nephew was winning on the racetrack, Battista "Pinin" Farina had been winning worldwide acclaim for his automotive designs. With seed money from an aunt and a contract from Turin automaker Vincenzo Lancia, Carrozzeria Pinin Farina officially opened in 1930. Pinin Farina designs featured radiators moved off the vertical and angled back toward the windshield. Soon he would curve those radiators and mold them into the shape of the car's hood. His 1935 Alfa Romeo 6C "Pescara" and a 1936 and 1937 custom-bodied Lancia Aprilias explored the edges of automotive aerodynamics. At the same time, he was creating ultra-luxury cars for royalty, and thus earning the crown that topped the company's emblem, a lower-case "f" set against a diagonal stripe.

90 TOP GIUSEPPE "NINO" FARINA (CENTER) AND MIKE HAWTHORN (RIGHT) DROVE A FERRARI 375MM PININ TO VICTORY IN THE 24-HOUR RACE AT SPA-FRANCORCHAMPS, BELGIUM IN 1953. THE EVENT WAS THE FIRST OFFICIAL EVENT IN THE WORLD SPORTS CAR RACING CHAMPIONSHIPS. FARINA WAS A SON OF GIOVANNI FARINA AND NEPHEW OF BATTISTA "PININ" FARINA.

90 BOTTOM REIGNING WORLD DRIVING (GRAND PRIX) CHAMPION GIUSEPPE FARINA MAKES HIS POINT AT THE FRENCH GRAND PRIX AT RHEIMS IN 1951.

90-91 GIUSEPPE "NINO" FARINA IS CONGRATULATED IN ROME DURING THE 1934 MILLE MIGLIA RALLY.

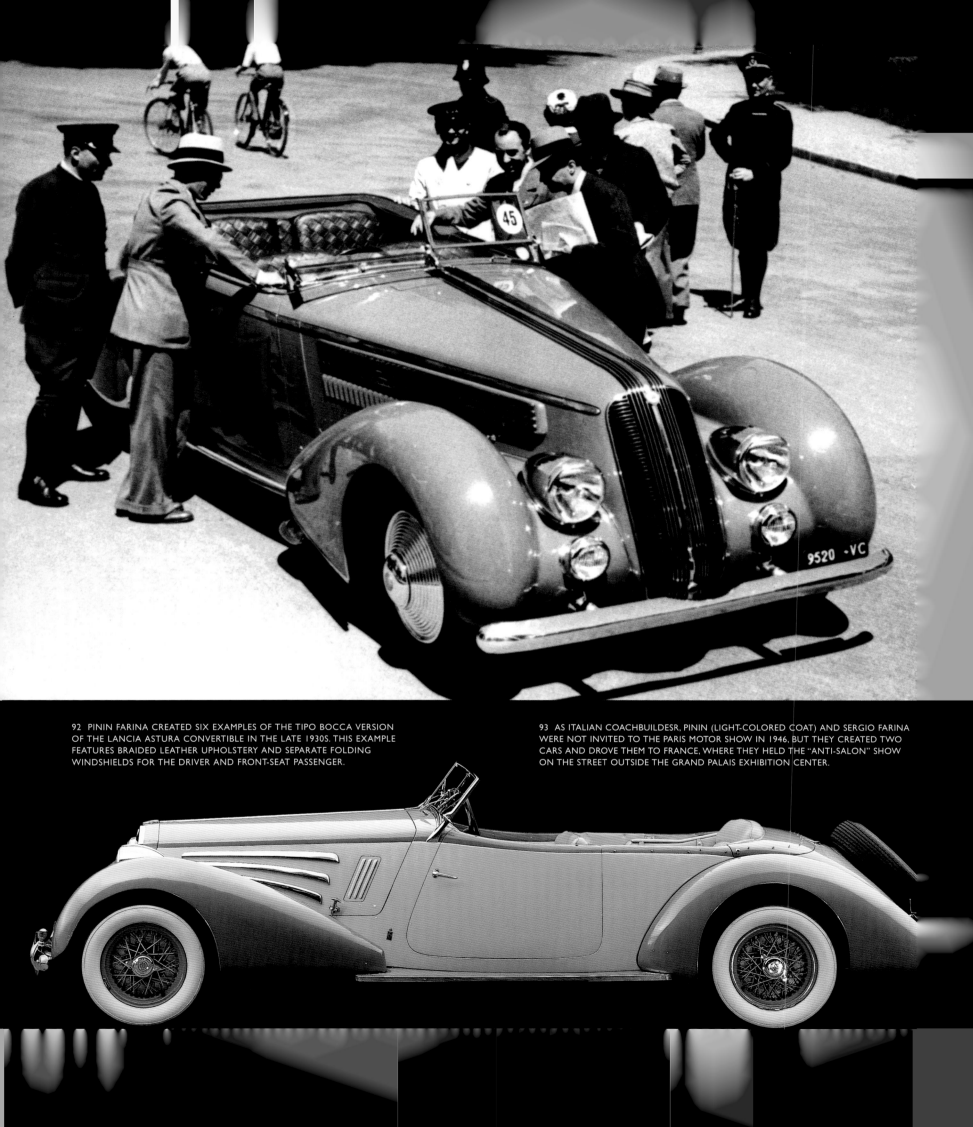

92 PININ FARINA CREATED SIX EXAMPLES OF THE TIPO BOCCA VERSION
OF THE LANCIA ASTURA CONVERTIBLE IN THE LATE 1930S. THIS EXAMPLE
FEATURES BRAIDED LEATHER UPHOLSTERY AND SEPARATE FOLDING
WINDSHIELDS FOR THE DRIVER AND FRONT-SEAT PASSENGER.

93 AS ITALIAN COACHBUILDESR, PININ (LIGHT-COLORED COAT) AND SERGIO FARINA
WERE NOT INVITED TO THE PARIS MOTOR SHOW IN 1946, BUT THEY CREATED TWO
CARS AND DROVE THEM TO FRANCE, WHERE THEY HELD THE "ANTI-SALON" SHOW
ON THE STREET OUTSIDE THE GRAND PALAIS EXHIBITION CENTER.

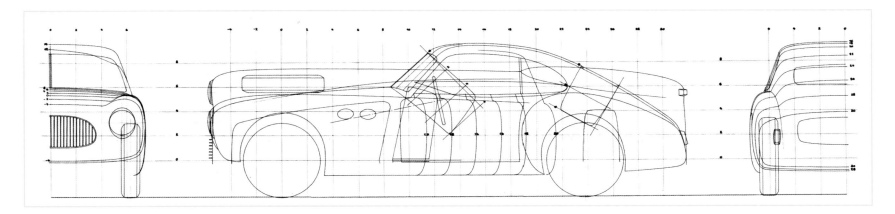

The carrozzeria was both an artistic and an industrial undertaking. Pinin Farina's designs were winning automotive beauty contests and his shop was building so many car bodies that by 1939 he employed 500 people.

Pinin Farina was eager to gear up after World War II, but found a barricade across the road back to work: the 1946 Paris Auto Salon, where post-war European and American automakers and coachbuilders would showcase the products that could supply the pent-up demand after so many years without new vehicles, decided to punish Italy by barring any exhibit of its cars.

Undaunted, Pinin prepared two cars and headed for Paris. He drove a specially bodied Alfa Romeo 2500 S convertible and his 20-year-old son, Sergio, was at the wheel of a Lancia Aprilia cabriolet with Pinin Farina bodywork.

They stopped at the edge of Paris to thoroughly clean the cars, then drove to the Grand Palais exhibition center and parked the cars near the main entrance. Parisians and press alike praised the vehicles as well as the spirit of what they called the "Anti-Salon."

Pinin Farina was heralded for leading the rebirth of Italian automotive design.

Not long after returning to Turin, Pinin Farina would show that he not only was the leader of Italian automotive design, but of automotive design, period! Even though fire swept his factory late in 1946 and interrupted work for several months, Pinin Farina found time to create two amazing vehicles. The first was the Maserati Sport A6 1500 concept with a transparent sliding roof. The other was a car that would mark a sea change in automotive design.

Automaker Piero Dusio of Cisitalia was working on a new chassis and wanted his friend Pinin Farina to create its body.

"The new chassis allowed me to put into effect my ideas without restraint," Farina said.

The car they created was the Cisitala 202: art met automobile in its form. Indeed, the car was the centerpiece of the Museum of Modern Art's "8 Automobiles" exhibit of motorcar design in 1951, and was the first automobile to become part of the New York museum's permanent collection.

The Cisitalia 202 established a new direction in automotive design. Instead of a body with various parts, fenders and such, added on, the Cisitalia's body was a smooth envelope that appeared to be a single, sculptural shell shaped tightly to the chassis, with skillfully integrated cutouts provided for the wheels and with a hood that was lower than the car's front fenders.

"The openings Farina cuts into the jacket provide some of the most skillfully contrived details of automobile design," wrote MOMA curator Arthur Drexler.

"The grille opening is a modified cross section of the hood, which thus resembles the cut end of a cigar, while the rolled edge of the opening itself helps to suggest that the grille is part of a continuous structural framework beneath the metal surface.

"Because the sloping hood lies below the two front fenders it suggests low, fast power. This hood treatment has the additional merit of making the wheels seem larger. . . ."

94 TOP LAYOUT SKETCHES SHOW FRONT, SIDE, TOP AND REAR VIEWS OF THE CISITALIA, PININ FARINA'S STUNNING AND TREND-SETTING POST-WAR AUTOMOTIVE DESIGN.

94 BOTTOM OFFICIALLY KNOWN AS THE CISITALIA 202, THIS SCULPTURALLY GORGEOUS AUTOMOBILE MADE ITS PUBLIC DEBUT AT AN EXHIBITION OF COACHBUILDERS AT THE MILAN TRIENNALE IN 1947.

95 THE CISITALIA WASN'T ONLY PART OF THE EIGHT-CAR DISPLAY AT THE MUSEUM OF MODERN ART IN NEW YORK CITY, IT WAS THE FIRST AUTOMOBILE TO BE INCLUDED IN THE MUSEUM'S PERMANENT ART COLLECTION.

96-97 THE CISITALIA IS CONSIDERED PERHAPS THE FIRST TRULY MODERN AUTOMOTIVE DESIGN, WITH A BODY THAT APPEARS SCULPTED FROM A SINGLE PIECE OF METAL AND WITH FENDERS THAT RISE ABOVE THE HOOD'S ARC.

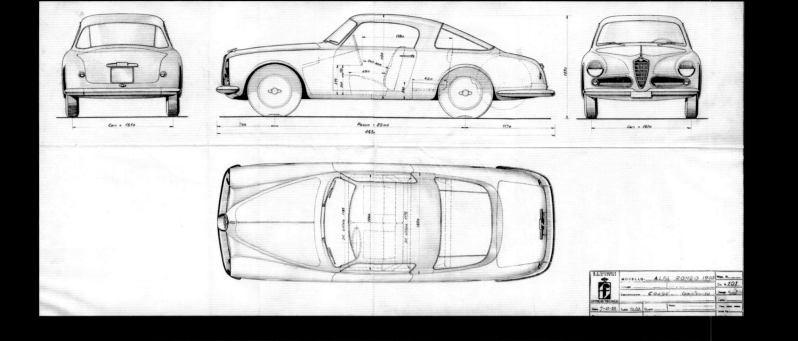

Soon there were contracts to design and build cars for American automaker Nash, for Peugeot of France and the British Motor Corporation, as well as for Italy's own Alfa Romeo and Fiat.

In 1952, Pininfarina started designing cars for Enzo Ferrari. Pinin Farina assigned responsibility for fulfilling the Ferrari agreement to his 25-year-old son, Sergio. A few years earlier, Pinin had turned over many of the business aspects of the carrozzeria to his son-in-law, Renzo Carli, an aeronautical engineer who, despite being only 10 years older than Sergio, became mentor to the young Farina who had just graduated with a degree in mechanical engineering.

With Pinin in his early 60s, Sergio became the family-owned company's general manager by the mid-1950s. Pinin continued to do much of the design work, including the creation of his personal car, the Florida, a Lancia Aurelia-based prototype that displayed his interpretation of an American-style sedan. Not that he hadn't been doing his versions of

American cars for quite a while, including the 1931 Cadillac V-16 Spider "Bateau" for the Maharaja of Orchha, the 1949 Berlina 5-Posti proposal for a sleek post-war Cadillac and the round-grille 1954 Cadillac Cabriolet Speciale, with others to follow, including the 1959 Starlight Coupe, the 1959 and 1960 Eldorado Brougham, 1961 Brougham "Jacqueline" concept named for American President Kennedy's wife and culminating in the Cadillac Allante that went into production in 1993.

Even more interesting, however, were the aerodynamic concepts Pinin Farina was creating with help from University of Turin aerodynamics professor Alberto Morelli.

These included the pf-X and pf-Y, both of which looked as though they might have been designed for intergalactic rather than highway travel.

The pf series also included Sigma, a concept designed to explore advances in active and passive safety technologies.

99

100 TOP DRAWINGS DETAIL THE ALFA ROMEO 1600 SPIDER DUETTO. THE DESIGN CAN BE TRACED BACK TO A PININ FARINA CONCEPT CAR FROM 1956. THE CAR FEATURED A SCOOP THAT RAN THE FULL LENGTH OF ITS SIDE PANELS.

100-101 THE PININFARINA-DESIGNED ALFA ROMEO 1600 SPIDER DUETTO WOULD BECOME POPULAR AND SOUGHT AFTER AROUND THE WORLD, NOT ONLY BECAUSE OF HOW IT LOOKED, BUT BECAUSE OF ITS ROLE IN THE AMERICAN MOVIE, *THE GRADUATE*.

102 TOP THE DESIGN AND PRODUCTION OF THE ALFA ROMEO GIULIETTA SPIDER WAS A MILESTONE FOR PININ FARINA AS

AN INDUSTRIAL RATHER THAN SIMPLY A DESIGN COMPANY. SOME 27,000 COPIES OF THE TWO-SEAT ROADSTER WOULD BE PRODUCED.

102-103 DESIGN CUES USED IN THE ALFA ROMEO GIULIETTA SPIDER CAN BE IDENTIFIED IN SEVERAL CONCEPT CARS ACTUALLY PRODUCED BY PININ FARINA. THE CAR'S FRONT END DESIGN FEATURES A PROMINENT GRILLE WITH SPLIT FRONT BUMPERS.

104-105 PININFARINA CREATED A VARIETY OF BODIES FOR THE FERRARI 250 GT. IN 1957, IT UNVEILED THE CALIFORNIA SPYDER. THE CAR WAS SPECIALLY DESIGNED TO FIT THE NEEDS OF FERRARI CUSTOMERS IN SUNNY SOUTHERN CALIFORNIA.

By the mid-1950s, Pinin Farina needed a new and larger production facility to build nearly 6000 car bodies a year for its clients. Indeed, Pinin Farina had become so well known around the world that most people assumed that Pinin Farina was one word, and, in 1961, the president of Italy signed a decree merging the words into a new family surname – Pininfarina. Late in 1966, just before the introduction of the Alfa Romeo 1600 Spider Duetto, the car that would become famous after its role in the movie *The Graduate*, 73-year-old Batista "Pinin", now Pininfarina, died leaving his son as chairman, his son-in-law as managing director and studio veteran Franco Martinengo as chief designer.

LEONARDO FIORAVANTI

The portfolio of "Pinin's" work spanned the transition of the automobile from upright and open coaches to sleek and exotic sports cars, and from futuristic concept vehicles to everyday cars for the modern motorist.

The boy who had polished his mother's cooking pots not only created wondrous moving metallic sculptures, but had founded a company that advanced from coachbuilder to industrial producer of vehicles for a variety of international automakers. That company would build on his legacy as it continued to design and build the world's most beautiful and dynamic automobiles.

In the mid-1990s, an article in *Automobile Quarterly* offered a list of some of Italy's leading auto designers, a list that included Scaglione, Michelotti, Boano, Formenti, Giugiaro, Fioravanti and Gandini. Fioravanti is Leonardo Fioravanti, who was hired by Pinin Farina in the mid-1960s soon after earning his degree in mechanical engineering from Milan Polytechnic University.

While Fioravanti was trained as an engineer, with specialties in vehicle construction and aerodynamics, he would make his mark as the designer who would style more Ferraris than anyone else, as well as other production and concept vehicles.

Fioravanti's first assignment at Pininfarina was to create not only a Ferrari, but a Ferrari that would bear the name of Ferrari's late son, Dino. The car, the Ferrari Dino 206 GT had high rounded fenders that curved back on either side of a long and low hood, beautifully sculpted side air vents and a roofline that bracketed flying buttress rear pillars around the mid-mounted V6 engine.

Almost immediately, Fioravanti followed with the Ferrari 365 Daytona, a car that took Pinin Farina's "superfast" styling cues to a new level that one British writer termed a "poem in steel." Such poetry could be fine-tuned in Pininfarina's own full-scale wind tunnel, which had been designed by Fioravanti, Professor Morelli and Pininfarina aerodynamics engineer Antonello Cogotti.

Such facilities typically were built by the military or major automakers, but Pininfarina recognized that the expense was a wise investment for its design and coachbuilding businesses.

106 AND 106-107 FERRARI FAITHFUL WERE DISAPPOINTED IN THE COMPANY'S 275 GTB4 MODEL SHOWN AT PARIS IN 1967, SO PININ FARINA TURNED TO ITS YOUNG DESIGNER LEONARDO FIORAVANTI, WHO IN A WEEK CREATED THE DESIGN OF THE CAR'S SUCCESSOR, THE 365 GTB4 "DAYTONA".

107 TOP TODAY, LEONARDO FIORAVANTI AND HIS SONS HAVE THEIR OWN DESIGN CONSULTING BUSINESS, AND CREATED THE FLIP-TOP ROOF FOR THE NEW FERRARI 575 SUPERAMERICA.

107 BOTTOM LEONARDO FIORAVANTI DID MORE THAN JUST TOUCH THE FERRARI 365 GTB4 BB BERLINETTA BOXER, HE DESIGNED BOTH THAT CAR AND ITS MID-ENGINED INSPIRATION, THE P6 PROTOTYPE PARKED NEXT TO IT, AS WELL AS SIX OTHER FERRARIS.

108 TOP FERRARI PRODUCED THE 365 GTB4 FROM 1969 TO 1974. THE CAR WAS KNOWN AS THE "DAYTONA" AFTER FERRARIS FINISHED FIRST, SECOND AND THIRD IN THE 24-HOUR RACE AT DAYTONA INTERNATIONAL SPEEDWAY IN FLORIDA IN 1967.

108-109 LEONARDO FIORAVANTI'S FIRST ASSIGNMENT AT PININFARINA WAS TO CREATE THE CAR THAT WOULD BEAR THE NAME OF THE LATE SON OF ENZO FERRARI. THE CAR WAS THE 206 GT "DINO," THE FIRST ROAD-GOING MID-ENGINE FERRARI. SHOWN HERE IS THE 1970 "DINO."

109 TOP A DRAWING OF THE CAR THAT WOULD BECOME THE FERRARI 365 GTB4 DAYTONA.

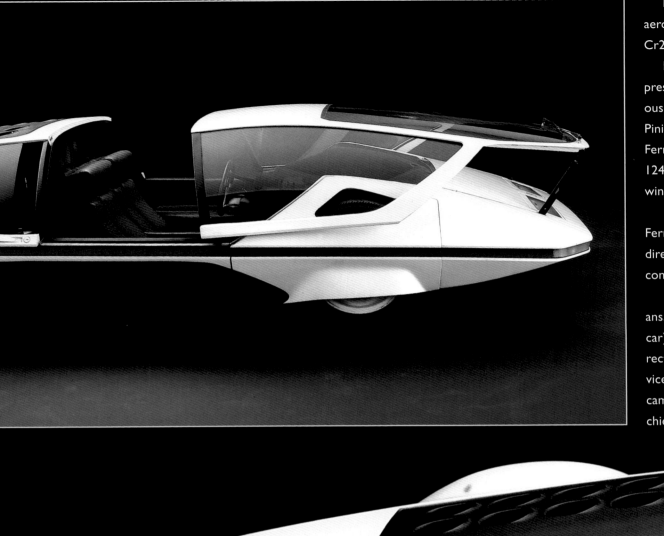

In the 1970s Pininfarina took automotive aerodynamics to the extreme with its Modulo, Cr25 and CNR prototypes.

For its 50th anniversary in 1980, Pininfarina presented the Ferrari Pinin, an exotic and luxurious four-door sedan. Production cars created by Pininfarina ranged from the Peugeot 205 to the Ferrari Testarossa and from Pininfarina's own Fiat 124-based Spider Europa roadster to the high-winged Ferrari F-40.

Fioravanti left in 1987 to work directly for Ferrari and, after Enzo's death, to become design director at Fiat until he opened his own design consulting business with his sons.

He was succeeded by two Pininfarina veterans, Lorenzo Ramaciotti for prototype (concept car) construction and Diego Ottina as design director. Ramaciotti would become Pininfarinia's vice president of design in 1988, and in 2007 he came out of retirement to accept a position as chief of design at Fiat.

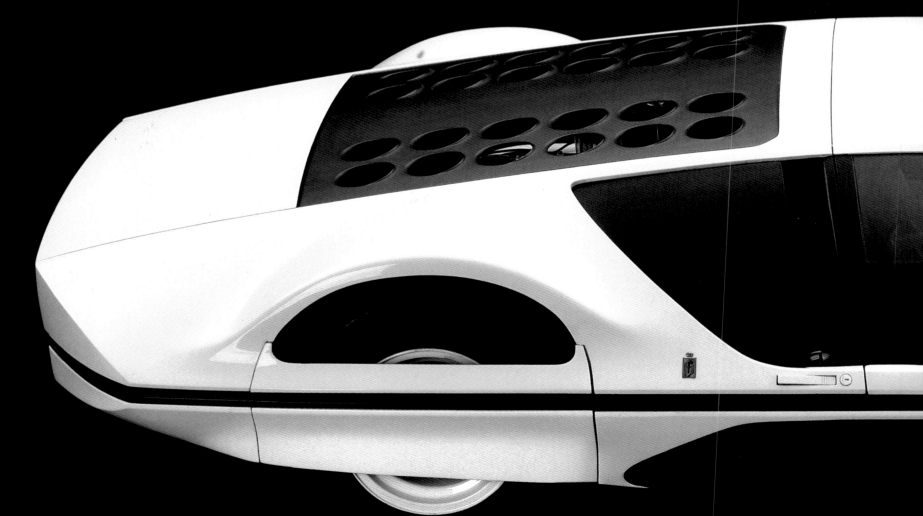

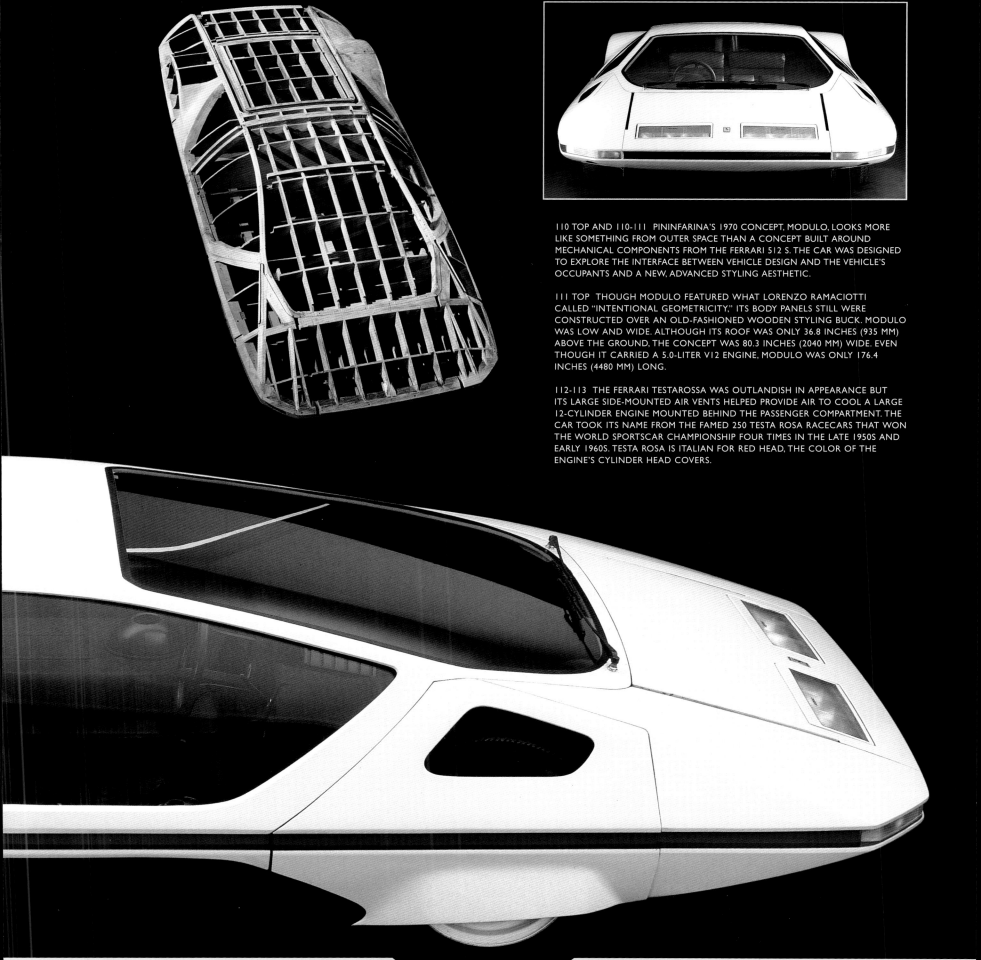

110 TOP AND 110-111 PININFARINA'S 1970 CONCEPT, MODULO, LOOKS MORE LIKE SOMETHING FROM OUTER SPACE THAN A CONCEPT BUILT AROUND MECHANICAL COMPONENTS FROM THE FERRARI 512 S. THE CAR WAS DESIGNED TO EXPLORE THE INTERFACE BETWEEN VEHICLE DESIGN AND THE VEHICLE'S OCCUPANTS AND A NEW, ADVANCED STYLING AESTHETIC.

111 TOP THOUGH MODULO FEATURED WHAT LORENZO RAMACIOTTI CALLED "INTENTIONAL GEOMETRICITY," ITS BODY PANELS STILL WERE CONSTRUCTED OVER AN OLD-FASHIONED WOODEN STYLING BUCK. MODULO WAS LOW AND WIDE. ALTHOUGH ITS ROOF WAS ONLY 36.8 INCHES (935 MM) ABOVE THE GROUND, THE CONCEPT WAS 80.3 INCHES (2040 MM) WIDE. EVEN THOUGH IT CARRIED A 5.0-LITER V12 ENGINE, MODULO WAS ONLY 176.4 INCHES (4480 MM) LONG.

112-113 THE FERRARI TESTAROSSA WAS OUTLANDISH IN APPEARANCE BUT ITS LARGE SIDE-MOUNTED AIR VENTS HELPED PROVIDE AIR TO COOL A LARGE 12-CYLINDER ENGINE MOUNTED BEHIND THE PASSENGER COMPARTMENT. THE CAR TOOK ITS NAME FROM THE FAMED 250 TESTA ROSA RACECARS THAT WON THE WORLD SPORTSCAR CHAMPIONSHIP FOUR TIMES IN THE LATE 1950S AND EARLY 1960S. TESTA ROSA IS ITALIAN FOR RED HEAD, THE COLOR OF THE ENGINE'S CYLINDER HEAD COVERS.

114 TOP LEFT AND 114-115 BOTTOM PININFARINA WORKED WITH AERODYNAMICS EXPERTS FROM TURIN POLYTECHNIC UNIVERSITY ON THE DETAILS OF THIS 1969 CONCEPT VEHICLE. THE CAR'S WIDE BUT THIN MOUTH ACTS AS A DYNAMIC AIR INTAKE FOR THE OIL COOLERS AND THE PASSENGER COMPARTMENT. THE COVERS FOR THE RETRACTING HEADLAMPS INCLUDE AIR VENTS TO COOL THE CAR'S FRONT BRAKES.

114-115 TOP THE CAR STANDS LESS THAN A METER HIGH AT 982 MM (38.6 INCHES).

115 TOP RIGHT THE REAR SECTION OF THE BODYWORK AND THE CANOPY OVER THE PASSENGER COMPARTMENT TIP OPEN TO PROVIDE ACCESS TO THE 12-CYLINDER ENGINE AND THE SEATS.

KEN OKUYAMA

Beginning in 1989, Pininfarina would unveil another stunning series of concept cars, including the Ferrari-powered, Opel-based Chronos, a succession of Ethos concepts that combined low emissions with high emotional appeal, and the Peugeot-powered Nautilus luxury sedan. Even Pininfarina production designs such as the Peugeot 406 coupe and Alfa Romeo Spider and GTV (coupe). And, of course, there were more Ferraris, including the F50 and 360 Modena. Ken Okuyama, a Japanese-born but American-educated designer, joined Pininfarina after working at General Motors and Porsche. He would draw not only the Ferrari "rossa" concept to celebrate Pininfarinia's 70th anniversary in 2000, but the Ferrari Enzo supercar in 2002. Okuyama left Pininfarina to lead the transportation design department at the prestigious Art Center College of Design in Pasadena, California, but returned two years later as Pininfarina's creative director and designer of the Maserati Birdcage concept on the occasion of the 75th anniversary of Pininfarina's company.

116 TOP AND 116-117 BORN IN JAPAN AND EDUCATED IN THE UNITED STATES, KEN OKUYAMA LED PININFARINA DESIGNERS AT THE TURN OF THE 21ST CENTURY, WHEN AUTOMOTIVE DESIGNERS WITH ASIAN HERITAGE WERE EMERGING STARS ON A GLOBAL STAGE. THE FERRARI "ROSSA" CONCEPT VEHICLE WAS DESIGNED TO CELEBRATE PININFARINA'S 70TH ANNIVERSARY. THE STYLING DREW ON SOME FAMILIAR PININFARINA/FERRARI CUES, SUCH AS THE FRONT-MOUNTED 12-CYLINDER ENGINE, BUT ALSO FORESHADOWED NEW DESIGN DIRECTIONS FOR THE PARTNERSHIP'S FUTURE.

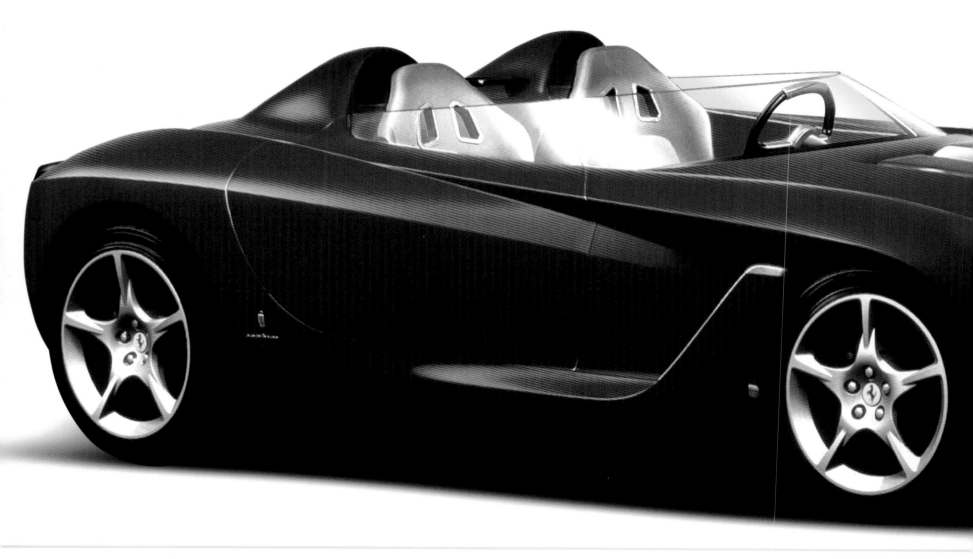

117 TOP LEFT IN 1991, PININFARNIA PRESENTED THE GENERAL MOTORS CHRONOS CONCEPT CAR AT THE NORTH AMERICAN INTERNATIONAL AUTO SHOW IN DETROIT. THE CAR HAD A TWIN-TURBOCHARGED V6 ENGINE MOUNTED IN FRONT, A REMOVABLE HARDTOP AND CELEBRATED THE GM/PININFARINA RELATIONSHIP THAT DATED BACK TO A 1931 CADILLAC V16 SPIDER CREATED FOR THE MAHARAJAH OF ORCCHA AND INCLUDED SEVERAL CADILLAC CONCEPTS IN THE 1950S AND THE CADILLAC ALLANTE MODEL IN THE 1980S.

117 TOP AND CENTER RIGHT ETABETA WAS A 1996 CONCEPT DESIGNED BY PININFARINA FOR THE ITALIAN NATIONAL RESEARCH COUNCIL. THE CAR WAS INTENDED FOR URBAN USE, WAS BASED AROUND A LOW-EMISSIONS HYBRID POWERTRAIN AND CONSTRUCTED ENTIRELY OF RECYCLABLE MATERIALS.

117 BOTTOM RIGHT ETABETA WAS DESIGNED TO PROVIDE MODULAR ASSEMBLY FROM BODY PANELS MADE OF RECYCLABLE MATERIALS. IT ALSO WAS DESIGNED WITH A REAR SECTION THAT TELESCOPED 7.8 INCHES (200 MM) TO PROVIDE ADDITIONAL CARGO CAPACITY.

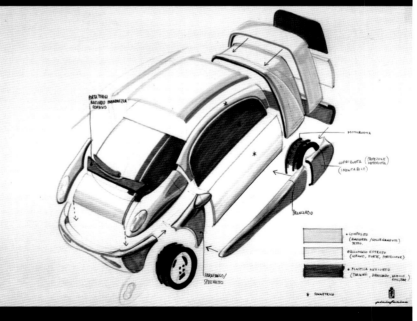

118 TOP MEMBERS OF THE FERRARI FORMULA ONE RACING TEAM WERE DRAWN INTO THE DEVELOPMENT OF THE ENZO FERRARI, WITH F1 RACING CHAMPION MICHAEL SCHUMACHER HELPING WITH TEST-DRIVING DUTIES.

118-119 TEN YEARS AFTER ENZO FERRARI'S DEATH, THE COMPANY THAT BEARS HIS NAME BEGAN WORK ON A NEW CAR THAT WOULD SURPASS THE F40 AND F50 AS THE ULTIMATE SPORTS CAR, A ROAD-GOING VEHICLE WITH ELEMENTS OF A FORMULA ONE RACER AND A STEALTH FIGHTER JET. THAT CAR WOULD BEAR FERRARI'S OWN NAME, AND THUS THE 2002 ENZO FERRARI.

119 TOP LEFT UNLIKE THE HIGH-WINGED F40 AND F50, THE ENZO'S WING IS MORE DISCREET, RISING UPWARD ONLY AT HIGHER SPEEDS TO PROVIDE THE DOWNFORCE NEEDED TO KEEP A CAR STABLE AT SPEEDS OF 350 KM/H (217 MILES PER HOUR).

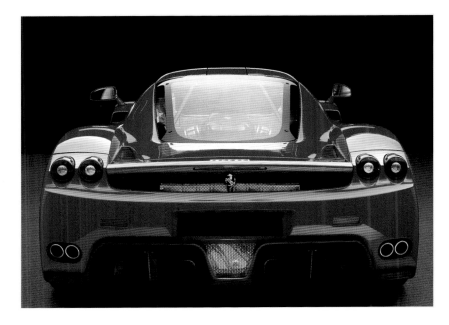

119 TOP RIGHT KEN OKUYAMA'S DESIGN WAS NOT ONLY AESTHETICALLY PLEASING, BUT AERODYNAMICALLY FUNCTIONAL AS WELL, WITH UNDER-CAR TUNNELS HELPING TO CREATE ROAD-GRIPPING DOWNFORCE. WITH A 6.0-LITER V12 ENGINE GENERATING 660 HORSEPOWER, THE ENZO SPRINTS TO 200 KM/H (124 MILES PER HOUR) IN 9.5 SECONDS.

120 TOP THE BIRDCAGE 75TH TAKES ITS NAME FROM THE FAMOUS "BIRDCAGE" MASERATI RACECARS OF A BYGONE ERA. THE CARS WERE SO-CALLED BECAUSE OF THEIR INTRICATE NETWORKED TUBULAR-FRAME CHASSIS. THE NEW BIRDCAGE WAS A CAR AND A HI-TECH SCULPTURE WITH MOTOROLA JOINING PININFARINA AND MASERATI TO ENVISAGE FUTURE TECHNOLOGIES FOR THE ROAD.

120-121 BIRDCAGE 75TH WAS THE OFFICIAL NAME OF A PININFARINA CONCEPT CAR CREATED IN 2005 FOR THE COMPANY'S 75TH ANNIVERSARY AND WAS DESIGNED TO RECALL THE EXTREME SPORTS CAR OF THE 1950S, '60S AND EARLY '70S, INCLUDING THE MASERATI A6 GCS, WITH SIX CARS PRODUCED IN THE MID-150S, FOUR OF THEM WITH COUPE BODIES DESIGNED BY PININ FARINA.

121 TOP THIS DRAWING HINTS AT THE CAR'S PERFORMANCE POTENTIAL WITH A FLAME-LIKE REPRESENTATION OF THE EXHAUST EMERGING FROM THE STACKED AND CENTRALLY POSITIONED TAIL PIPES. THE POWERTRAIN FOR THE CONCEPT INCLUDES A MORE THAN 700-HORSEPOWER V12 ENGINE BORROWED FROM THE MASERATI MC12 SUPERCAR. THE TOP HALF OF THE CAR IS TRANSPARENT, ALLOWING THE VARIOUS MECHANICAL COMPONENTS TO BE SHOWCASED AND GIVING THE DRIVER AND OCCUPANT OUTSTANDING VISIBILITY AS WELL. THE CAR MADE ITS DEBUT AT THE GENEVA MOTOR SHOW IN 2005.

ITALIAN JOBS:
THE GRAND MASTER
GIORGETTO GIUGIARO

THE WORLD'S BEST STAYS MOTIVATED BY LOOKING DAILY AT HIS "ERRORS"

*J*ust before the close of the 20th century, an international panel of automotive writers and editors was assembled to select the most important car designer of what many consider to be the automotive century — the century during which the automobile had more impact on society than perhaps any other invention. That jury of more than 130 experts from more than 30 nations selected Giorgetto Giugiaro.

Grandson of an artist who painted frescoes in Italian churches and in the homes of the wealthy and son of an artist who did oil painting as well as frescoes, Giorgetto Giugiaro learned at an early age how to exploit light and shadow and the nuance of surface. When Giorgetto was 14, Mario Giugiaro encouraged his son to move from the family's hometown at Garessio, a village located in Cuneo province, between Monaco and Genoa, and known for its dominating Saracen castle. Mario told his son to go some 75 miles north, to Turin, to study art by day and technical drawing at night. Mario was insistent that an artist needed marketable skills as well as artistic passion. As the home of the Savoy dynasty, Turin had a strong appreciation for art and craftsmanship, but as the industrial center of northern Italy, it also needed and could support artists with technical drawing skills.

Giorgetto did as his father suggested, moving to Turin in 1952. To prepare for his formal application to Turin's Academy of Fine Arts, he studied with Eugenio Colmo, a leader in Turin's considerable circle of art and culture. Each year, Colmo staged a showing of his students' work. Giugiaro's presentation included watercolors, some of them of automobiles, and these were so skillfully done that they caught the eye of Colmo's nephew, Dante Giacoso, technical director at automaker Fiat and designer of the Topolino and other cars. Giacosa offered Giugiaro an apprenticeship. Giugiaro accepted, not because

he wanted to design cars, but because he needed money to pay for the supplies he would have to buy for art school. But the young artist soon became fascinated not only by the process of designing cars, but by all the other processes involved in their creation and production. He also became frustrated because his role was such a very small part of those processes.

This situation changed in 1959 when Giugiaro was introduced to Nuccio Bertone at the Turin Motor Show. Bertone ran one of the most famous automotive design studios in the world and asked to see some of Giugiaro's sketches. Giugiaro had not brought any of his work to the show, but dashed off some drawings right there on the stand. Bertone selected one and asked the 21-year-old to work it into more detail and to bring it to him a week later. Giugiaro did, but when Bertone saw the finished art work he became upset, charging that Giugiaro had not done the drawings, that they were much to accomplished for someone of so young and with so little experience. Giugiaro convinced Bertone that the work, indeed, was his. Bertone hired him, and immediately assigned him to the design of not just a small component, but of an entire new car for Alfa Romeo.

Giugiaro's design would become the 1960 Alfa Romeo 2000 Sprint, a car praised for its seemingly perfect proportions. But there was no time for Giugiaro to savor his sudden success; he had to hustle to create a sports coupe, the Gordon-Keeble, for the 1960 Geneva show. The time pressure intensified when Giugiaro was called up for military duty. Because of his artistic skills, he was able to spend much of his time after an initial round of serious Alpine Corps basic training doing portraits for officers and their families while stationed at a barracks some 40 miles south of Turin. With Bertone shuttling back and forth with new assignments and to pick up Giugiaro's sketches, the young soldier styled a succession of sports coupes – the Ferrari 250 GT, the Aston Martin DB4 GT Jet, the BMW 32000 CS, the Maserati 5000 GT and the ASA 1000 GT – all while on active duty!

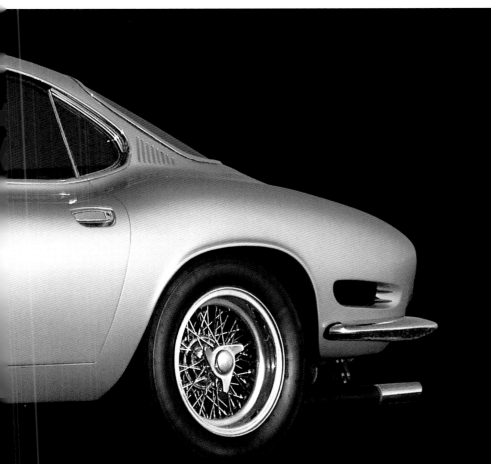

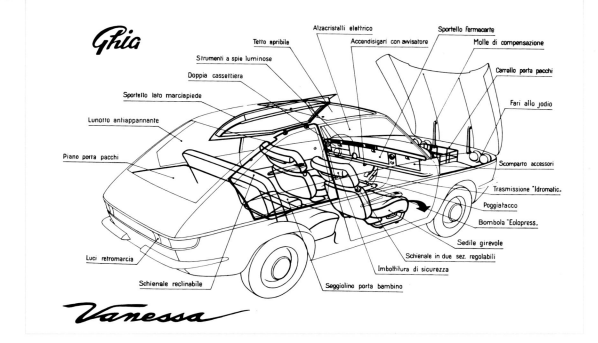

Ghia

Tetto apribile
Alzacristalli elettrico
Accendisigari con avvisatore
Sportello fermacarte
Molle di compensazione
Strumenti a spie luminose
Doppia cassettiera
Sportello lato marciapiede
Lunotto antiappannante
Carrello porta pacchi
Fari allo jodio
Piano porta pacchi
Scomparto accessori
Trasmissione "Idromatic.
Poggiatacco
Bombola "Eolopress.
Sedile girevole
Schienale in due sez. regolabili
Luci retromarcia
Imbottitura di sicurezza
Schienale reclinabile
Seggiolino porta bambino

Vanessa

His 16-month stint in the armed services over, Giugiaro returned to Bertone's studio and created an astounding concept vehicle. Testudo was built around mechanical components from the rear-engine Chevrolet Corvair, but instead of that car's chunky body, Giugiaro designed a car that was long and low, with a clean beltline crease punctuating is smoothly curving surface, with delicately thin bumpers, no front grille, pop-up headlamps and a clear canopy roof that was hinged along the base of the windshield.

Bertone and Giugiaro also began design work for the Japanese auto industry, doing projects for Toyo Kogyo before and after it changed its name to Mazda. Giugiaro designed Canguro, a racy Alfa Romeo-based coupe, and the Fiat 850 Spider and began drawings for what would become the Fiat Dino coupe. Someone else would finish the Dino, however. Giugiaro and his wife had their first child and he left Bertone for both more responsibility and more money at Ghia.

Giugiaro started at Ghia in December 1965 and within a year he had created five significant vehicles. The first – shown at Geneva less than four months after Giugiaro joined Ghia – was the Isuzu 117, which would go into production in 1968 and would continue to be built – as the 117 and Florian sedan and wagon – until late spring of 1981. Next came the Turin show and Giugiaro had not

one but two exotic sports cars on display – the De Tomaso Mangusta and the Maserati Ghibli. Less famous but certainly significant were the other two vehicles Giugiaro designed that year. The Rowan Elettrica – named for the new owners of Ghia and its electrical rather than gasoline-fueled power source – was Giugiaro's first small and boxy – though boxy with an artistic flair – economy car.

The other car Giugiaro did that year was the Vanessa, a car presumably designed for women, and Giugiaro says that it was his own wife and child he had in mind as he made his sketches. Based on a Fiat 850 sedan, Vanessa had a larger windows to provide better visibility for parking and other maneuvers. Instead of a rear bench seat, there were two bucket seats designed to provide better protection for children. Instead of the typical fixed rear window, on the passenger's side was a gullwing-style fixture that swung up to ease loading cargo – or even a very young child – into the back seat. Additionally, the driver's seat cushion slid outward to make entry and exit easier in a skirt.

Friction developed between Giugiaro and Alejandro De Tomaso, whose brother-in-law ran the American electronics company that owned Ghia. Giugiaro set up his own design consulting business, Ital Styling, and soon would leave Ghia, working independently until joining with long-time Fiat engineer and production specialist Aldo Manto-

vani to launch SIRP (Italian Society for the Realization of Prototypes), more commonly and later officially known as Ital Design, then Italdesign and eventually Italdesign Giugiaro. The new company was more than a design studio; it would provide design and engineering solutions to the auto industry. Japanese automakers were early clients, with Mantovani and his engineering partners helping Isuzu put the 117 into production. Alfa Romeo offered the firm a contract to design the Alfasud that launched in 1971.

Giugiaro also continued his string of stunning and innovative concept cars, the new company making its auto show debut at Turin in 1968 with the Bizzarrini Manta, which had three seats just ahead of its rear-mounted Chevrolet Corvette engine. To celebrate the success in racing of its 33 Competizione, Alfa asked three coachbuilders to design concepts for the Turin show in 1969. They were Bertone, which did the Carabo, Pininfarina, which did the P33, and Giugiaro, who did the Iguana, and somehow also found time to create the Abarth 1600 concept for the same show. Later that year, Volkswagen contracted Giugiaro to design the car that would replace its venerable Beetle, the Golf that would go into production in 1974. He also was commissioned to do the VW Passat and Scirocco, the Maserati Bora and Merak, the Lotus Esprit and the De Lorean.

127 BOTTOM RIGHT A TECHNICAL DRAWING SHOWS DETAILS OF THE PACKAGING OF THE GOLF, WHICH PROVIDED ROOM FOR PASSENGERS AND CARGO UNDER ITS HATCHBACK ROOFLINE.

128 TOP LEFT GIORGETTO GIUGIARO SITS AT HIS EASEL AS HE SKETCHES THE SHAPE AND DETAILS OF THE VOLKSWAGEN/PORSCHE TAPIRO, WHICH MADE ITS DEBUT IN 1970.

128-129 TOP THE TAPIRO MADE ITS DEBUT AT THE 1970 TURIN MOTOR SHOW. THE FOLLOWING YEAR GIUGIARO SHOWED THE VW/KARMANN CHEETAH CONCEPT AND SOON ALSO HAD AN AUDI KARMANN ASSO DI PICCHE CONCEPT AND PRODUCTION VERSIONS OF THE VW PASSAT, GOLF AND SCIROCCO, A GOLF-BASED SPORTS COUPE.

128-129 BOTTOM TAPIRO WAS BUILT ON THE FLOOR PAN OF THE PORSCHE 914/6 AND THUS WAS BUILT AROUND A 2.4-LITER SIX-CYLINDER ENGINE. BUT UNLIKE THE CHOPPED-BOX DESIGN OF THE PORSCHE, TAPIRO WAS WEDGE SHAPED.

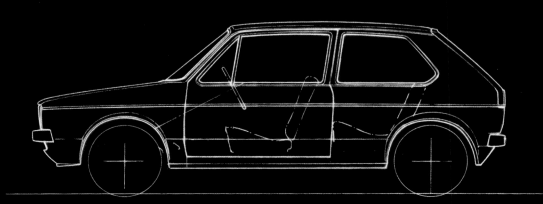

130-131 GIORGETTO GIUGIARO AND HIS SON, FABRIZIO, LOOK AT WHAT REMAINS OF THE TAPIRO CONCEPT, NOW SITTING ELEVATED LIKE A PIECE OF SCULPTURE.

131 TAPIRO'S ARCHITECTURE INCLUDED A FIXED BACKBONE THAT SERVED TO SUPPORT THE TOP OF THE WINDSHIELD AS WELL AS TWO DOORS THAT OPENED GULL-WING STYLE AND THE TWO DOORS THAT PROVIDED ACCESS TO THE CAR'S ENGINE.

By the mid-1970s, Ital Design also had presented such concept vehicles as the Porsche Tapiro, Alfasud Caimano, Audi Karmann Asso di Picche, Maserati Boomerang, Hyundai Pony Coupe (signaling the start of a long-term relationship with the South Korean automaker) and the New York Taxi, a concept for the Museum of Modern Art that presented Giugiaro's ideas for a small but roomy six-seat urban vehicle solution that could easily accommodate someone in a wheelchair or baby stroller.

Ital Design not only designed but built the M1 for BMW. It designed the Lancia Delta, the Audi 80, and what many claim was the inspiration for the minivan, NY Taxi-inspired Lancia Megagamma concept. In 1982, Giugiaro would take the minivan to new levels with the tiny but tall and double-decker looking Capsula.

A decade later, he would turn minivan into maxivan with his Columbus concept.

132 TOP IN 1976, THE MUSEUM OF MODERN ART STAGED AN EXHIBITION OF POTENTIAL NEW NEW YORK TAXI DESIGNS AND GIUGIARO CREATED THIS ALFA ROMEO-BASED VEHICLE COMPLETE WITH A REMOVABLE SLIDE TO MAKE IT EASIER TO ENTER WITH A WHEELCHAIR OR CHILDREN'S STROLLER.

132 BOTTOM GIUGIARO AND HIS TEAM WORK ON A WOODEN SEATING BUCK, WHICH DESIGNERS BUILD TO ASSESS THE INTERIOR SPACE IN THEIR DESIGNS BEFORE COMMITTING TO BUILDING FULL-SIZE VEHICLE MODELS.

There were designs for Renault, Saab, Fiat, Subaru, Toyota and others — and more envelope-pushing concepts — Machimoto, the part car/part motorcycle — and, in 1988, Asgard, Aspid, Aztec, which were as stunning for their day as Bertone's B.A.T.s had been some three decades earlier. A few years later, Giugiaro's 26-year-old son, Fabrizio, made his design debut with his own Nazca concept trio.

The proposed revival of Bugatti took the form of several gorgeous concepts of the course of several years in the 1990s, and they were joined by more production vehicles as well as concepts including the Jaguar Kensington, Lucciola, Lamborghini Cala, Formula 4 and Formula Hammer, Alfa Romeo Scighera and Volkswagen W12 Synchro. Late in the decade, Italdesign celebrated its 30th anniversary with the Structura concept with its aluminum space frame external skeleton.

133 TOP GIUGIARO IS THE SON AND GRANDSON OF ARTISTS, AND IS SKILLED IN SKETCHING IN VARIOUS MEDIA, INCLUDING CHALK. HERE HE WORKS ON A RENDERING OF THE FIAT PANDA.

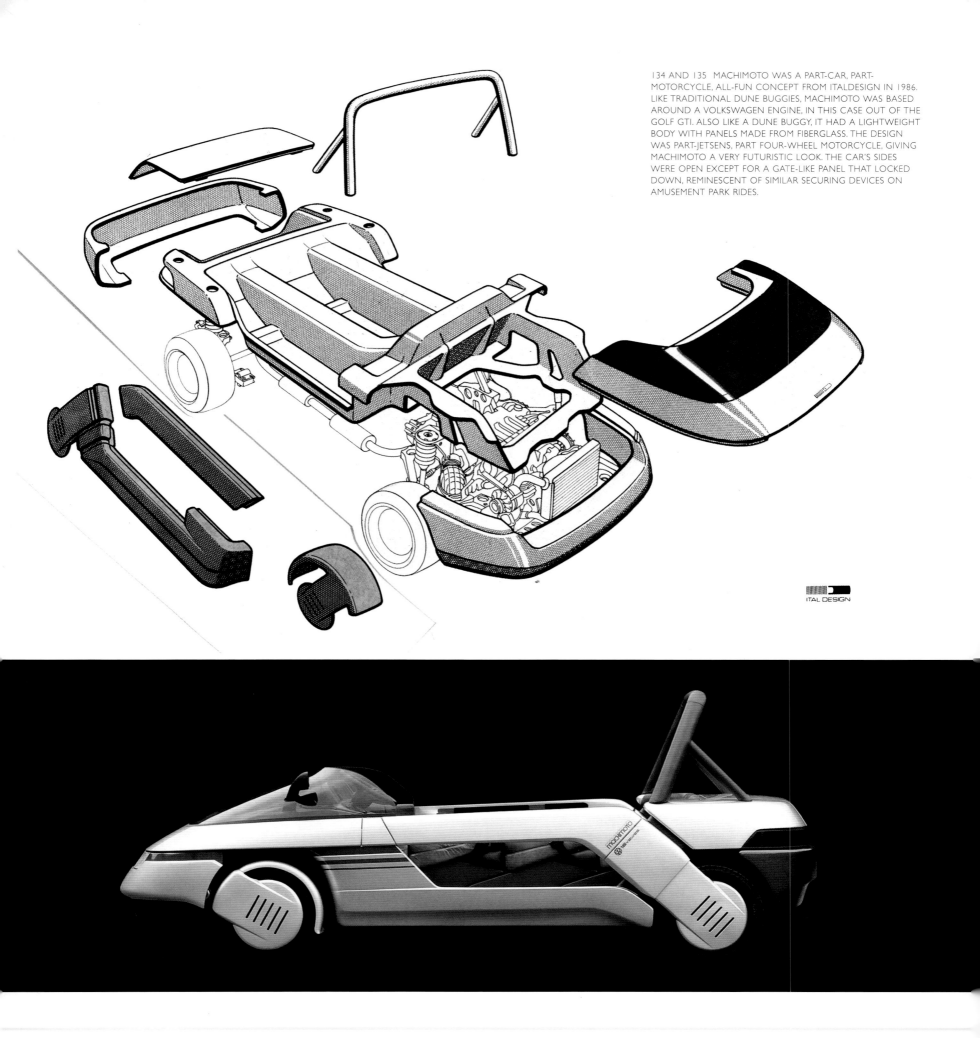

134 AND 135 MACHIMOTO WAS A PART-CAR, PART-MOTORCYCLE, ALL-FUN CONCEPT FROM ITALDESIGN IN 1986. LIKE TRADITIONAL DUNE BUGGIES, MACHIMOTO WAS BASED AROUND A VOLKSWAGEN ENGINE, IN THIS CASE OUT OF THE GOLF GTI. ALSO LIKE A DUNE BUGGY, IT HAD A LIGHTWEIGHT BODY WITH PANELS MADE FROM FIBERGLASS. THE DESIGN WAS PART-JETSENS, PART FOUR-WHEEL MOTORCYCLE, GIVING MACHIMOTO A VERY FUTURISTIC LOOK. THE CAR'S SIDES WERE OPEN EXCEPT FOR A GATE-LIKE PANEL THAT LOCKED DOWN, REMINESCENT OF SIMILAR SECURING DEVICES ON AMUSEMENT PARK RIDES.

ITAL DESIGN

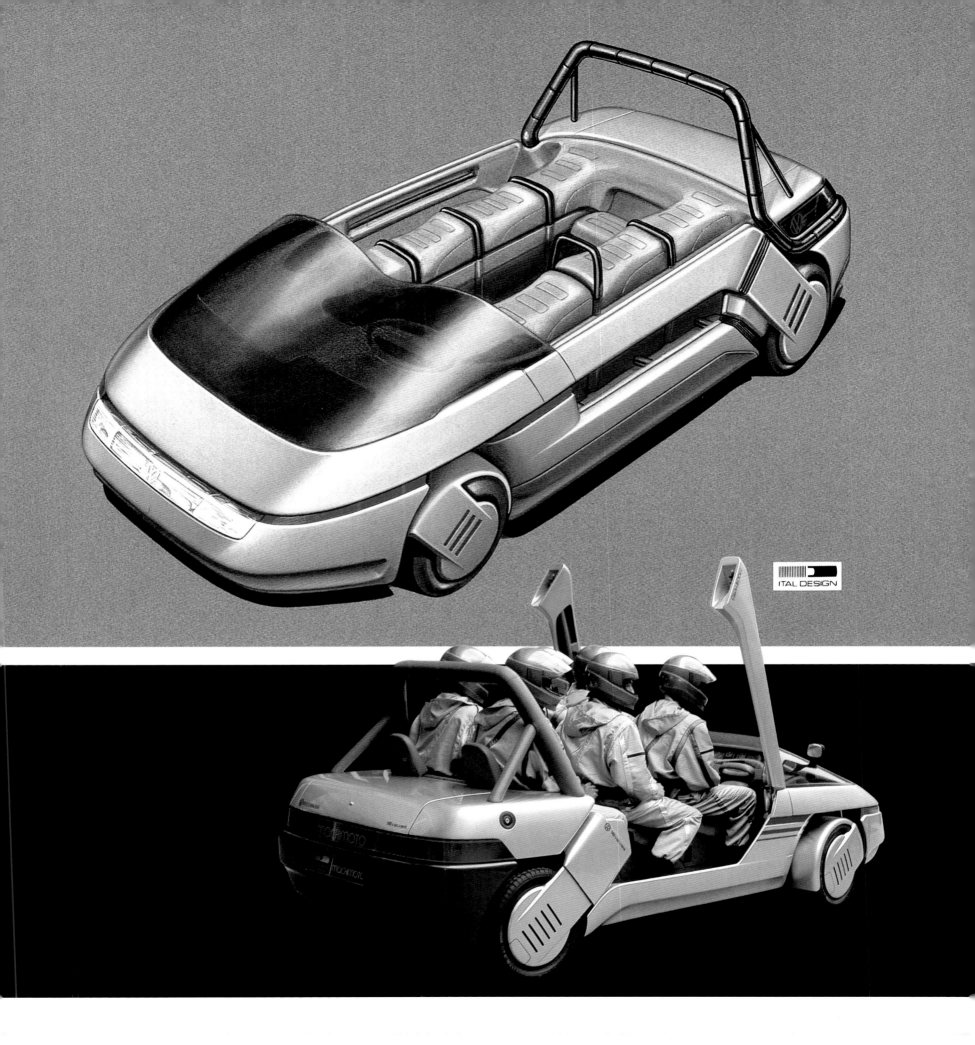

ITAL DESIGN

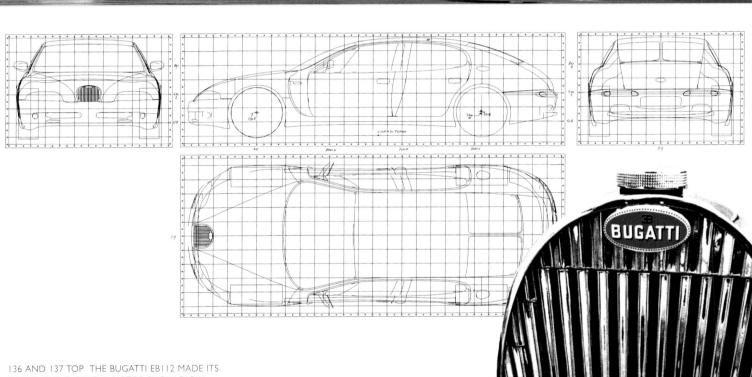

136 AND 137 TOP THE BUGATTI EB112 MADE ITS
DEBUT AT THE GENEVA MOTOR SHOW EARLY
IN 1993. IT WAS A FOUR-DOOR SEDAN THAT
COMBINED LUXURY WITH SPORTS CAR DYNAMICS
AND STYLING.

137 CENTER THE PACKAGING SKETCHES SHOW
DETAILS OF THE BUGATTI EB112 FROM SEVERAL
VIEWS. SOMEHOW, DESIGNERS ARE BLESSED WITH
AN ARTISTIC EYE THAT ALLOWS THEM TO SEE SUCH
DRAWINGS AND TO PROJECT THEM INTO THREE-
DIMENSIONAL AUTOMOTIVE SCULPTURE.

137 BOTTOM WHEN ROMANO ARTIOLI DECIDED
TO RESURRECT BUGATTI AS A MODERN BRAND,
GIUGIARO WAS COMMISSIONED TO CREATE A
SERIES OF INSPIRATIONAL CONCEPT CARS, WHICH
ITALDESIGN DID FROM 1993 UNTIL 1999,
INCLUDING THE EB112, SHOWN HERE AS
AN ARTIST'S ILLUSTRATION.

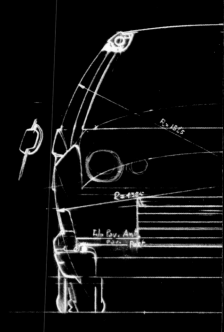

138 TOP LEFT LUCCIOLA WAS A 1993 CONCEPT DESIGNED AROUND A HYBRID POWERTRAIN AND DESIGNED TO BE A FUN IF COMPACT CAR FOR USE AROUND TOWN. IT'S INTERIOR WAS DESIGNED FOR EASY CHANGES IN SEAT POSITIONS AND COLORFUL COVERINGS. FRONT SEATS COULD SWIVEL TO FACE THE REAR, WHERE REAR SEATS COULD BE ELEVATED TO PROVIDE A VIEWING PLATFORM WITH THE PASSENGER'S HEAD EXTENDING ABOVE THE ROOFLINE.

138 CENTER LEFT LUCCIOLA WAS DESIGNED AS A PLAYFUL WAY TO SUCCUMB TO THE SEDUCTION OF LEISURE TIME. SEATS NOT ONLY SWIVELED, BUT COULD BE FOLDED FLAT FOR A SNOOZE OR, WITH THE TOP OPEN, FOR RECLINING IN THE SUNLIGHT.

138 BOTTOM LEFT LUCCIOLA MAY HAVE BEEN SMALL IN DIMENSIONS, BUT IT WAS AS LARGE AS ALL OUTDOORS THANKS TO FABRIC ROOF PANELS THAT SLID OPEN.

138-139 TOP BY USING AN EXTERNAL SPACEFRAME CHASSIS, ITALDESIGN'S STRUCTURA CONCEPT OF 1998 COULD EXPLORE WAYS TO EXPAND A VEHICLE'S INTERIOR WITHOUT EXPANDING ITS EXTERIOR FOOTPRINT.

138-139 CENTER STRUCTURA WAS A MAJOR PROJECT FOR ITALDESIGN, AND MARKED THE COMPANY'S 30TH ANNVERSIARY. GIUGIARO USED STRUCTURA TO EXPLORE THE INTEGRATION OF DESIGN AND STRUCTURE WITH THE SKELETAL ALUMINUM SPACEFRAME CHASSIS ITSELF BECOMING PART OF THE DESIGN AESTHETIC.

139 BOTTOM GIUGIARO SAW STRUCTURA AS A SHORT BUT TALL AND ROOMY AND LUXURIOUS LIMOSINE-LIKE VEHICLE, ALBEIT A SPORTY PERFORMING LIMO WITH ALL-WHEEL DRIVE DRAWING POWER FROM EITHER VOLKSWAGEN'S W12 OR AUDI'S V8 ENGINE.

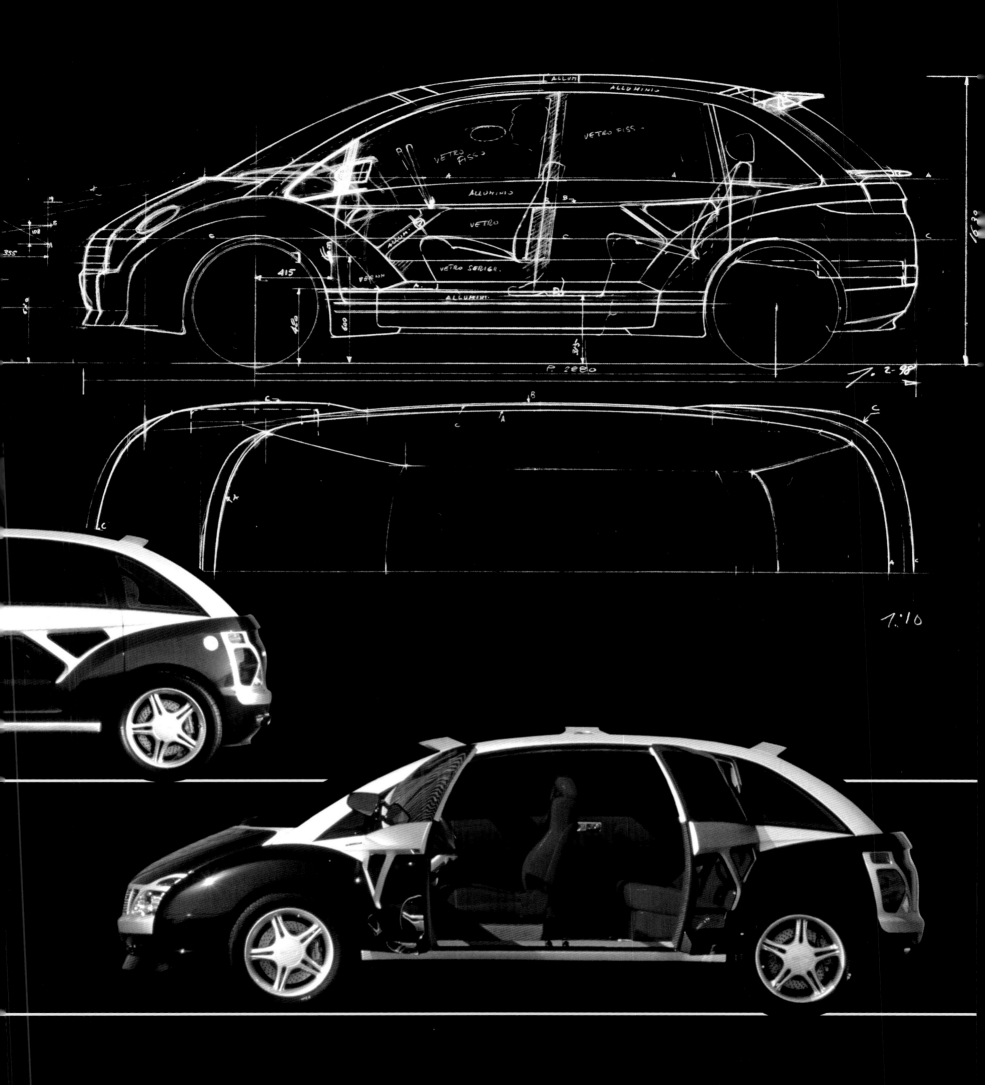

Winning "designer of the century" accolades didn't mean Giugiaro was ready to retire. Not only was he instrumental in Turin's successful bid to become host to the 2006 Winter Olympics, but he and his Italdesign studio presented such concepts as the Maserati Buran, Alfa Romeo Brera, Corvette Moray and Toyota Alessandro – a hybrid vehicle disguised as a supercar. Then, to celebrate his 50 years in automotive design, he created the Ferrari GG50.

Many of Giugiaro's stunning concept vehicles are parked in a showroom not far from his office. They span the decades and evolutions in his style. They would be the focal point of any collection or museum display, and each day, Giugiaro walks past them, though not to gloat on his genius or the beauty of his creations. Instead, he views his work through perhaps the most critical of eyes. "Every day," he says, "it is good to see all the errors."

Giorgetto Giugiaro's eyes are focused not on the past, but on the future, and he is motivated to make it not only better, but also more beautiful.

140 TOP LEFT TO CELEBRATE THE 40TH ANNIVERSARY OF HIS FIRST ALFA ROMEO DESIGN, THE 2000/2600 SPRINT, GIORGETTO GIUGIARO CREATED THE ALFA ROMEO BRERA CONCEPT CAR, WHICH WAS UNVEILED TO INTERNATIONAL ACCLAIM AT THE GENEVA MOTOR SHOW IN 2002.

140 TOP RIGHT ARTIST AND AUTOMOTIVE DESIGN MASTER, GIUGIARO DRAWS BY HAND AS HE WORKS ON VEHICLE DESIGN.

140 CENTER RIGHT THE BRERA TAKES THREE-DIMENSIONAL FORM IN THE SHAPE OF A FULL-SCALE CLAY MODEL.

140 BOTTOM RIGHT SKILLED CRAFTSMEN AT ITALDESIGN COVER THE CLAY MODEL WITH A PLASTIC MATERIAL THAT CAN BE PAINTED TO LOOK LIKE A REAL CAR MADE OF METAL. SUCH MODELS ARE STUDIED AND, WHEN COMPLETED, ARE USED TO CREATE COMPUTER MODELS SO PARTS CAN BE PRODUCED TO CONSTRUCT THE FULLY FUNCTIONAL CONCEPT VEHICLE.

141 TOP DRAWINGS SHOW THE PACKAGING OF THE ALFA ROMEO BRERA CONCEPT CAR, A 2+2 SPORTS COUPE THAT ALFA ROMEO SUBSEQUENTLY PUT INTO SERIES PRODUCTION.

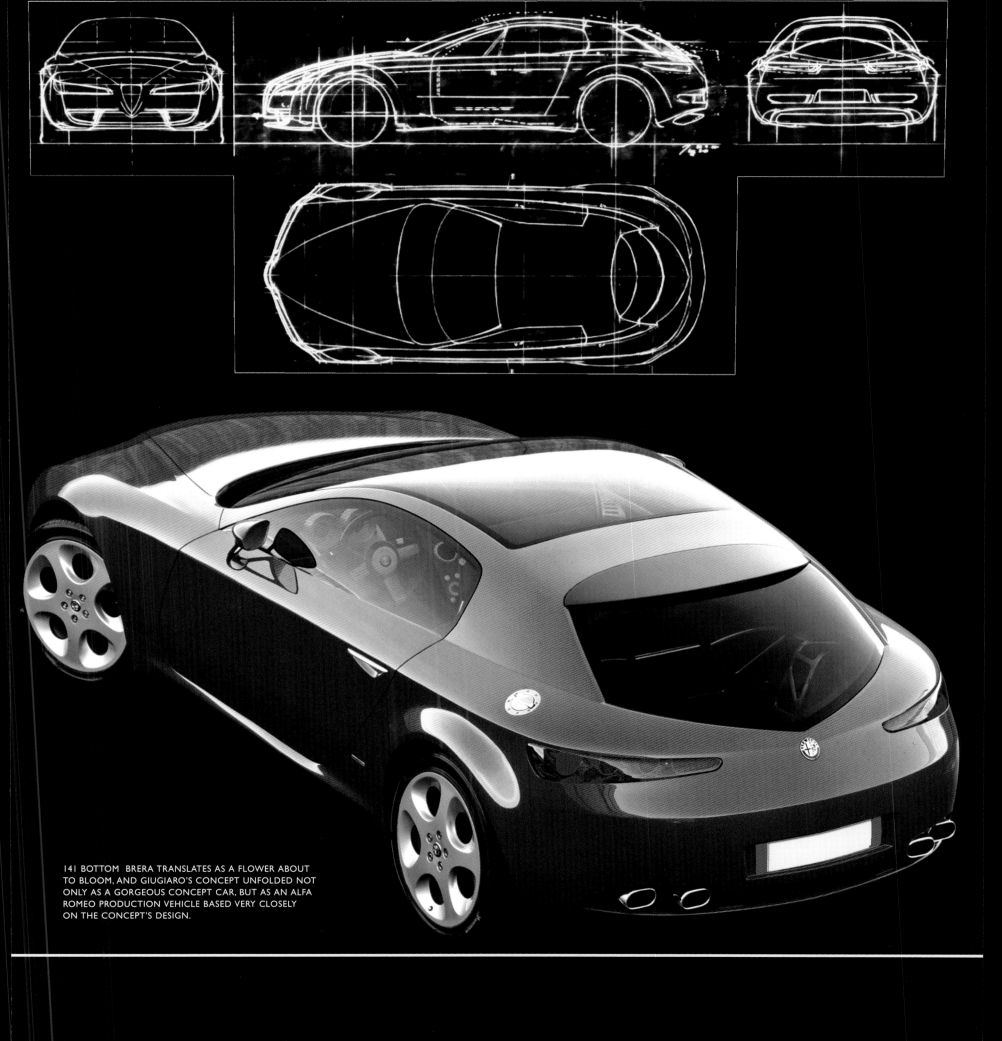

141 BOTTOM BRERA TRANSLATES AS A FLOWER ABOUT
TO BLOOM, AND GIUGIARO'S CONCEPT UNFOLDED NOT
ONLY AS A GORGEOUS CONCEPT CAR, BUT AS AN ALFA
ROMEO PRODUCTION VEHICLE BASED VERY CLOSELY
ON THE CONCEPT'S DESIGN.

142-143 TO CELEBRATE THE 50TH ANNIVERSARY OF
AMERICA'S SPORTS CAR, THE CHEVROLET CORVETTE,
GIUGIARO TOOK THE LEAD IN THE DESIGN OF THE
CORVETTE MORAY, NAMED FOR THE MORAY EEL AND ALSO
NAMED IN KEEPING WITH CHEVROLET'S OWN CORVETTE
CONCEPT VEHICLES, INCLUDING THE MAKO SHARK AND
STING RAY. THE MORAY CONCEPT MADE ITS DEBUT AT THE
GENEVA MOTOR SHOW IN 2003.

143 TOP SEMI-DOME ROOF PANELS ARE HINGED LIKE A
GULL'S WINGS TO AN ARCHED CENTRAL SPINE AND CAN
BE REMOVED TO TRANSFORM THE MORAY FROM A CLOSED
COUPE TO AN OPEN ROADSTER. THE SPLIT-WINDOW EFFECT
ALSO RECALLS THE MOST FAMOUS OF ALL CORVETTES, THE
1963 "SPLIT WINDOW" COUPE.

144-145 IN 2005, GIORGETTO GIUGIARO CELEBRATED HIS 50TH ANNIVERSARY AS AN AUTOMOTIVE DESIGNER BY UNVEILING THE FERRARI GG 50 AT THE TOKYO MOTOR SHOW. ALTHOUGH HE WAS CREDITED WITH THE FERRARI 250 GT WHEN HE WORKED AT BERTONE, GIUGIARO HAD NEVER OFFICIALLY UNDERTAKEN A FULL FERRARI DESIGN UNTIL THE CAR THAT BEARS HIS INITIALS. GIUGIARO'S FERRARI GG 50 IS BUILT OVER THE MECHANICAL COMPONENTS OF FERRARI'S 612 SCAGLIETTI. THE GG 50 HAS ALUMINUM BODYWORK AND IN ADDITION TO BEING A CONCEPT CAR, IS WHAT GIUGIARO DRIVES EVERYDAY, MUCH AS PININ FARINA DROVE HIS LANCIA FLORIDA II OR AS HARLEY EARL OF GENERAL MOTORS USED THE BUICK Y-JOB AND LATER THE LE SABRE CONCEPT AS HIS PERSONAL CAR.

144 BOTTOM AND 145 BOTTOM PACKAGE DRAWINGS STARTED WITH FIXED POINTS FROM THE FERRARI PLATFORM, OVER WHICH GIUGIARO CREATED HIS OWN BODYWORK AND OTHER FEATURES.

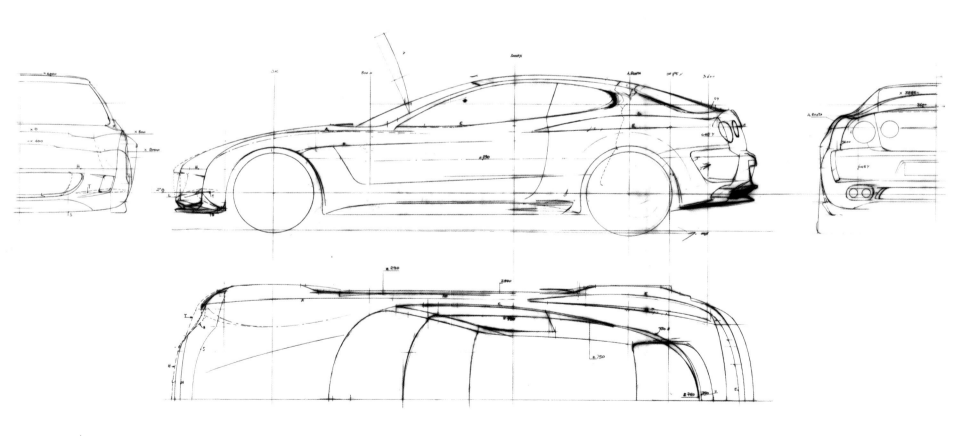

ENGLAND:
FROM EXPORTING CARS
TO EXPORTING DESIGNERS

WILLIAM LYONS

*I*n England, the most notable car designers of the mid-20th century weren't styling specialists at all, but engineers with an eye for what we now would call shrink-wrapping sheetmetal around precisely placed and tuned mechanical components. Thus William Lyons, concerned with the aerodynamics that would enhance performance on the racetrack, designed such gorgeous Jaguars as the XK120, and Alex Issigonis created the Mini, a car that transcended status as an automotive design statement to become a fashion and indeed a cultural icon.

Like several masters of design, Lyons was born into a musical family. He worked as a trainee at Crossley Motors by day and studied engineering at night. With William Walmsley, he founded the Swallow Sidecar Company to build sidecars so motorcycle riders could take a passenger along. In 1925, Lyons bought an Austin Seven but didn't like its design and decided he could do better. With coachbuilder Cyril Holland, he created the Austin Seven Swallow. Others also thought his design was better and orders were taken for 500 such cars. Thus Swallow, builder of sidecars, became Standard Swallow, builder of motorcars. Standard Swallow would change its name to Jaguar after World War II and would build a succession of curvaceous sedans and sports cars, including C-, D- and E-type roadsters

based on Lyons' lines and also strongly influenced and enhanced for motorsports competition by the aerodynamicist Malcolm Sayer.

146-147 TRIUMPH WANTED A POST-WAR SPORTS CAR THAT WAS A LITTLE MORE ELEGANT IN APPEARANCE THAN ITS BRITISH RIVALS, SO WALTER BELGROVE STYLED THE DELIGHTFUL TR2 FOR 1952. THE CAR EVOLVED INTO THE TR3 IN 1955 (A 1960 TR3A IS SHOWN HERE).

148-149 WILLIAM LYONS WAS AN ENGINEER, BUT HE HAD AN ARTIST'S EYE AND CREATED SOME OF THE MOST GORGEOUS AUTOMOBILES IN HISTORY. AMONG THOSE CARS SUCH AS THE 1954 JAGUAR XK120 ROADSTER LAUNCHED IN 1949.

149 TOP WILLIAMS LYONS (SECOND FROM THE RIGHT) IS AMONG THOSE CONGRATULATING PETER WHITEHEAD AND PETER WALKER AFTER THEIR VICTORY IN THE 24 HOURS OF LE MANS RACE IN 1951. THE WINNING JAGUAR XK120 C FINISHED NEARLY 80 MILES AHEAD OF THE COMPETITION, WHICH INCLUDED ENTRIES FROM TALBOT, ASTON MARTIN, HEALEY AND FERRARI, LANCIA, CUNNINGHAM AND PORSCHE.

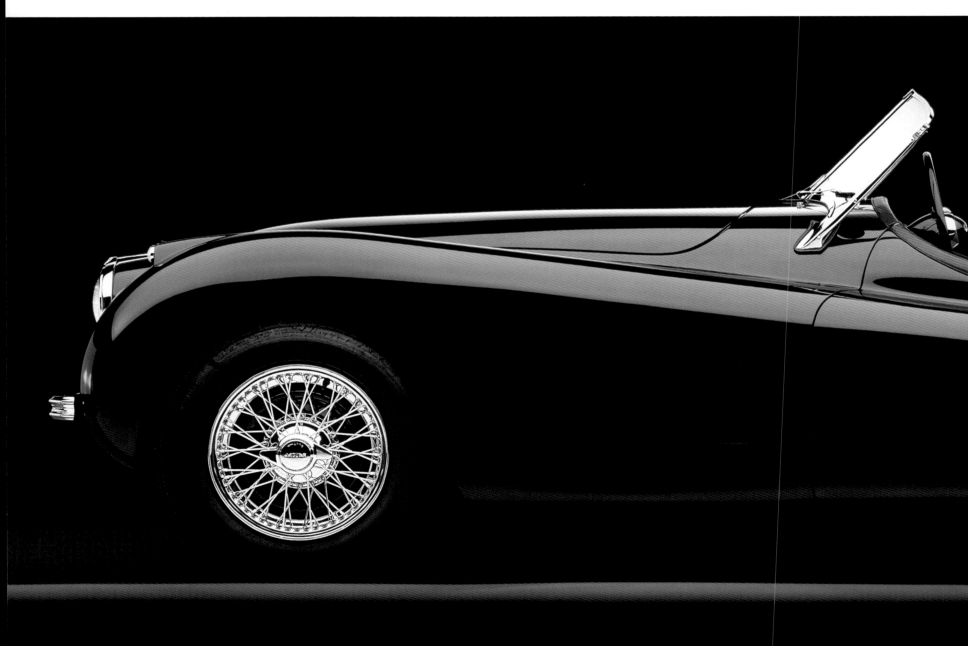

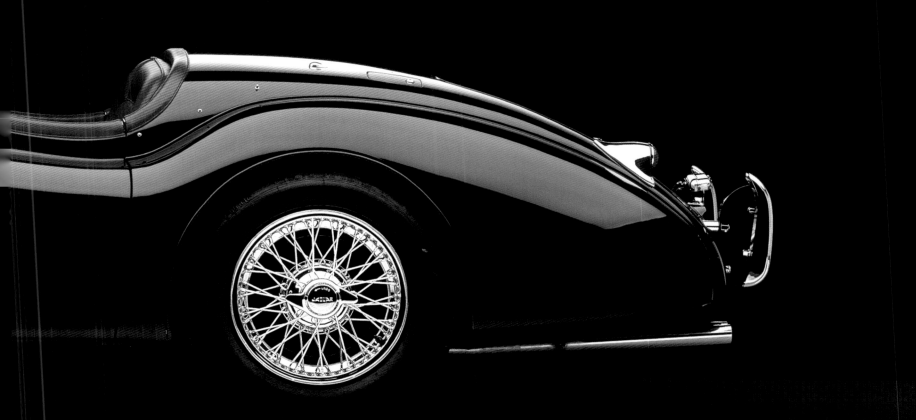

150-151 TOP KEN WHARTON CROSSES THE FINISH LINE TO WIN THE 12-HOUR RACE AT RHEIMS, FRANCE IN 1954 IN A JAGUAR D-TYPE RACER.

150-151 BOTTOM AERODYNAMICIST MALCOM SAYER WORKED WITH WILLIAM LYONS ON THE RACING VERSIONS OF JAGUAR SPORTS CARS. SHOWN HERE IS A 1955 XKD OR D-TYPE RACER.

151 TOP JAGUAR WON THE FERODO TROPHY FOR OUTSTANDING CONTRIBUTION TO BRITISH MOTOR RACING IN 1953. WILLIAM LYONS HOLDS THE TROPHY, PRESENTED BY FERODO'S WILLIAM SMITH (CENTER) AND G.S. SUTCLIFFE (RIGHT).

152 AND 152-153 IN THE EARLY 1960S, LYONS AND JAGUAR PRODUCED ONE OF THE MOST BEAUTIFUL SPORTS CARS EVER, THE E-TYPE. THE CAR WAS AMONG LYONS' LAST DESIGNS. JAGUAR WAS SOLD TO THE BRITISH MOTOR CORPORATION IN 1966, WITH LYONS TAKING THE TITLE OF CHAIRMAN, BUT NO LONGER AS DIRECTLY INVOLVED IN CAR DESIGN AND DEVELOPMENT. THE E-TYPE WAS UNVEILED AT THE GENEVA MOTOR SHOW IN 1961. STYLING WAS BASED ON THE D-TYPE RACECAR.

ALEXANDER ISSIGONIS

Issigonis was born in Turkey. His mother was the daughter of a German brewery owner and his father, though born in Greece, was a British subject who worked as an engineer.

The family spent much of World War I in a German internment camp and young Alexander and his mother fled to England soon after his father died. Issigonis believed that engineering and design were unified and he was particularly fascinated by efficient packaging. With the exception of purpose-built racecars, perhaps no motor vehicle was ever as efficiently packaged as Issigonis' Mini, which he created for the British Motor Corporation in anticipation of the Suez Crisis and the resulting gasoline shortages in Europe.

For England, the Mini filled a role very similar to the Volkswagen "Beetle" in Germany and the Fiat Topolino/500 in Italy by providing a vehicle that took up little room but offered a surprisingly generous amount of space inside.

154 TOP WITH THE SUEZ CRISIS AND GASOLINE SHORTAGES LOOMING, THE BRITISH MOTOR CORPORATION TURNED TO ENGINEER ALEXANDER ISSIGONIS TO CREATE A CAR THAT WOULD BE SMALL AND FUEL EFFICIENT, COMPACT ON THE OUTSIDE BUT ROOMY INSIDE. THAT CAR WAS THE AUSTIN SEVEN, MORE WIDELY KNOWN AS THE "MINI."

154 BOTTOM AN EARLY ADVERTISEMENT FOR THE MORRIS VERSION OF THE MINI, THE MINI-MINOR, PROCLAIMS THE CAR AS "WIZARDRY ON WHEELS." ISSIGONIS' CHALLENGE WAS TO CREATE A CAR NO MORE THAN 10 FEET LONG, FOUR-FEET WIDE AND FOUR-FEET TALL THAT COULD COMFORTABLY CARRY FOUR PEOPLE AND THEIR LUGGAGE.

155 TOP INCREDIBLE INDEED! THIS AUSTIN DISPLAY SHOWCASES JUST HOW MUCH LUGGAGE AND OTHER GEAR COULD BE PACKED INSIDE THE "MINI."

155 BOTTOM THE ORIGINAL MINI REMAINED IN PRODUCTION FOR MORE THAN 40 YEARS. OF THE MORE THAN 5.3 MILLION BUILT, SEVERAL WERE USED FOR MOTOR RACING. HERE, JOHN COOPER AND THE COMPETITIONS DEPARTMENT PREPARE MINIS FOR THE 1966 MONTE CARLO RALLY, WHICH THE UNDER-POWERED BUT DYNAMICALLY DELIGHTFUL MINIS WON IN 1965, 1966 AND AGAIN IN 1967.

CAR WITH A SURPRISING AMOUNT OF ROOM INSIDE, BUT ALSO A CAR WITH STYLE THAT, WHILE UNUSUAL, WAS NONETHELESS AESTHETICALLY PLEASING IN ITS OVERALL FORM AND PRACTICALITY.

157 TOP ALEXANDER ISSIGONIS' ORIGINAL SKETCHES SHOW HIS IDEAS FOR (FROM LEFT) SUCH THINGS AS THE DETAILS OF THE FUEL-FILLER HOSE, THE CARS TAIL LAMPS AND EVEN THE LICENSE PLATE HOLDER; THE CAR'S INTERIOR WITH COLD-AIR VENTS, DASHBOARD PADDING AND BEAR-SHIFT LEVER; AS WELL AS THE CAR'S BODY WITH ITS FUEL TANK LOCATED IN FRONT BUT UP AND OUT OF THE WAY OF THE ENGINE SHOULD THE CAR BE INVOLVED IN A CRASH.

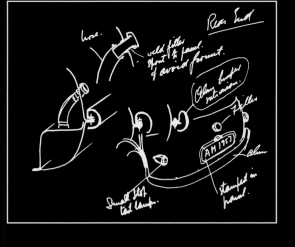
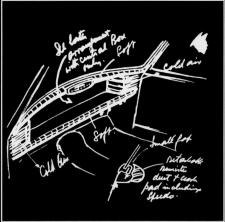
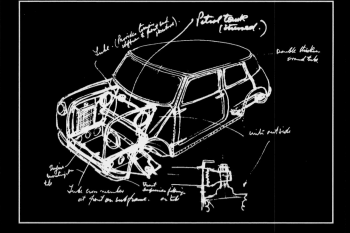

AFTER WORLD WAR II

In the years immediately after World War II, English was second only to the United States in automotive production, with the bulk of that output, including Lyons' Jaguars and Issigonis' Mini, destined for export to overseas markets. Two of England's largest mass-market automakers, Ford and Vauxhall, had been controlled for many decades by American automakers Ford and General Motors, respectively, and by the mid-1960s America's Chrysler Corporation had bought Britain's Rootes Group, an amalgamation of once proudly independent automakers such as Sunbeam. Smaller automakers, such as MG, Triumph and Healey, specialized in low-volume production of sports cars.

But the boom was short-lived as the British auto industry was struck from two sides. One on hand, there was increasingly strong competition from overseas automakers, particularly from Japan. On the other, the British government's economic and social policies made manufacturing in England ever more expensive and difficult. British car companies either closed or consolidated or, in many cases, simply sold out to foreign ownership, such as Rover to Honda; Jaguar, Aston Martin and Land Rover to Ford; Rolls-Royce to BMW; and Bentley to Volkswagen. In a sad irony, the demise of the British auto industry coincided with the rise of British automotive design. Like Jaguar and Mini, many British cars had been "styled " by engineers, or, in the case of Rolls-Royce or Bentley, often carried bodies created by British coachbuilding specialists, or, in later cases, took their styling from Italian design houses. For example, despite its long and proud history, Rolls-Royce didn't have a real in-house designer until after World War II, when it hired John Blatchley from the London-based coachbuilder Gurney Nutting to

design vehicles such as the Silver Dawn, Silver Cloud and Silver Shadow. Blatchley also had influence over design at Bentley, which had been part of the Rolls family for two decades.

158-159 LIKE SO MANY BRITISH SPORTS CARS OF THE ERA, THE AUSTIN HEALEY 100 (A 1956 100M LE MANS MODEL IS SHOWN HERE) WAS DESIGNED FOR THE AMERICAN MARKET, TO FILL A GAP BETWEEN BASIC MGS AND EXPENSIVE JAGUARS. THE HEALEY 100 WAS DESIGNED BY GERRY COKER AND WAS PUBLICIZED BY A SERIES OF SPEED-RECORD RUNS BY COMPANY HEAD DONALD HEALEY.

159 TOP AFTER RELYING ON COACHBUILDERS FOR MUCH OF ITS CARS' BODYWORK, ROLLS-ROYCE BROUGHT JOHN BLATCHLEY OF COACHBUILDER GURNEY NUTTING IN HOUSE TO CREATE BODIES SUCH AS THE ONE FOR THIS 1963 SILVER CLOUD III COUPE.

PETER STEVENS

But while Britain built and exported fewer and fewer cars, it began producing and exporting people who designed cars. Their training took place at the Royal College of Art in London and at other schools that added automotive design instruction to the curriculum. For many years, the British school system had provided young men with a very practical, almost engineering-oriented education. Those who could draw and had an interest in the three-dimensional art of the automobile now could combine the two at places such as the Royal College of Art. As a result, such graduates became very attractive to the world's automakers. Among the first transportation design graduates from the college was Peter Stevens, who worked at Ford, then designed the Lotus Espirit and Elan, the Jaguar XJR-15 and, in the early 1990s, the amazing McLaren F1.

160-161 TOP PETER STEVENS WAS AMONG THE FIRST GRADUATES TO HAVE STUDIED TRANSPORTATION DESIGN AT THE ROYAL COLLEGE OF ART. AMONG HIS FIRST POST-GRADUATE PROJECTS WAS A HANDLE FOR THE SLIDING SUNROOF ON A FORD GRANADA, BUT HE SOON WAS WORKING AT LOTUS, WHERE HE UPDATED THE ESPIRIT, A MODEL ORIGINALLY DESIGNED IN 1972 BY GIORGETTO GIUGIARO.

160-161 BOTTOM AND 161 TOP STEVENS' MOST FAMOUS DESIGN WAS THE EXOTIC BODY FOR THE MCLAREN F1, A CAR BASED ON FORMULA ONE RACING TECHNOLOGY AND CAPABLE OF SPEEDS IN EXCESS OF 240 MILES PER HOUR IN STANDARD GUISE.

ROYAL COLLEGE GRADUATES

Among the early design stars emerging from the Royal College of Art was Geoff Lawson, who joined Jaguar in 1984, a year after the death of William Lyons. Lawson would be responsible for creating cars that reflected and updated the style and grace that had marked the company's products some 30 years earlier. Lawson died in 1999 but the quality of Jaguar design continued under fellow Royal College of Art alumnus Ian Callum, who had been design director at Aston Martin. Callum's brother, Moray, also a graduate of the college, would become head designer for Japanese automaker Mazda, making the Scottish-born Callums the first brothers to head design departments at two international automakers (Moray Callum later became a design director for Ford, which holds a controlling interest in Mazda).

Both of the Callum brothers had worked for a period after college for Ghia, and in 2003 another Royal College of Art graduate and former Ghia and Ford designer, David Wilkie, became design director for another of the legendary Italian styling companies, Stile Bertone.

Among the many other Royal College of Art graduates who left the UK were Turkish-born Murat Gunak, who worked at Mercedes-Benz and Peugeot before becoming head of design for Volkswagen; Ken Melville, a Scotsman who worked at Mercedes-Benz before going to French automaker Renault; Henrik Fisker, Danish born but British educated and designer of the Z8 for BMW, who succeeded Ian Callum at Aston Martin and then founded his own coachbuilding business, Fisker Coachbuild, in southern California. Meanwhile, Simon Cox stayed in the UK to head General Motors' British design studio.

162-163 THE C-XF WAS JAGUAR'S CONCEPT CAR FOR THE 2007 AUTO SHOW SEASON AND PREVIEWED THE NEW 2009 XF MODEL, A FOUR-DOOR SEDAN WITH SLEEK, COUPE-STYLE DESIGN.

163 BEFORE BECOMING DESIGN DIRECTOR AT JAGUAR, ROYAL COLLEGE OF ART GRADUATE IAN CALLUM WAS DESIGN MANAGER AT ASTON MARTIN, WHERE HIS WORK INCLUDED THE LUSCIOUS DB7 COUPE.

PETER HORBURY

One talent such British designers often brought to their non-British employers was an outsider's eye for identifying each company's particular and in many cases previously uncodified design DNA, especially as formerly strong national design influences increasingly gave way to an emphasis on corporate styling and brand identity. For example, said Horbury, "There was a time in the 1960s when people bought a Pininfarina design or a Bertone design or whatever else and then you'd find Austins and Morrises and Peugeots and Fiats looking suspiciously similar [because] you got the house design with whatever badge you were selling."

While working for MGA Developments, a British design consultancy, "what we didn't want to do was to sell everyone of our clients an MGA design or a Peter Horbury design," Horbury recalls. "What we wanted to do was to get into the soul of their company and give them a design which was obviously theirs alone. Companies want a strong identity of their own." When Horbury became design director at Volvo, he revolutionized the styling of vehicles known for being safe if aesthetically uninspiring by discovering and then emphasizing their Swedish and corporate heritages. Horbury believes that being an outsider was cru-

cial to the process. "It wasn't just me drawing a car that's beautiful and saying 'make it,'" Horbury explained of his effort to translate the Volvo brand values into a visual design statement.

His designers studied both national and brand heritage. "Often they have a lot to do with each other anyway," he added. Horbury and his designers looked beyond Volvo to Swedish furniture, architecture, fashion, even the country's landscape for clues to the nation's unique visual identity and for ideas that might make a Volvo vehicle just as unique, if just not quite so box-like. As so often happens in the auto industry, the designers got their chance when the company needed to showcase its gas turbine-electric hybrid powertrain (the Volkswagen New Beetle and Chrysler Neon both were designs presented to the public as a way to showcase new technology). Volvo

executives anticipated putting the new drive system into an existing vehicle and sending it off on the auto show circuit. But Horbury and his design staff saw an opportunity and convinced the company to showcase the technology in a show vehicle, a concept car that would incorporate their new national/corporate design identity. "The head of Volvo saw the clay [model] and said 'I don't like it,'" Horbury recalls. "I told him, 'You will, I promise you.'" The concept would be unveiled at the Paris Motor Show as the ECC – the Environmental Concept Car – and executives wanted to paint it green, to underscore its eco-friendly technology. Horbury said that was too obvious. Instead, he was inspired by a photo he saw on an office wall, a photo of a polar bear with the low sun casting pink and blue light across the ice. "This combination of pink and blue on the white ice, this was it,"

Horbury knew. "This represents the cleanest air in the world." Fortunately, Volvo's paint supplier created a similar effect on the car, "and people got it immediately. It was Scandinavia!" Horbury remembers, and while the powertrain has yet to enter production, the lines of the concept car can be seen in every Volvo since, and those cars, while strongly reflecting Volvo and its Swedish heritage, are selling well and around the world. Horbury is involved in trying to do the same thing with the cars Ford Motor Company designs for its primarily American domestic market. Just as with Volvo in Sweden, he said, "there are certain things about America which are common through the entire land. There's one word that said 'America' to me and its optimism, and it's outgoing and it's faith in the future. People didn't come from all over Europe and other parts of the world be-

cause they thought things were going to get worse. It was always because it was going to get better, and people went from the East Coast to the West in wagon trains not because they were leaving the better life behind. It was always going to get better over the next ridge and then the next ridge and then the next ridge and they never stopped. The future was everything."

164 TOP ROYAL COLLEGE OF ART GRADUATE PETER HORBURY LEFT THE BRITISH ISLES TO BECOME DESIGN DIRECTOR FOR SWEDISH AUTOMAKER VOLVO. HORBURY BELIEVES NON-NATIVE DESIGNERS CAN BRING A FRESH EYE TO HELP IDENTIFY THE SOUL OF AN AUTOMAKER'S STYLING HERITAGE.

164 BOTTOM AND 165 VOLVO HAD A REPUTATION FOR BUILDING SAFE BUT BOXY CARS. HORBURY AND HIS DESIGN STAFF, INCLUDING THOSE WORKING IN A VOLVO STUDIO FAR AWAY IN CALIFORNIA, SAW MORE AESTHETICALLY PLEASING ELEMENTS IN SWEDEN'S DESIGN HERITAGE AND LANDSCAPE AND TRIED TO INCORPORATE THEM INTO AN IMAGE-CHANGING CONCEPT CAR, THE ECC, UNVEILED AT THE PARIS MOTOR SHOW IN 1992.

GERMANY:
THE ENGINEER'S MIND,
THE ARTIST'S EYE

FERDINAND PORSCHE

*I*talian automotive designer Leonardo Fioravanti notes that his long career, which includes the styling of a record number of Ferraris, has been a constant pursuit of beauty. But, he added, beauty is more than merely in the eye of the beholder. He quotes Plato when he said he believes that "Beauty is the splendor of the truth."

For Fioravanti, whether he's designing cars, yachts or buildings, that splendor is produced only when innovative engineering is enfolded within the aesthetic design. That also is the case when it comes to automotive design in Germany with its strong roots in the Bauhaus movement, its belief that form follows function, and an underlying principle that ornaments look best on Christmas trees.

Another considerable influence on German automotive design has been the presence of the autobahns, a series of carefully engineered highways that still disdain speed limits over substantial portions of pavement. Thus aerodynamic efficiency enhanced by precise and well-executed surface treatments have been hallmarks of German automotive design, and have produced their own unique form of beautiful automobiles. It was an engineering team led by Ferdinand Porsche which produced the Volkswagen "Beetle" while Porsche's son, Ferry, an engineer, and his grandson, F.A. "Butzi" Porsche, a designer, created the sports cars that bore the family's name.

169 TOP FERDINAND PORSCHE SHOWS A MODEL OF THE PEOPLE'S CAR TO ADOLF HITLER AT THE FÜHRER'S 40TH BIRTHDAY PARTY.

166-167 MURAT GUNAK, A NATIVE OF TURKEY, A GRADUATE OF THE ROYAL COLLEGE OF ART IN ENGLAND AND FORMER HEAD OF DESIGN AT PEUGEOT, LED THE TEAM AT MERCEDES-BENZ THAT DESIGNED THE MERCEDES-BENZ SLR MCLAREN.

168 TOP A FAMILY'S PRIDE IN ITS NEW VW SHOWS IN THIS ADVERTISEMENT FROM THE LATE 1950S.

168-169 THOUGH OFFICIALLY THE VOLKSWAGEN TYPE ONE, THE CAR DESIGNED BY ENGINEER FERDINAND PORSCHE, WITH ERWIN KOMENDA RESPONSIBLE FOR THE BODY'S BEETLE-LIKE SHAPE, WOULD BECOME KNOWN AROUND THE WORLD SIMPLY AS THE BEETLE AND WOULD SURPASS THE FORD MODEL T AS THE BEST-SELLING VEHICLE OF ALL TIME WITH NEARLY 22 MILLION OF THEM PRODUCED.

170 TOP FERDINAND PORSCHE NEVER CREATED A CAR WITH HIS NAME ON IT, BUT HIS SON, FERRY, AND HIS FRIENDS KARL RABE AND ERWIN KOMENDA, DESIGNED THE PORSCHE 356, SHOWN HERE IN ITS RACY CARRERA GUISE. CARRERA IS THE SPANISH WORD FOR "RACING," AND THE 356 MADE ITS DEBUT AT LE MANS IN 1951.

170 BOTTOM FERDINAND PORSCHE SHOWS A MODEL OF THE CAR THAT BEARS HIS NAME TO HIS GRANDSONS, F.A. PORSCHE (LEFT), WHO WOULD DESIGN THE PORSCHE 911, AND FERDINAND PIËCH (RIGHT), WHO WOULD GROW UP TO GUIDE PORSCHE'S RACING PROGRAM, THEN LEAD AUDI AND FINALLY VOLKSWAGEN GROUP.

170-171 THOUGH BASED ON THE VOLKSWAGEN TYPE ONE, THE PORSCHE GOT A MUCH SLEEKER BODY AND ALSO MANY MECHANICAL UPGRADES THAT MADE IT EXTREMELY NIMBLE AND ABLE TO COMPETE ON THE ROAD OR RACETRACK WITH MUCH MORE POWERFUL MACHINES.

Porsche, of course, is almost synonymous with design. Though Porsche Design, which does the styling of a variety of goods, is a separate company from the automaker, both trace their ancestry back to Ferdinand Porsche and his children and their offspring. Ferdinand's grandson, F.A. "Butzi" Porsche, designed the original 911 in the early 1960s, and then launched Porsche Design. Tony Lapine, an American who worked for Harley Earl at General Motors and Opel, was Porsche's automotive design leader for the 1970s and '80s. He hired Harm Lagaay, a Dutchman who left for Ford and then went to BMW before returning as Porsche's design director in 1989 to help Porsche expand its vehicle portfolio with the Boxster roadster, Cayenne sport utility and Carrera GT supercar.

172 TOP THE VOLKSWAGEN GROUP'S SUPERVISORY BOARD GATHERS AROUND A PORSCHE 911 2.0 COUPLE AS THEY CELEBRATE FERDINAND PORSCHE'S 70TH BIRTHDAY.

172-173 FERDINAND PORSCHE'S GRANDSON, F.A. "BUTZI" PORSCHE, DESIGNED THE REPLACEMENT FOR THE PORSCHE 356, A CAR THAT WENT INTO PRODUCTION IN 1965 AS THE PORSCHE 911. ALTHOUGH IT WOULD BE REFINED THROUGH THE YEARS, THE CAR'S BASIC SILHOUETTE CARRIES ON INTO THE 21ST CENTURY, GIVING THE 911 ICONIC STATUS AMONG AUTOMOTIVE DESIGNS.

Perhaps the most famous of all German car designs — that of the 1954 Mercedes-Benz 300 SL with its "Gullwing" doors — was designed for the company's racing program by Walter Hacker from the company's body-engineering department, where engineers, albeit those with artistic talent, worked under Hermann Ahrens as they styled both commercial and passenger vehicles. However, Karl Wilfert certainly played a role. Wilfert was Mercedes' first real design director and brought Mercedes into the modern design age, a move begun in 1953 when he moved the radiator cap from its traditionally prominent position to a place beneath the hood of the Mercedes' 180 model.

174-175 LIKE THE VOLKSWAGEN BEETLE AND THE PORSCHE 911, THE MERCEDES-BENZ 300 SL WITH ITS GULL-WING DOORS HAS BECOME AN ICON OF GERMAN AUTOMOTIVE DESIGN. THE CAR WAS DESIGNED BY MERCEDES' RACING DEPARTMENT. THE CAR HAD A SPACE FRAME CHASSIS AND THE DOORS WERE DESIGNED TO CUT AS SLIGHTLY AS POSSIBLE INTO THE SIDE STRUCTURE AND WERE HINGED TO AN OVERHEAD BEAM THAT ENHANCED THE CAR'S S STRENGTH. IT WAS AN ELEGANT AND ARTISTIC SOLUTION TYPICAL OF THE FORM FOLLOWS FUNCTION SCHOOL OF DESIGN.

175 TOP THE 300 SL WAS DEVELOPED FOR RACING, AND IN ITS FIRST SEASON POSTED VICTORIES IN BOTH THE 24 HOURS OF LE MANS AND THE FAMED PANAMERICANA ROAD RACE THROUGH MEXICO. GULLWING 300 SL COUPES WERE BUILT FROM 1954 TO 1957 WITH ROADSTERS IN PRODUCTION FROM 1957 TO 1963.

new model would be seen clearly as the successor to its previous version. Sacco called this evolution versus revolution, this method of updating the new without outdating the old, "vertical affinity."

Speaking of corporate or brand identity, Sacco once explained that it goes beyond the grille and three-pointed star, adding that; "It isn't necessary to be a designer in order to recognize [the elements]." For example, he said, photos of a new Mercedes model would be shown to non-Mercedes drivers. "The first photos were blurred, then we showed clearer and clearer ones." But, he added, "even with the first blurred photos, the majority recognized that the car, which they had never seen before, was a Mercedes."

While maintaining and even strengthening the Mercedes brand design, Sacco accelerated the evolutionary changes as one generation begat the next. He also guided the unprecedented diversity of the Mercedes-Benz lineup, with a succession of sports cars, from the small SLK roadster to the Mercedes-Benz SLR McLaren supercar; from sedans and coupes in a variety of new sizes and categories; from the urban Smart to the urbane S-Class, as well as the creation of sport utility vehicles.

In 1958, Wilfert hired a young Italian designer, Bruno Sacco, who had studied mechanical engineering but would focus on body design at Ghia and Pinin Farina. At Mercedes, Sacco immediately worked on vehicles ranging from the huge 600 sedan to the 230SL sports car, and led the aesthetic design of two major projects, the ESV and the C111 and their successors. Both were experiments on wheels, and beautiful for the way they incorporated engineering within design. The Experimental Safety Vehicle was a project to enhance vehicle safety, and the C111, a series of vehicles to explore the extremes of high-speed dynamic performance.

Sacco admits that it took several years for him to absorb Mercedes' corporate culture, but by 1975 he was in a position to give that culture a visible form when he became the head of design for the world's oldest car company. Sacco would lead the Mercedes design department until the turn of the 21st century, when he retired.

Regardless of what other German automakers were doing, all Mercedes vehicles, regardless of model, would be recognizable not only as part of the greater Mercedes family – Sacco called this "horizontal homogeneity," expressed especially in the face, the grille and headlight design and details. Also, however, each

176 ITALIAN NATIVE BRUNO SACCO, SHOWN HERE GOING OVER THE DETAILS OF THE CLASSIC MERCEDES-BENZ GRILLE, JOINED MERCEDES DESIGN DEPARTMENT IN 1958. HE BECAME DESIGN DIRECTOR IN 1975. SACCO SAYS IT TOOK HIM YEARS TO ABSORB MERCEDES' CORPORATE CULTURE, BUT HE TRANSLATED THAT CULTURE INTO STYLISH CAR DESIGNS UNTIL HIS RETIREMENT AT THE TURN OF THE 21ST CENTURY.

176-177 EVEN AT A YOUNG AGE, BRUNO SACCO HELPED DEFINE AND THEN FINE TUNE MERCEDES-BENZ DESIGN. SHOWN HERE IS A 1971 280 SE COUPE.

178 TOP THE MERCEDES-BENZ SLR MCLAREN WAS A COOPERATIVE SUPERCAR EFFORT THAT INVOLVED MERCEDES-BENZ AND ITS FORMULA ONE RACING TEAM, MCLAREN. ALTHOUGH ITS DOORS HAVE "SWING-WING" RATHER THAN GULLWING HINGES, THE CAR IN MANY WAYS IS A CONTEMPORARY INTERPRETATION OF THE 300 FROM THE 1950S.

178-179 UNLIKE THE MCLAREN RACECAR, THE SLR HAS ITS ENGINE, A 617-HORSEPOWER, 5.5-LITER SUPERCHARGED V8, POSITIONED IN FRONT OF THE DRIVER'S COMPARTMENT, THUS THE CAR HAS THE TRADITIONAL LONG HOOD OF THE CLASSIC SPORTS CAR. BUT IT ALSO HAS A FULL ARRAY OF STATE-OF-THE-ART BRAKES AND OTHER SYSTEMS THAT HELP THE DRIVER MAINTAIN CONTROL AT VERY HIGH SPEEDS, OR WHILE STOPPING SAFELY FROM SUCH SPEEDS.

HARMUT WARKUSS

Though their companies and their design histories were very different, Harmut Warkuss played a role at Volkswagen similar to Sacco's at Mercedes-Benz, that of creating and building and guiding a modern design department. In Warkuss' case, that design staff would deal with a group of brands as diverse as Volkswagen, Audi, Bugatti and Lamborghini.

When it came time for Volkswagen to create a successor to the original Beetle, which had replaced Henry Ford's Model T as the world's best-selling car of all-time, it turned, in the early 1970s, to Italian designer Giorgetto Giugiaro, who created the Golf, as well as the sportier Scirocco, which joined an expanding VW fleet that already included the Giugia-ro-designed Passat/Dasher. At the time, Harmut Warkuss was working at Audi.

Warkuss's father had been killed in World War II and with his mother and brother had been deported and interned by the Soviets before finding a way into West Germany. Warkuss loved to draw, and his mother pointed him toward work as an engraver, though in the process he became more interested in model making in three dimensions. Still, he was headed to an engraving job in Sweden in 1964 when he received an offer to join the design department at Mercedes-Benz. He left for Ford after two years, but soon returned to Mercedes and before very long accepted an invitation to join Au-di, where he helped create the Audi 100 coupe and then, in 1972, did his first complete design, the Audi 80, a car praised by one author as marking "the birth of what has come to be recognized as the quintessential Germany automotive style: essential, concrete, retrained and always, well balanced."

Four years later, he was head of Audi design, working closely with Ferdinand Piëch, grandson of Ferdinand Porsche and an engineering and managerial dynamo with expertise not only in such things as turbocharging race cars and developing quattro four-wheel-drive, but an appreciation for the importance of effective and aesthetic design. Piëch wanted to take Audi upscale, to compete with BMW and

180-181 ONE OF THE WAYS THAT AUDI SIGNALED ITS INTENTION TO MOVE MORE UPSCALE CAME IN 1991 WHEN IT UNVEILED THE AVUS CONCEPT CAR AT THE TOKYO MOTOR SHOW. DESIGNED BY AMERICAN J. MAYS, WHO LATER WOULD BECOME HEAD OF DESIGN FOR THE FORD MOTOR COMPANY, AVUS TIED TOGETHER AUDI'S AUTO UNION RACING HERITAGE AND ITS TRANSITION INTO A PRODUCER OF MODERN CARS THAT COMBINED LUXURY AND DYNAMIC PERFORMANCE.

Mercedes, and Warkuss and his design staff showed the way with concept vehicles such as the Avus and Quattro Spyder, with production vehicles such as the Avant, a very sporty wagon, and with what were acclaimed as the world's best-designed automotive interiors.

Then, in 1993, Piëch moved from the head of Audi to lead its parent, Volkswagen Group, and he took Warkuss with him to guide VW design – the "New Beetle" was created under his watch – and eventually to oversee not just VW but all of its brands, including Bugatti.

181 TOP WHEN VOLKSWAGEN NEEDED A CAR TO WRAP AROUND AN ALL-ELECTRIC POWERTRAIN IT WANTED TO SHOWCASE, THE VW DESIGN DEPARTMENT TOOK ADVANTAGE OF THE OPPORTUNITY BY CREATING CONCEPT 1, A PROPOSAL FOR A CONTEMPORARY NEW BEETLE BY AMERICAN DESIGNERS J. MAYS AND FREEMAN THOMAS. UNLIKE THE POWERTRAIN, THE CAR PROVED SO POPULAR THAT IT SOON WENT INTO PRODUCTION.

Warkuss had been succeeded at Audi by Peter Schreyer, a German who studied at Britain's Royal College of Art. His efforts at Audi included working with American Freeman Thomas on the Audi TT and then, in 2001, creating the Rosemeyer supercar concept. After more than 25 years at Audi and VW, Schreyer became design director of Korean automaker Kia. Succeeding Warkuss after his retirement from VW was Murat Gunak, Turkish-born and British-educated former head of design at Peugeot, who then oversaw the design of the Maybach and SLR for Mercedes-Benz before joining VW.

Murak's rein at VW was brief and he was succeeded by Walter de Silva, formerly head of design for Alfa Romeo and then Audi.

182-183 BEFORE LEAVING VOLKSWAGEN/AUDI FOR IMPORTANT JOBS IN THE ADVANCED DESIGN STUDIOS OF CHRYSLER AND THEN FORD, FREEMAN THOMAS WORKED WITH AUDI DESIGN DIRECTOR PETER SCHREYER TO CREATE THE TT, A SPORTS CAR AVAILABLE IN COUPE OR ROADSTER ARCHITECTURES. MUCH AS THE PORSCHE 356 HAD BEEN BASED ON THE ORIGINAL VW BEETLE, THE TT SHARED SOME OF ITS UNDERPINNINGS WITH THE NEW BEETLE, BUT LIKE THE PORSCHE GOT A BOOST IN POWER AND CARRIED A MUCH SPORTIER BODY.

183 TOP AUDI'S RACING HERITAGE THROUGH AUTO UNION, ONE OF THE FOUR RINGS ON THE AUDI LOGO, WAS UNDERSCORED BY THE ROSEMEYER CONCEPT CAR, A MODERN INTERPRETATION OF THE CLASSIC 1930S RACER AND NAMED FOR BERND ROSEMEYER, ONE OF THE SPORT'S EARLY SUPERSTAR DRIVERS. THE CONCEPT CARRIES A 700-HORSEPOWER 16-CYLINDER ENGINE MOUNTED BENEATH THE LONG SLOPING REAR END WITH A VERY UPRIGHT FACE AND A DYNAMIC PROFILE.

DESIGN ORIENTED BMW

Among the German automakers, BMW was historically the most design oriented, with Wilhelm Meyerhuber as styling director in the 1930s. The emblematic double grille first appeared in 1933 on the BMW 303. Soon afterward, Kurt Joachim, Peter Szymanowski and engineer Fritz Fielder created the stunning 1936 BMW 328 roadster. As BMW rebuilt from the devastation of World War II, it turned to designers such as Paul Bracq of France, Giovanni Michelotti, Ercole Spada, Giorgetto Giugiaro and the Bertone studio of Italy, and to Count Albrecht Goertz, a German who had been based in the United States, for design. Like other automakers, BMW also had its own design studio, led for many years by Claus Luthe, who had styled the rotary-powered Ro80 for NSU in the late 1960s.

Die großen europäischen Achtzylinder

184 TOP AMERICAN IMPORTER MAX HOFFMAN CONVINCED BMW TO HIRE COUNT ALBRECHT GOERTZ TO DESIGN A NEW SPORTS CAR WHICH DEBUTED AT THE FAMED WALDORF-ASTORIA HOTEL IN 1955. THE BMW 507 ROADSTER EXTENDED THE DOUBLE-KIDNEY GRILLE THE FULL WIDTH OF THE CAR'S FRONT AND HAD A LONG AND LOW HOOD SET BETWEEN FENDERS THAT SWEPT BACK TO A KINK JUST AHEAD OF THE REAR FENDERS.

184-185 WITH A 3.2-LITER V8 ENGINE, THE 507 WAS BEAUTIFUL, BUT ALSO EXPENSIVE. THE CAR HAD A STRONG FOLLOWING AMONG CELEBRITIES, INCLUDING ELVIS PRESLEY, WHO LATER GAVE THE CAR TO MOVIE CO-STAR URSULA ANDRESS. BMW, WHICH WAS IN A STATE OF CORPORATE FINANCIAL WOE, PRODUCED ONLY SOME 250 UNITS IN THE COURSE OF THREE YEARS.

185 TOP WHEN THE 507 ROADSTER DEBUTED IN EUROPE AT THE 1955 FRANKFURT MOTOR SHOW, IT WAS JOINED ON THE STAND BY A NEARLY IDENTICAL TWIN, BUT THIS ONE HAD A REMOVABLE HARDTOP THAT GAVE THE CAR AN EVEN MORE ELEGANT PROFILE.

CHRIS BANGLE

In 1992, BMW took a dramatic step in its design direction by hiring Chris Bangle, an American who had worked at Opel before becoming head of design at Fiat. Under Bangle's direction, BMW styling, with a now heightened degree of surface tension and concave sculpturing that Bangle calls "flame surfacing," has become controversial but also influential. For example, the high rear deck of the 2002 BMW 7 Series, actually created by Dutch designer Adrian Van Hooydonk working in BMW's American design studio in California, was derided by critics as the "Bangle butt," but was copied quickly by other automakers' studios for their cars. Van Hooydonk succeeded Bangle as head of BMW automotive design as Bangle moved up to oversee all of BMW Group design, where he continued to oversee BMW, Mini and Rolls-Royce design while working on a revolutionary plan with BMW engineers to change the way cars are built in the coming decades. Once again, the blending of design and engineering to emphasize corporate culture cues have become more important in a world in which brands are marketed around the globe. Bangle explained: "The whole idea of national identity is being usurped by corporate identities and some companies, which have a sense of national origin and corporate origin which lie on top of each other very well, like German companies or French companies, tend to make a national look come across when, in reality, that trend can also fulfill a corporate look."

Bangle was one of many Americans and other non-Germans who worked in the Opel studio. General Motors took control of the German automaker in 1929 and used Opel's design studio as a training ground for many of its most talented young designers, including people such as Wayne Cherry, who would go on to head all GM design, and more recently Bryan Nesbitt, who designed the PT Cruiser for Chrysler, was hired away by GM, sent to Opel for overseas experience before returning to run one of GM's key studios in Michigan. Ford's German design facilities played a similar role, and were where Jack Telnack worked before returning to the United States to oversee all Ford automotive design and where he and the others learned from Uwe Bahnsen, the German-born head of Ford's European studio for several decades.

186 TOP BMW DESIGN TOOK A BOLD TURN IN THE EARLY 1990S WHEN AMERICAN CHRIS BANGLE (BLUE SHIRT) TOOK OVER THE STUDIO.

186-187 THE BMW 7 SERIES FEATURED A VERY HIGH REAR DECK LID THAT MANY THOUGHT LOOKED AWKWARD. THE DESIGN BECAME KNOWN AS THE "BANGLE BUTT." BMW DESIGNERS HAD THE LAST LAUGH, HOWEVER, AS DESIGNERS FROM OTHER AUTOMAKERS RECOGNIZED THE VISUAL APPEAL THE NEW TAIL TREATMENT CREATED IN SEDANS. SOON, MANY AUTOMAKERS WERE COPYING THE "BUTT" FOR THEIR OWN VEHICLES.

187 TOP THE FACE OF THE 2006 BMW M6, A HIGH-PERFORMANCE COUPE, SHOWS THE FACE OF BMW DESIGN UNDER CHRIS BANGLE. ALTHOUGH THE RANGE EXTENDS FROM TWO-SEAT ROADSTERS THROUGH COUPES AND SEDANS, WAGONS AND HATCHBACKS, TO FULL-SIZE SPORT UTILITY VEHICLES, EACH BMW CLEARLY ANNOUNCES ITS PRESENCE AND HERITAGE WITH FEATURES SUCH AS THE DOUBLE-KIDNEY GRILLE.

FRANCE:
ARTISTIC EXPRESSION
ISN'T JUST ALLOWED,
IT'S ENCOURAGED

A WAVE OF BLUE CARS

If purely artistic decoration and ornamentation have not been part of German design, they seem to have been almost vital ingredients in French automotive styling. "The other day we had a seminar with the members of the design management in this fantastic hall [a collection of racing cars in the National Automobile Museum of France at Mulhouse] where there is a wave of blue cars [French, mainly Bugattis] and a wave of red cars [Italian, mainly Ferraris and Maseratis] and a wave of silvery cars [German, mainly Mercedes]," said Patrick Le Quément, head of design at Renault and a man heralded as one of the masters of automotive design at the turn of the 21st century. "One of our design directors, who is Italian, made the

remark that he found that the French cars were interesting, aesthetically not the most pleasing, but very innovative and yet in some ways a little sort of not thought through, with a lot of experimental work, a lot of do-it-yourself fixes needed. I must say there is a lot of truth there."

"One of the things I've always been struck by is the fact that the notion of nationality is sometimes relevant and is sometimes looked on as being irrelevant," Le Quément continued. "I think the environment influences the designers in a way, for example, that Saoutchik in his work was very French [even though Saoutchk was born in Russia] and Ettore Bugatti, despite the fact of his Italian origin, his cars were very French in approach and not at all Italian.

There is this sort of inspiration of lightness, which is constantly present in French design."

Le Quément added that he "used to find the notion of Frenchness very, very important when I arrived back from abroad to France in late 1987. But more recently, I am not 100-percent sure that the national design approach is as much relevant today as it was a few years ago." Instead, corporate culture cues have become more important than strict national heritage in a world in which brands are marketed not just across the country but around the world. For example, Le

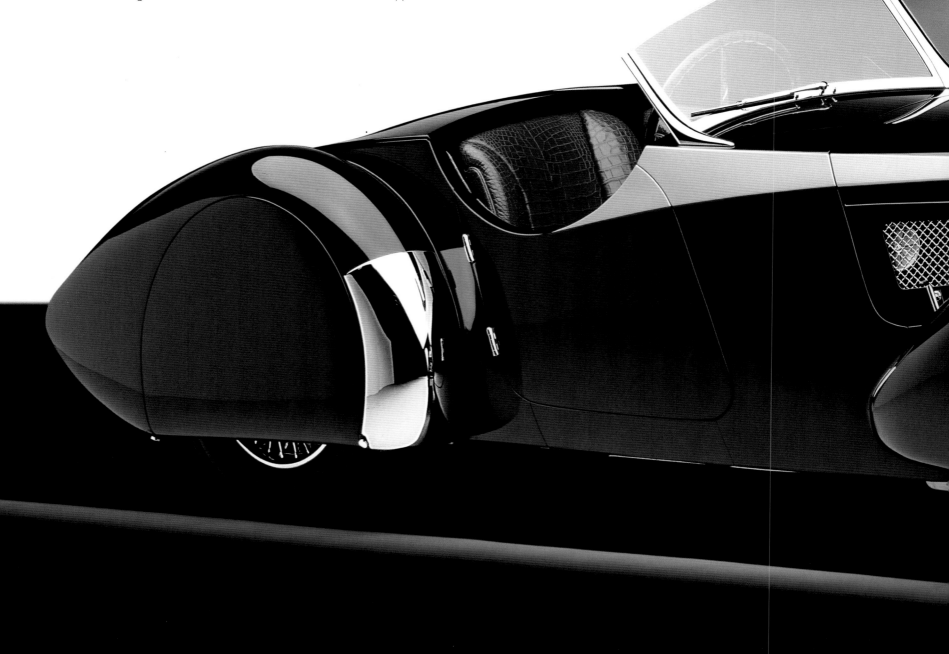

Quément pointed out that only half of Renault's designers are French, and those who are not come from some two dozen nations around the globe. But, he added, that while the designers may not be French, "they are Renault through and through."

"Those designers all come to us because of the reputation we have for allowing an enormous amount of freedom that allows designers to express themselves, and secondly because there has been an awful lot of very interesting cars coming out of France," he explained. Le Quément said that at *Renault*, and across French automotive design in general, there have been things that have worked well, and things that have not worked at all. But at least the effort, the risk is allowed. "There are very few designers around the world who

can say that everything they have been involved with has been a success," he said. "If they are in that situation, it's probably because they never tried hard enough. Failure is always associated with movement. You cannot stumble unless you are in motion." French automotive design certainly has been in motion, influenced at various times by French architects — for example, Le Corbusier and Pierre Jeanneret developing ideas for a "people's car," the so-called *Voiture Minimum*, as well as overcoming its own occasional stumble, and the ebbs and flows of French politics and societal change.

The resulting automotive designs sometimes, even often, may have appeared strange, if not outrageous, to non-French eyes.

188-189   THOUGH DESIGNED BY ITALIAN SCULPTOR FLAMINIO BERTONI, THE CITROËN DS, INTRODUCED IN 1955, EPITOMIZES THE SOMETIMES OUTRAGEOUS ARTISTIC EXPRESSION ALLOWED IN FRENCH AUTOMOTIVE DESIGN.

190-191   THE BUGATTIS WERE AN ARTISTIC FAMILY. CARLO WAS A FAMOUS 19TH-CENTURY FURNITURE MAKER. HIS SON REMBRANDT WAS AN ACCLAIMED SCULPTOR AND THEN THERE WAS HIS OTHER SON, ETTORE, A MULTI-FACETED ARTIST WHO SPECIALIZED IN METALWORK WITH A SUCCESSION OF CARS THAT BORE THE FAMILY NAME. ETTORE'S SON JEAN ALSO HAD A BRILLIANT IF BRIEF CAREER IN AUTOMOTIVE DESIGN (HE DIED AT THE AGE OF 30 WHEN HE VEERED OFF THE ROAD TO AVOID A DRUNKEN BICYCLE RIDER). SHOWN HERE IS A 1938 BUGATTI TYPE 57SC ROADSTER, THE WORK OF FATHER AND SON.

SIMCA, PEUGEOT, CITROËN

Bertone; and the compact 2004 C3 Pluriel that is both open coupe and convertible.

The Traction Avant, 2CV, DS and other early Citroëns were designed by Flaminio Bertoni, an Italian sculptor (and not related to the Bertone design company). Robert Opron joined Citroën's design staff in the mid-1960s and stayed until Peugeot took over, when he went to Renault. Opron's work included the Maserati-engined SM and many others, with Michel Harmand doing Citroën's innovative interiors. After Opron, many of Citroën's designs were created by a young Italian, Donato Coco, who moved to Ferrari in 2005. At the turn of the 21st Century, Jean-Pierre Ploue joined Citroën after working at Ford, Volkswagen and Renault, where he designed the Twingo with Patrick Le Quément. Citroën presented its ideas for its future design language in 2002 with the C-Airdream concept car.

None of the French automakers had modern, American-style design studios until the mid 1950s, when Simca established one under the leadership of Count Mario Revelli de Beaumont, who had worked in several Italian studios and had done freelance work for a variety of automakers.

(Simca later would be purchased by Chrysler, and then by Peugeot.)

Peugeot, some argue, is actually the world's oldest car company, because it was the first to sell cars to customers, in 1889. In the late 1920s, Peugeot had a drawing office comprising Alfred Giauque and Louis Dufresne, who specialized in racing cars and "advanced" (possible future product) design. By the early 1930s, Peugeot hired artist Henri Thomas to help with body design and also brought in aerodynamics engineer Jean Andreau. Thomas would lead Peugeot's design efforts until 1948. Though he was succeeded by George Boschetti, Jean-Pierre Peu-geot turned increasingly to Pinin Farina in Italy for new designs, from the 403 in 1955 through to the 406 in 1997, though in consultation with Peugeot's Paul Bouvot and later Gerard Welter, who joined Peugeot as an 18-year-old in 1960 and managed the design program for many years, finally bringing the design of several models in-house with a staff that included Murat Gunak and Jerome Gallix.

In 1976, Peugeot took control of Citroën, a French company with a strong if quirky design tradition that includes such interesting vehicles as the 1934 7CV, or Traction Avant, which combined a sporty, low-slung body with an effective and affordable front-wheel drive powertrain; the 1939 2CV, a snail-shaped vehicle that was the "people's car" of France; the 1955 DS, with its elegant but egg-like body and height-adjustable hydropneumatic suspension; the 1970 SM, designed in conjunction with Maserati; the 1982 BX and 1989 XM, both with

192 TOP SIMCA WAS THE FIRST FRENCH AUTOMAKER WITH ITS OWN AMERICAN-STYLE DESIGN STUDIO, ESTABLISHED IN THE MID-1950S. SHOWN HERE IS PART OF THE SIMCA ARONDE LINEUP FOR 1955, INCLUDING BEAULIEU, COUPE DE VILLE AND GRAND LARGE MODELS.

192 BOTTOM PEUGEOT'S 201 MODEL MAY NOT HAVE COVERED THE WORLD, BUT BETWEEN 1929 AND 1937 THE FRENCH AUTOMAKER BUILT MORE THAN 140,000 OF THE CAR THAT WAS THE FIRST TO FEATURE INDEPENDENT FRONT WHEELS.

193 ITALIAN SCULPTOR FLAMINIO BERTONI DESIGNED THREE OF CITROËN'S MOST IMPORTANT VEHICLES, THE DS (ABOVE), THE 2CV (LOWER LEFT) AND THE TRACTION AVANT (LOWER RIGHT).

PATRICK LE QUÉMENT

Renault took its first adventure in automotive design in the late 1920s, hiring coachbuilders Hibbard and Darrin to work on the Reinastella. Then, in 1934, Marcel Riffart created Renault's Viva Grand Sport. Renault emerged from World War II with the 4CV and in 1956 succeeded it with Roger Barthaud's popular Dauphine. Barthaud, Gaston Juchet and Robert Opron led the Renault design staff and worked with both internal and Italian designers on various projects. Then, in 1987, Patrick Le Quément arrived.

Like French design itself, Le Quément has been innovative, and while he may have stumbled on occasion, his designs have been internationally acclaimed. Indeed, he has learned that some of his 25-year-old sketches remain on the wall of the Ford design studio in Germany.

Le Quément is the son of a French army physician and a British nurse. When his father died in an accident, his mother sent Patrick to school in England, where he eventually studied product design. He returned to France to work at Simca, which was moving from Fiat's to Chrysler's corporate portfolio. He stayed only a year, then he and a co-worker launched their own short-lived design firm before he signed on with Ford, where his design skills and mastery of English earned him a series of international assignments. At age 36 he became the youngest of Ford's design studio managers and worked closely with Ford's European design chief Uwe Bahnsen on the Probe concept car series as well as several successful production cars.

Le Quément was in line to succeed Bahnsen, but corporate politics changed and after a brief stint in the United States he returned to Europe to oversee advanced design at Volkswagen-Audi. Then, in 1987, he was recruited to Renault, where his was given authority unknown for any automotive design director, reporting directly to the company's chairman, and where he has led the design of a succession of vehicles that are very French, though in ways that differentiate them from those designed for Citroën or Peugeot.

As far as his non-French designers being able to design very French vehicles, Le Quément explained, "Sometimes foreign designers are better able to capture what Frenchness is than those who live naturally here." He offered the historic examples of Bugatti and Saoutchik and the team of Figoni et Falaschi, non-Frenchmen who established French curves and ornamentation as a national design tradition.

194 DESIGNERS AND MODEL MAKERS WORK IN CLAY (TOP) TO CREATE A SCALE MODEL IN THE RENAULT STUDIO. WHEN THAT MODEL'S DETAILS ARE APPROVED, A FULL-SCALE MODEL IS CREATED (CENTER), AGAIN IN CLAY, THOUGH COVERED WITH MATERIAL THAT MAKES IT APPEAR TO HAVE A COMPLETE METALLIC BODY. FINALLY, THE FULL-SIZE CAR, IN THIS CASE THE AVANTIME CONCEPT, IS READY FOR ITS DEBUT AT THE 1999 GENEVA MOTOR SHOW.

195 TOP PATRICK LE QUÉMENT (FAR RIGHT) JOINS A GROUP OF HIS DESIGNERS AROUND A
COMPUTER SCREEN THAT ALLOWS THEM TO MAKE ELECTRONICALLY GENERATED DRAWINGS.
RENAULT DESIGNERS (RIGHT) WORK ON A SCALE MODEL OF THE Z06 CONCEPT CAR PROJECT.

195 BOTTOM PATRICK LE QUÉMENT USED A SUCCESSION OF CONCEPT CARS – VEL SATIS,
AVANTIME, TALISMAN AND ELLYPSE – TO INTRODUCE A NEW DESIGN THEME AT RENAULT.
THE NEW ARCHITECTURE CULMINATED IN THE LAUNCH OF THE MEGANE II.

AMERICAN STYLE:
FROM HOLLYWOOD TO
THE HIGHWAY WITH HARLEY EARL
AND GENERAL MOTORS

HARLEY EARL

arley Earl's story has early parallels to those of some of the great European automotive designers. Like Nuccio Bertone and Battista Farina, Harley Earl grew up as part of a family in the coachbuilding business.

But while Bertone and Pininfarina were able to build family businesses into international institutions, Earl followed another route.

He built the first and the largest and the prototypical automotive manufacturer's design operation at what would become — with considerable credit going to Earl and his design staff — the word's largest automaker, General Motors.

Harley Earl advanced automotive design not through coachbuilding, but by taking design out of the coachbuilder's garage and into the very mainstream of automotive manufacturing.

As automotive historian Michael Lamm wrote in *Automobile Quarterly*, Harley Earl was the person who would "integrate the art, science, and showmanship of automobile design," establishing not just an influential design house but the very foundation of the automobile manufacturer's car design studio itself. And to think, it may all have traced back to a family camping trip and the clay cars that a teenaged Harley Earl crafted for himself and his brother.

Harley Earl was born in 1893 in Hollywood, California, though it would be years before the movie industry would establish its base in what at the time was a farming community. J.W. Earl, who would become Harley's father, had moved to the West Coast of the United States from Michigan, where he worked as a lumberjack and operated a sawmill.

At the age of 23, J.W. Earl opened a carriage shop in downtown Los Angeles. His business did well and he married into a prominent family. In 1908, the Earl Carriage Works became the Earl Automobile Works, at first producing windshields, and then other components for the new motorcars. By 1911, Earl Automobile Works was doing complete custom bodywork.

Each summer from 1896 until 1914, when his mother, Abbie (Taft) Earl, died, Harley Earl's family spent its time camping at Bailey's Ranch in the mountains north of Los Angeles.

There was a lot of rain the summer of Harley Earl's 16th year and the rain created natural clay that the teenager used to fashion some two dozen toy cars for himself and his younger brother, Art. "What Harley J. Earl began in the clay of Bailey's Ranch, he later shaped into an industry of tremendous economic and social important," Lamm wrote.

"He wasn't the first man to 'style' a car, but he did create the business or industry of designing cars. He fathered it, formed it, systematized it, saw its tremendous potential in terms of car sales, and to his everlasting credit, Harley Earl had the personality to convince the engineering-dominated auto industry to recognize its importance.

"Making styling more than the frosting on the engineer's cake was Harley Earl's great contribution to the American economy." And to automotive design and designers around the world.

By the time of his retirement in the mid-1950s, Harley Earl would have his hand in the creation not just of a few cars made of clay, but of some 50 million vehicles produced by General Motors.

From a global perspective, he developed the techniques and organizational structure that would produce seemingly every mass-produced car for the past eight decades – and for decades yet to come.

Though he showed an artistic interest in motorcars at a young age, Harley Earl was even more interested in sports and other activities in his teenage years.

Among those other activities was auto racing, and Earl raced his father's car without per-

196-197 THE 1959 CADILLAC ELDORADO CONVERTIBLE IS ONE OF THE LAST VEHICLES DESIGNED IN HARLEY EARL'S STUDIO AT GENERAL MOTORS.

198 TOP IN THE 1930S, GENERAL MOTORS WOULD

SHOWCASE ITS NEW VEHICLES IN NEW YORK CITY FOR WALL STREET INVESTORS.

199 TOP A POSTCARD, CIRCA 1911, SHOWS A PEDESTRIAN'S SURPRISE AS A NEW BUICK ROLLS DOWN THE ROAD.

mission. But it was more typical sports in which he excelled. He set a pole vault record at the University of Southern California, and although he was sent to Stanford University with his family's hopes that he'd concentrate long enough to become an attorney, he didn't. Instead, he was sent home to recuperate from a severe leg injury suffered on the athletic field.

Back in Los Angeles, he worked with his father and in 1918 he started designing custom bodywork – long, low and sporty bodywork – much of it for the stars of Hollywood's fledgling movie industry (Cecil B. DeMille was by now a neighbor and friend of the Earl family).

After J.W. Earl remarried, he sold his automotive business to Don Lee, the West Coast distributor for Cadillac.

As design director for the Don Lee Coach and Body Works, Harley Earl designed more than 100 custom car bodies in 1919 and 1920. In 1921, Cadillac president Richard Collins, who wintered in the Los Angeles area, met Earl through Don Lee and asked the young stylist if

he'd design six new Cadillacs and produce scale models that Collins could show to dealers.

Earl went to work on the designs, but in the meantime, Collins soon quit Cadillac to work for another car company. While Earl's models didn't leave Los Angeles, word of his design talents did reach Detroit.

Hollywood stars loved the custom cars designed by Harley Earl. In 1925, Don Lee placed an order for 100 Cadillac chassis, an order that Cadillac's new president, Lawrence Fisher, had no intention of fulfilling.

Cadillac was in the business of selling cars with Cadillac bodies on them.

Still, Fisher traveled to California to see Don Lee's operation. Fisher and Earl hit it off well, in part because Earl introduced the flamboyant Fisher to his Hollywood neighbors.

Even before Fisher's trip, General Motors executives realized they needed a new car line that would slot between the Buick and Cadillac brands, and that they wanted that new model to have more flair in its design.

200 EVEN BEFORE HE BECAME A FULL-TIME EMPLOYEE, GENERAL MOTORS HIRED A YOUNG HARLEY EARL TO DESIGN THE 1927 LASALLE, THE FIRST AMERICAN CAR CREATED BY A DESIGNER INSTEAD OF BY ENGINEERS AND TECHNICIANS. GM PRESIDENT ALFRED SLOAN WAS SO IMPRESSED WITH EARL'S WORK ON THE LASALLE (BELOW) THAT HE INVITED HIM TO SEE THE PARIS MOTOR SHOW AND TO VISIT FRENCH COACHBUILDERS. SLOAN ANTICIPATED THAT HE COULD USE DESIGN TO MAKE GENERAL MOTORS' CARS MORE APPEALING THAN THOSE BASICALLY BLACK AND BOXY VEHICLES BEING PRODUCED BY FORD AND HE MADE EARL, THEN 34 YEARS OLD, THE FIRST DESIGN DIRECTOR OF ANY MAJOR AUTOMAKER.

Harley Earl went to work for General Motors in 1927 and stayed until he retired in 1958. But that was Earl's second stint at the company. His first lasted only three months, early in 1926, when Earl and a GM model maker created what would become the 1927 LaSalle, the car that did much more than span the gap in the GM model lineup between Buick and Cadillac. Earl admitted that he was inspired by and borrowed heavily from Europe's Hispano-Suiza; nonetheless, that 1927 LaSalle is considered the first American car built from a design created by a designer rather than by engineers and technicians.

GM president Alfred Sloan liked Earl and his quick work so much that he invited him to attend the upcoming Paris auto show.

Not only did they attend the motor show, but they stopped to see coachbuilders such as Hibbard & Darrin. After the trip, Earl stopped in Detroit to make sure work on the LaSalle was progressing, then he returned to Los Angeles and his wife and their young child.

By the following summer, however, Sloan was ready with a plan he believed would help General Motors in its effort to overtake crosstown rival, Ford, which had ridden the black and boxy Model T to its position as the world's largest carmaker. Sloan saw styling, with new and colorful designs each year encouraging dissatisfaction in the marketplace for last year's vehicles, as a crucial element in selling more cars.

201 ART & COLOUR WAS THE TITLE GIVEN TO GM'S DESIGN DEPARTMENT AND IT USED ARTISTIC DESIGNS AND A VARIETY OF COLORS TO ENHANCE THE APPEAL OF PRODUCTS SUCH AS THE BUICKS SHOWN IN THIS POSTER FROM 1936.

Sloan decided that General Motors should establish what he called an Art & Colour Section within its central office and Sloan wanted 34-year-old Harley Earl to hire the 50-person staff and head the new group.

To everyone's surprise, Art & Colour's first car was a disaster. Earl and his team's initial effort would become the 1929 Buick, which immediately became known as the "pregnant" Buick after production engineers changed the cars shape. A battle ensued. At 6.4 ft and with his Hollywood-style personality and dress sense, Earl was an intimidating figure in his own right, plus he had established a strong relationship with Sloan should he need additional support.

Earl won the right to have a say in any changes to designs needed by the production department. He also realized that he needed engineers of his own within the styling studio to help head off such problems.

Earl brought integrated vehicle design to General Motors. He also insisted that two-dimensional drawings be transformed into three-dimensional and full-size clay models (built over wooden forms) so everyone from designers to executives — and production engineers as well — could clearly see vehicle design proposals.

Such clay modeling would become the standard in the industry and allowed much better development of shapes and surfaces than was possible by trying to interpret a metal shape directly from a drawing.

Earl also filled his section with talent. Among the early hires were Gordon Buehrig, who would go on to design much-heralded Cords; John Tjaarda, who later would do Lincolns and Packards; Frank Hershey, who long before designing the 1955 Thunderbird at Ford would do the 1935 Pontiac with Earl; even Virgil Exner, who in the 1950s would lead Chrysler's design studio and become perhaps the only challenger

to Earl's supremacy among American designers. Tom Hibbard, of Hibbard & Darrin in Paris, was recruited to GM.

Richard Teague, who would become chief designer at Packard and then a vice president at American Motors, worked in Earl's studio, and so did Strother MacMinn, who would become one of the most influential of all designers because of his long reign as chief instructor at the Art Center College of Design.

Early on, Earl also hired Bill Mitchell, a 23-year-old racer and advertising illustrator who would design a succession of outstanding GM vehicles — starting with the 1936 Cadillac 60-Special, which had an integrated coupe-style trunk and shunned the now-traditional running boards. Eventually, it would be Mitchell who would succeed Earl as head of the GM design staff.

By 1937, Earl and his staff of designers, modelers and engineers were so firmly entrenched

that Art & Colour became GM Styling (just three years later, Earl became a GM vice president, an unprecedented job title in the auto industry). In 1938, Earl created the first of what would become yet another of his major contributions to automotive design – the concept or "dream" car.

The first was the Buick Y-Job, which borrowed its name from experimental aircraft being developed by the aviation industry.

There had been earlier concept vehicles, and on both sides of the Atlantic Ocean, but they primarily had been aerodynamic rather than design studies.

The Y-Job was aerodynamic, but also incorporated technology and styling designed to propel vehicle art and science into the future.

For example, the Y-Job was the first car with a power convertible top and electric power windows. It also served as Earl's personal car for his daily commute to GM headquarters.

202-203 HARLEY EARL AND HIS DESIGNERS CREATED WHAT IS GENERALLY ACCEPTED AS THE WORLD'S FIRST CONCEPT OR "DREAM" CAR, THE BUICK Y-JOB, IN 1938. THE CAR LOOKED AHEAD TO THE FUTURE OF AUTOMOTIVE DESIGN AND TECHNOLOGY, INCLUDING ELECTRIC WINDOWS, A POWER CONVERTIBLE TOP, HIDDEN HEADLIGHTS AND MORE.

203 TOP THE CHICAGO WORLD'S FAIR IN 1933 WAS CALLED A "CENTURY OF PROGRESS" AND MANY OF THE DISPLAYS SHOWCASED PROGRESS IN TRANSPORTATION. AMONG THE CARS AT THE FAIR WERE THE PIERCE-ARROW SILVER ARROW, BUCKMINSTER FULLER'S DYMAXION, THE CHRYLSER AIRFLOW AND THE CADILLAC WORLD'S FAIR V-16 FASTBACK COUPE.

203 BOTTOM ALFRED SLOAN HAD REASONS TO ENJOY HIMSELF AS HIS STRATEGIES FOR GENERAL MOTORS BOOSTED VEHICLE SALES AND OVERTOOK FORD AMONG NOT ONLY AMERICAN BUT THE WORLD'S AUTOMAKERS. AMONG SLOAN'S STRATEGIES WAS USING ANNUAL DESIGN CHANGES TO CREATE DEMAND FOR THE LATEST VERSIONS OF GM CARS.

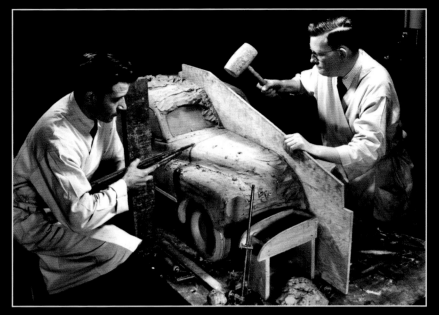

Aircraft would influence more than the name of Earl's next major concept car. Earl and his designers were allowed to visit a military air base near Detroit to see the Lockheed P-38 "Lightning" fighter plane. Then, soon after World War II, the U.S. unveiled the jet-powered F-86 Sabre fighter. They'd already introduced aircraft-inspired tail fins on the 1948 Cadillac and they loaded their next big dream car – the 1951 Le Sabre – with aviation-inspired design. The car also featured aviation-inspired technology, such as gauges (including an altimeter) and heated seats like those in military aircraft. The car also featured a convertible top that would automatically close when rain hit a sensor on the center console. Like the Y-Job, the Le Sabre became Earl's favored means of transport. It also renewed his interest in creating inspirational vehicles. After the war, Americans were eager to look ahead with optimism and Earl and his studio were there to point the way.

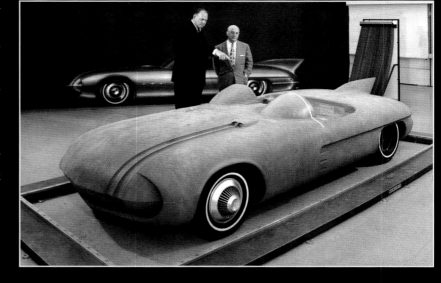

204 TOP MODELERS IN THE GM STYLING DEPARTMENT USE A VARIETY OF TOOLS TO SHAPE THE CLAY SURFACE OF A SCALE MODEL THAT SHOWS THE ANTICIPATED DESIGN OF THE 1947 CHEVROLET. RATHER THAN A DETAILED TECHNICAL DRAWING, THESE MODEL MAKERS ARE WORKING OFF A TEMPLATE TAKEN FROM A DESIGNER'S DRAWING ON A BLACKBOARD.

204 CENTER WHILE A TECHNICIAN SMOOTHES THE ROOF OF THE CLAY MODEL OF A SLEEK SEDAN, OTHERS GATHER AROUND A MODEL FOR WHAT APPEARS TO BE A SLEEK SPORTS CAR BEING DESIGNED IN THE GM STYLING STUDIOS IN 1948.

204 BOTTOM DESIGNERS CHECK SAMPLES FROM A BOARD THAT SHOWS A VARIETY OF COLORS BEING CONSIDERED FOR A FUTURE GENERAL MOTORS MODEL.

204-205 HARLEY EARL POSES WITH THE LE SABRE, GM'S FIRST MAJOR POST-WAR CONCEPT CAR. UNVEILED IN 1951, THE CAR TOOK STYLING CUES FROM JET FIGHTER AIRCRAFT AND FEATURED A RAIN SENSOR THAT COULD AUTOMATICALLY CLOSE THE CONVERTIBLE TOP WHEN THE CAR WAS PARKED.

205 TOP HARLEY EARL POINTS OUT DESIGN DETAILS ON A FULL-SIZE CLAY MODEL OF THE PONTIAC CLUB DE MER, A CONCEPT CAR WITH BOTH A SHARK-LIKE MOUTH AND DORSAL FIN. THE FINISHED CONCEPT CAR, WHICH STOOD ONLY 38.4 INCHES (97.5 MM) TALL, HAD AN ALUMINUM BODY AND 300-HORSEPOWER V8 ENGINE, WAS FEATURED AT THE 1956 GM MOTORAMA.

In the 1930s, Sloan had offered the New York financial community a preview of GM vehicles at an annual luncheon in the ballroom of the famed Waldorf-Astoria Hotel.

To celebrate the launch of its new post-war models, GM held public showings at the hotel in 1949 and 1950.

Then, in 1953, the company went all out, reviving the Parade of Progress, a tour of technology it discontinued during the war, and launching Motorama, part Broadway show, part auto show that not only unveiled the new GM models but that featured the future in the form of dream cars designed in Earl's studios.

Motorama began at the Waldorf, where people lined up around the building waiting to get in, and then traveled to other major American cities, where people also lined up for a glimpse of Earl's exotic creations, cars such as the Chevrolet Corvette, Buick Wildcat and Centurian, Pontiac Strato Streak, Strato-Star and Club De Mer, the Oldsmobile Golden Rocket, Cadillac La Espada and El Camino, and a new series of LaSalles. "People came to expect the excitement [of the concept vehicles]," says Chuck Jordan, a young designer at GM in the 1950s who later in his career would become vice-president of design.

"There was pent up demand and they were fascinated … they were ripe for this sort of thing." And nothing drew their attention quite like the Firebirds. Just as the trio of B.A.T. cars marked the high point of European dream car design, three Firebird concepts epitomized Harley Earl's vision of the American automotive spirit and the blending of design and technology, and of automotive and aerospace.

Like jet fighters, the Firebirds were powered by gas turbine engines.

Firebird I, or XP-21 as it was originally named, debuted at the Motorama in 1954 and not only looked like a jet fighter fuselage, complete with its exhaust emerging beneath a high central tail fin, but with clipped wings and oversized wheels. Inside the "cockpit," the driver controlled the vehicle not with a steering wheel but with an aircraft-style joystick.

In 1956, GM showed off Firebird II, the "family car" of the series with room for four under its clear canopy roof.

Firebird II not only had a steering wheel, but power windows and air conditioning. It also had an automatic guidance system that would steer itself by following electronic beams built into the highways of the future.

Earl wanted something very special for the Motorama in 1959 and thus Firebird III with its huge dorsal fin – Earl told designers it had to be tall enough to be seen over the crowd of people – several other auxiliary fins and twin bubble canopies.

The car also featured a centrally mounted stick-style controller so either of its two occupants could do the driving. "Harley Earl was fascinated with concepts.

"He got us going so hard on Motorama cars that we hardly had time to work on the production cars," says Jordan.

But GM designers not only found time to work on those production vehicles, with cars such as late 1950s Chevrolets, chrome-laden Oldsmobiles and, of course, the big-finned and bejeweled Cadillac Eldorado, which reached its extreme of excess with the 1959 Biaritz convertible in cake-frosting pink paint, they created the designs that embodied the post-war American spirit of optimism and confidence and the accompanying economic boom.

At the same time that the Firebirds and other concepts and finned and chromed production vehicles were being created, Earl was guiding the architects for the new GM Tech Center, a campus-style complex with buildings to house engineering and design functions.

A key part of the complex was the Styling Dome, where full-size models could be viewed in privacy indoors or outside in natural light.

Earl would spend only three years in his impressive office overlooking the man-made lake in the middle of the Tech Center campus.

In 1958, at the age of 65 — mandatory for retirement — he would leave General Motors, though his influence over automotive design would continue to extend around the world through the sheer volume of his vehicles and through the influence of those who worked under him through the decades.

207 TOP TO CREATE INTEREST IN ITS NEW POST-WAR MODELS, GENERAL MOTORS WOULD STAGE A MOTORAMA SHOW, USUALLY STARTING IN THE BALLROOM OF THE WALDORF-ASTORIA HOTEL IN NEW YORK CITY AND THEN TOURING OTHER MAJOR AMERICAN CITIES. THIS PHOTO SHOWS THE DISPLAY IN THE WALDORF'S BALLROOM IN 1950.

207 BOTTOM BILL MITCHELL, WHO SUCCEEDED HARLEY EARL AS HEAD OF GM'S DESIGN DEPARTMENT, POINTS TO A FORM THAT MAY BE USED TO CREATE A SCALE MODEL LIKE THOSE ON THE SHELF OF THE FIREBIRD I, II AND III CONCEPTS VEHICLES.

208-209 AND 209 TOP THE 1953 GM MOTORAMA INCLUDED A TWO-SEAT CHEVROLET ROADSTER CALLED THE CORVETTE AND THE FIBERGLASS-BODIED CAR SOON WENT INTO PRODUCTION. WHAT THE CHEVROLET CORVETTE HAD IN STYLE IT LACKED IN POWER, WITH AN ANEMIC INLINE SIX-CYLINDER AND TWO-SPEED AUTOMATIC TRANSMISSION. DESPITE ITS LOOKS, THE CORVETTE WAS A SPORTS CAR IN NAME ONLY AND GM WAS READY TO END PRODUCTION WHEN FORD LAUNCHED ITS RIVAL THUNDERBIRD. A V8 ENGINE AND MANUAL TRANSMISSION AND A RACING-ORIENTED AND BELGIAN-BORN ENGINEER NAMED ZORA ARKUS-DUNTOV TRANSFORMED THE CORVETTE INTO A TRULY WORLD-CLASS SPORTS CAR.

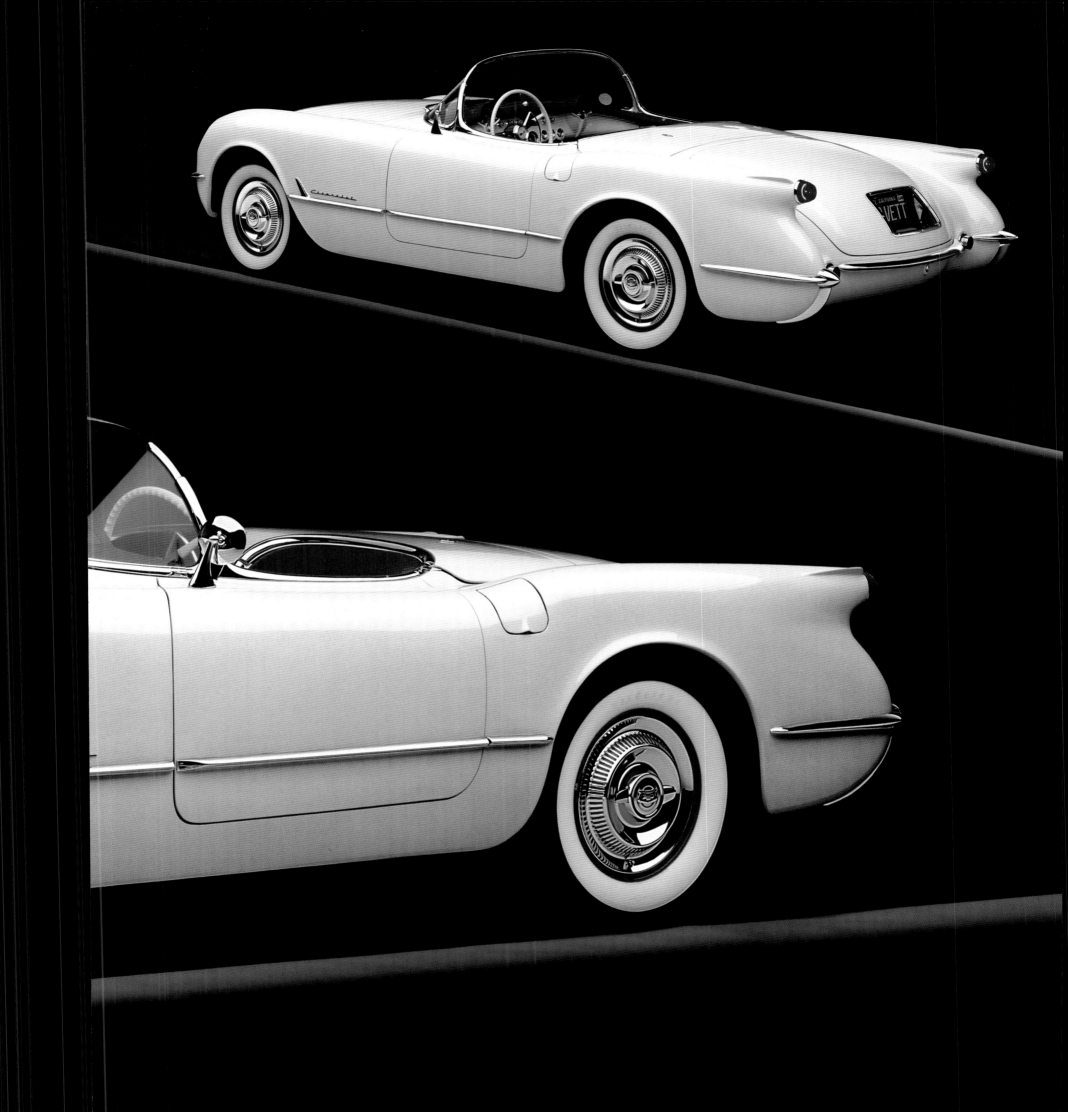

210 TOP FOR 1954, CADILLAC'S SUCH AS THIS ELDORADO CONVERTIBLE WITH ITS EXTRUDED ALUMINUM SKIRT AROUND THE REAR WHEEL, GREW LONGER AND LOWER, DISPLAYED A NEW EGG-CRATE GRILLE, A BUMPER WITH INVERTED GULL WINGS AND BULLET-LIKE "DAGWOOD" BUMPER PROTECTORS AND A LITTLE TALLER AND SHARPER REAR FINS.

210-211 THE WIDE GRILLE AND HUGE HOOD OF THE 1954 CADILLAC ELDORADO CONVERTIBLE COVER A 5.5-LITER (331 CUBIC INCH) V8 ENGINE THAT PUMPS OUT 230 HORSEPOWER. THE CADILLAC CONVERTIBLE WAS HANDSOME, BUT ALSO BIG AND HEAVY, WEIGHING IN AT MORE THAN 4800 POUNDS (2181 KILOGRAMS).

BILL MITCHELL

Earl was succeeded by Bill Mitchell, who as a teenager split his time between his father, a Buick dealer in Pennsylvania, and his mother, who worked for an advertising agency in New York City.

In New York, he started doing automotive illustrations for the ad agency and got involved in auto racing with the agency owner's sons, the Collier brothers who started a club that would evolve to become the Sports Car Club of America. Through a race fan whose company insured several of General Motors facilities, Mitchell was invited to send sketches to Harley Earl. Mitchell's drawings showed cars in motion.

"I've never made a drawing of a car standing still," Mitchell told an interviewer after he retired. Mitchell was only 23 years old when he went to work in the Art & Colour Section.

Earl liked him, assigned him to an experimental, rear-engine car project and soon put the then 24-year-old in charge of the Cadillac studio and worked closely with him on the design of the acclaimed 1938 Cadillac 60-Special.

Mitchell also designed the 1941 Cadillac (62 Series) that again boosted Cadillac sales and cemented his relationship with Earl, who took his protégé to California to expose him to the sort of car culture in which Earl had grown up.

Mitchell spent World War II making illustrations for the U.S. Navy, and then gained important management experience by running Earl's private industrial design company for four years before returning to GM as styling director under Earl. Although he wouldn't take over until Earl's retirement, the transition in leadership actually began in the summer of 1956 while Earl was traveling overseas. Out on his lunch break, GM designer Chuck Jordan drove past the Chrysler plant just six miles south of the GM Tech Center and saw the 1957 Plymouths parked behind a chain link fence. Jordan was shocked when he saw the cars, weeks before they were to be publicly unveiled, with their dramatically clean lines highlighted by well-proportioned tail fins. The cars made GM's designs look outdated. Jordan alerted Mitchell, and by the end of the day a succession of GM designers had made the trip to see the new Plymouths. With Mitchell leading the way, the GM design staff went to work on what would become its 1959 model lineup (the 1958 models already were too far along to be affected).

Earl was less than thrilled when he returned from Europe, but he realized a radically new design direction was necessary.

Not only would Mitchell lead the design staff in a new direction, but he would oversee the design of a radically new vehicle, one with its engine behind the passenger compartment.

In the face of small and fuel-efficient cars coming not only from overseas but from crosstown rival American Motors, GM, Ford and Chrysler each would launch a new compact car for the 1960 model year. However, the Chevrolet Corvair was unlike any of them. While Ford would need four years to find a way to transform the platform under its new compact Falcon sedan into the sporty Mustang coupe, the Corvair immediately provided GM with a low-slung sports car in compact car guise.

Though an artistic success, the Corvair, with its six-cylinder engine mounted behind the passenger compartment, would prove dynamically challenging for unskilled drivers and would become the focus of Ralph Nader's *Unsafe at Any Speed* crusade for strict new government safety regulations. The 1963 model year marked the launch of two of Mitchell's best designs – the "split-window" Corvette Sting Ray and the Buick Riviera. The Sting Ray was inspired by Mitchell's own racecar, while the Riviera had been intended as a new LaSalle model for the Cadillac brand. Many consider the 1965 model year the height of Mitchell's reign, though he later would lead the effort that produced such important designs as the 1966 Oldsmobile Toronado, the 1968 Corvette, the 1971 Riviera and even the 1980 Cadillac Seville – as well as concepts such as the mid-engined 1973 Aero Vette and 1977 Phantom – before retiring in 1977.

212 BILL MITCHELL SHOWS A SKETCH OF THE 1963 CHEVROLET CORVETTE DURING A DESIGN STAFF MEETING. MITCHELL, SON OF A BUICK DEALER, WORKED IN AN ADVERTISING AGENCY AND WAS 23 YEARS OLD WHEN HIRED BY HARLEY EARL, WHOM HE SUCCEEDED AS HEAD OF GM DESIGN WHEN EARL RETIRED IN 1959.

213 TOP A VEHICLE'S DESIGN TRAVELS A LONG ROUTE FORM THE DESIGNER'S PEN TO THE ROAD. THERE IS A LONG PROCESS OF VEHICLE DEVELOPMENT AND TESTING AND FINALLY DIES ARE MADE TO CREATE THE BODY PANELS AND OTHER COMPONENTS THAT ARE ASSEMBLED INTO THE FINISHED VEHICLE. THIS PHOTO SHOWS WORK IN A GM ASSEMBLY PLANT IN KANSAS CITY.

213 BOTTOM LEFT WORKERS AT GENERAL MOTORS' OLDSMOBILE ASSEMBLY PLANT ATTACH A FRONT SUB-ASSEMBLY THAT INCLUDES THE GRILLE AND HEADLIGHTS. WHEN THIS PHOTO WAS TAKEN IN 1973, THE OLDS PLANT WAS PRODUCING 91 VEHICLES AN HOUR, 16 HOURS A DAY, FIVE OR SOMETIMES SIX DAYS A WEEK.

213 BOTTOM RIGHT A V8 ENGINE AND TRANSMISSION ARE PREPARED FOR THEIR INSERTION INTO A 1973 MODEL OLDSMOBILE.

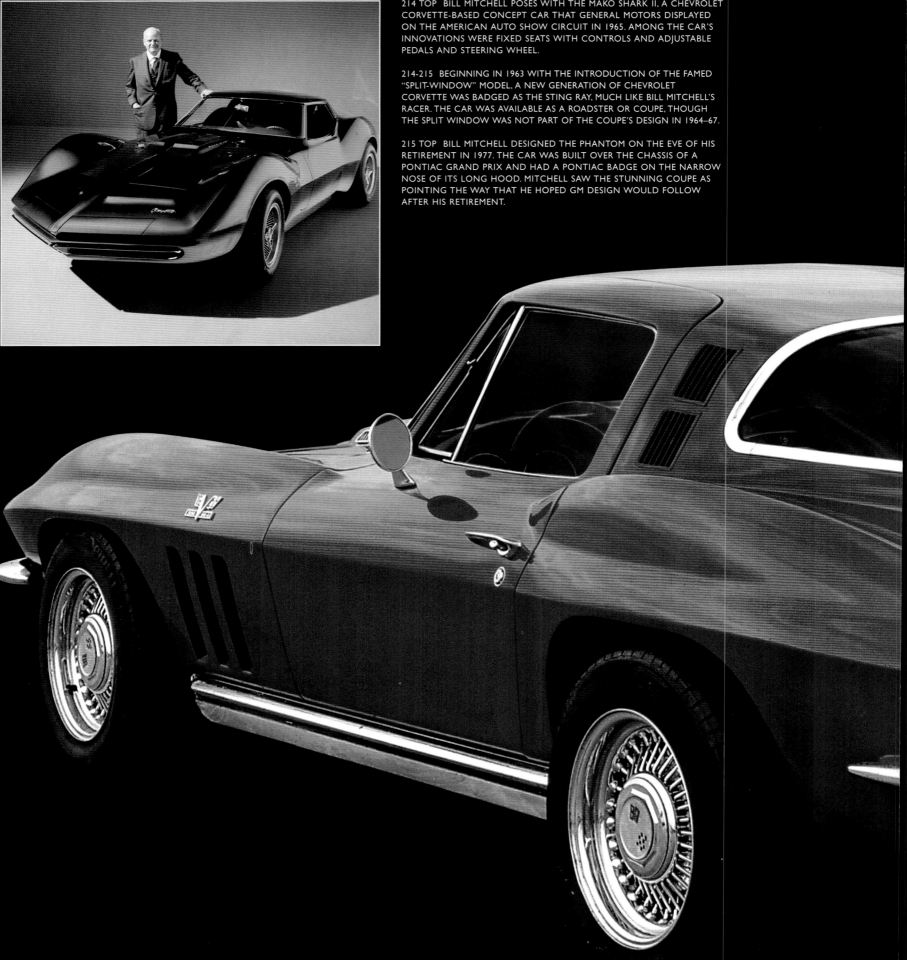

214 TOP BILL MITCHELL POSES WITH THE MAKO SHARK II, A CHEVROLET CORVETTE-BASED CONCEPT CAR THAT GENERAL MOTORS DISPLAYED ON THE AMERICAN AUTO SHOW CIRCUIT IN 1965. AMONG THE CAR'S INNOVATIONS WERE FIXED SEATS WITH CONTROLS AND ADJUSTABLE PEDALS AND STEERING WHEEL.

214-215 BEGINNING IN 1963 WITH THE INTRODUCTION OF THE FAMED "SPLIT-WINDOW" MODEL, A NEW GENERATION OF CHEVROLET CORVETTE WAS BADGED AS THE STING RAY, MUCH LIKE BILL MITCHELL'S RACER. THE CAR WAS AVAILABLE AS A ROADSTER OR COUPE, THOUGH THE SPLIT WINDOW WAS NOT PART OF THE COUPE'S DESIGN IN 1964–67.

215 TOP BILL MITCHELL DESIGNED THE PHANTOM ON THE EVE OF HIS RETIREMENT IN 1977. THE CAR WAS BUILT OVER THE CHASSIS OF A PONTIAC GRAND PRIX AND HAD A PONTIAC BADGE ON THE NARROW NOSE OF ITS LONG HOOD. MITCHELL SAW THE STUNNING COUPE AS POINTING THE WAY THAT HE HOPED GM DESIGN WOULD FOLLOW AFTER HIS RETIREMENT.

CHUCK JORDAN

Mitchell's chosen successor was Chuck Jordan, but he didn't get the job until 1986. Instead, Detroit-native Irv Rybicki, who had been Jordan's assistant, was selected by GM management, with Jordan serving as Rybicki's assistant.

Rybicki would oversee design during what at the time was the worst period in GM history, an era of financial and mechanical compromises that forced designs that looked as if they were done with cookie cutters rather than with artistic drawings and sculptural clay modeling.

Jordan became vice president of design as GM was making a comeback, and he helped the effort by making major changes, such as having interior and exterior designers work together on each vehicle, and by establishing distinct styling themes for each of the GM divisions.

When GM went to New York City in 1987 and put on a Motorama-style "Teamwork & Technology" show for investors and news media, Jordan and his studios provided a Motorama-style array of concept cars.

Jordan had grown up in southern California, knew at an early age that he wanted to design cars but decided that that to gain a competitive advantage over art school graduates, that he also would study mechanical engineering – and at MIT (the prestigious Massachusetts Institute of Technology).

He won a GM-sponsored design contest while in college and joined Harley Earl's staff after graduation.

He was in military service during the Korean War, but soon was designing heavy-duty tractors and trains.

Mitchell encouraged him to move quickly to cars and Jordan's first project was the Buick Centurian concept for the 1956 Motorama. Two years later, he became Cadillac's chief designer.

Mitchell assigned Jordan to Opel, GM's European brand, in 1967. In Europe, Jordan bought his first (of what would become many) Ferrari and created a new and much sportier styling theme for Opel.

Jordan returned to Michigan and was design director and heir apparent under Mitchell. One of many vehicles credited to Jordan's leadership and flair was the 1995 Oldsmobile Aurora, a vehicle that wasn't introduced until several years after his retirement.

"In 1989, I was the vice president and I decided that all the sedans on the road were dull, drab and boring," Jordan remembers.

"There was no character, no excitement." So Jordan put one of his advanced studios to work in secret, with an assignment to do an "emotional" four-door sedan, "a wow car," as he put it. The first attempt was, in Jordan's words, "double ugly."

The team started over "and that one developed into a beauty. It was exciting.

"You looked at it and said 'wow!'" But it also was a car no one had asked for, a car that was not in any of the GM division's product plans. So Jordan, borrowing a page from Harley Earl's design playbook, took the full-scale model of the car and placed it under wonderful lighting in a hallway where every GM manager would have to walk by it several times a day.

"One day the general manager of Oldsmobile came to me and said, 'we're going to drop the Toronado and we want to replace it with a sporty four-door sedan.

"Can we have that design you have out in the hall?'"

More than a decade later, that first-generation Aurora still looks fresh and modern, distinctive and even concept-car futuristic from every view.

216 TOP BILL MITCHELL HOPED THAT CHUCK JORDAN WOULD SUCCEED HIM JUST AS MITCHELL FOLLOWED HARLEY EARL, BUT GM MANAGEMENT MADE JORDAN WAIT NEARLY A DECADE TO MOVE INTO EARL'S OFFICE OVERLOOKING THE GM TECHNICAL CENTER.

216-217 CHUCK JORDAN CHECKS OUT THE PASSENGER SEAT IN A "SEATING BUCK," A FULL-SCALE MODEL CREATED TO SHOW HOW MUCH ROOM THE DRIVER AND OCCUPANTS WILL HAVE WITHIN A PROPOSED VEHICLE'S DESIGN PARAMETERS.

217 TOP SOME CONSIDERED THE 1966 OLDSMOBILE TORONADO TO BE AN UPDATED VERSION OF THE HERALDED AND CLASSIC 1936 CORD 810. CREATED UNDER MITCHELL'S DIRECTION, THE TORONADO LAUNCHED FRONT-WHEEL DRIVE AS A MAJOR FEATURE OF AMERICAN VEHICLES. THE CAR'S DESIGN NOT ONLY FEATURED A SUBSTANTICAL FRONT SECTION, BUT SUCH DETAILS AS THE ELIMINATION OF VENT WINDOWS, A C-PILLAR THAT WENT STRAIGHT INTO THE REAR QUARTERPANEL AND PROMINENT, MUSCULAR BLISTERS AROUND THE WHEELS.

WAYNE CHERRY

Jordan reached the mandatory retirement age in 1992 and again, the heir apparent did not get the job as GM chose Wayne Cherry over Jerry Palmer, who had designed Corvettes and Chevrolet Camaros and had managed GM's advanced design studios.

Cherry had spent most of his career in Europe. He grew up in Indianapolis and loved racecars, building his own cars to drag race and highly modifying those he drove on the street. He attended Art Center in Pasadena, California and joined GM in 1962. He soon was assigned to GM's British unit, Vauxhall, and in 1983 went to Opel, where his studio created several award-winning vehicles. After nearly 30 years abroad, Cherry returned to the U.S. in 1991, to head the Chevrolet studio, and after Jordan's retirement all GM studios. He skillfully directed an effort that used concept cars to carefully prepare consumers for major changes in vehicle styling.

For example, concept vehicles such as the Imag, Cien and Evoq introduced the "art and science" design theme that transformed Cadillac and restored its position as the American luxury car leader.

218 WAYNE CHERRY POINTS OUT FEATURES OF A MODIFIED VERSION OF THE HUMMER H2 TO GM'S NORTH AMERICAN PRESIDENT GARY COWGER (RIGHT). GM ACQUIRED RIGHTS TO DESIGN AND PRODUCE HUMMERS IN 1999, IN PART BECAUSE OF THE POSITIVE IMAGE OF THE HUMVEE MILITARY VEHICLE. BASED ON STANDARD GM TRUCK COMPONENTS.

219 SCULPTORS APPLY CLAY AND THEN SHAPE IT INTO THE PROPER FORM AS THEY CREATE A FULL-SIZE MODEL THAT WILL BE SHOWN TO GM EXECUTIVES AS THEY CONSIDER DETAILS AND POSSIBLE PRODUCTION. OFTEN SUCH MODELS HAVE DIFFERENT DETAILS ON THEIR LEFT AND RIGHT SIDES SO EXECUTIVES CAN SEE TWO VERSIONS OF THE CAR AT THE SAME TIME.

ED WELBURN

When Cherry retired in 2003, Ed Welburn became not only the sixth person to sit at Harley Earl's famed desk, but the first African-American to head any automaker's global design department.

Welburn had joined GM in 1972, had designed vehicles such as the 257 mile-per-hour Oldsmobile Aerotech prototype and had overseen GM's advanced styling studios that produced vehicles such as the Autonomy concept with its skateboard-style platform and interchangeable bodies.

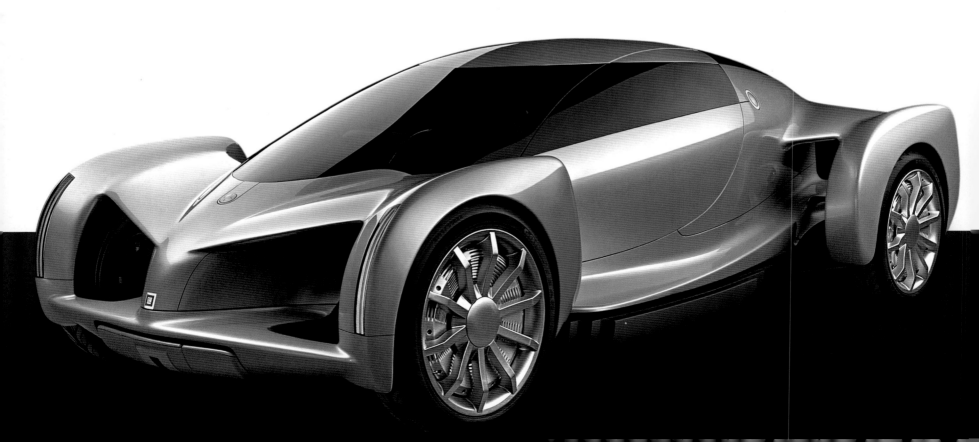

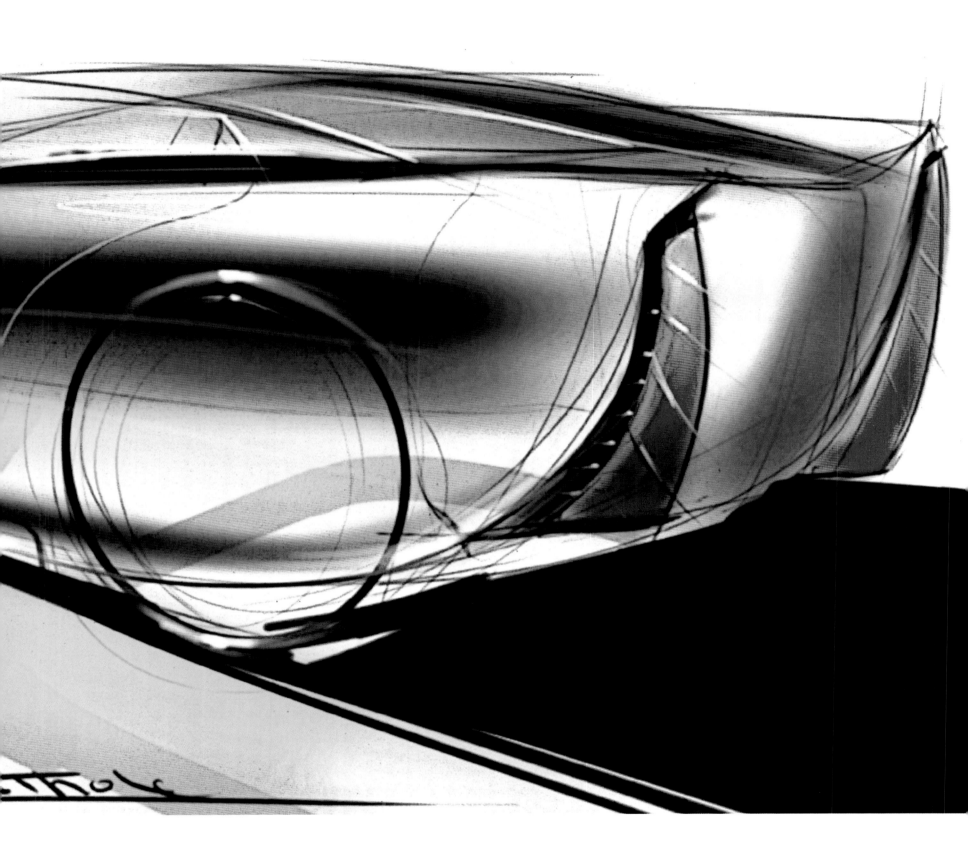

222 TOP DESIGNERS WORK ON THE ANGULAR DETAILS OF A SCALE MODEL OF THE CADILLAC EVOQ ROADSTER CONCEPT THAT WAS SEEN ON THE AUTO SHOW CIRCUIT IN 1999.

222 BOTTOM TO PAVE THE WAY FOR NEW SO-CALLED ART AND SCIENCE, A SET OF VERY ANGULAR DESIGN ELEMENTS FOR CADILLAC, GENERAL MOTORS CREATED THE EVOQ ROADSTER CONCEPT IN 1999, THE IMAJ LARGE SEDAN IN 2000, THE VISION WAGON IN 2001 AND THE CIEN

SUPERCAR IN 2002. THESE ELEMENTS SUBSEQUENTLY WERE APPLIED TO CADILLAC'S PRODUCTION VEHICLES.

222-223 THIS VERY STYLIZED DRAWING WAS PART OF THE DESIGN DEVELOPMENT FOR THE EVOQ ROADSTER, A CADILLAC CONCEPT CAR THAT STARTED TO INTRODUCE A NEW AND MORE ANGULAR DESIGN THEME TO GENERAL MOTORS' LUXURY BRAND.

224 TOP CAMARO WAS CHEVROLET'S COMPETITOR TO THE LEGENDARY FORD MUSTANG, BUT A SERIES OF FACTORS LED TO ITS DEMISE. HOWEVER, ITS ABSENCE WAS ONLY MOMENTARY AND CHEVROELT UNVEILED A NEW CAMARO CONCEPT CAR AT THE NORTH AMERICAN INTERNATIONAL AUTO SHOW IN DETROIT IN 2006.

224-225 THOUGH THE PRODUCTION VERSION WILL HAVE DOOR HANDLES AND A HIGHER ROOFLINE, THE CHEVROLET CAMARO CONCEPT VEHICLE FORMS THE BASIS FOR THE CAR THAT WILL BE AVAILABLE IN BOTH COUPE AND CONVERTIBLE ARCHITECTURES EARLY IN 2009.

CAMARO

AMERICAN STYLE:
'EX' MARKED THE SPOT AS DESIGN PROVES TO BE A TREASURE FOR CHRYSLER

CONCEPT CARS POWER CHRYSLER TO AUTOMOTIVE DESIGN EXCELLENCE

During his three-decade tenure over General Motors styling, Harley Earl reigned as the dominant force in American automotive design.

Certainly, there were other designers who created some sensational vehicles, for example, Gordon Buehrig's mid-1930s Cord and Studebakers from Raymond Loewy's studios.

But if Earl had any sort of genuine rival, a challenger for being able to set American automotive design standards, it was Virgil Exner at Chrysler. Ironically, Exner had begun his automotive design career in Earl's Art & Colour Section at General Motors,

and at age 27 was put in charge of the Pontiac design studio … but let's not get ahead of the story.

Exner came to prominence at Chrysler, a company founded by Walter Chrysler, who was what we would now call a manufacturing manager in the railroad industry. But Chrysler was curious about motorcars and in the early 1900s attended the Chicago Auto Show, where he fell in love with the Locomobile. As it turned out, Chrysler didn't want to drive the newfangled motorcar. In fact, he didn't know how to drive. He wanted to study the machine, to analyze how it worked. So he got a friend to co-sign on a loan and had the vehicle shipped to

his home in Iowa, where he took the car apart piece by piece and then reassembled it. To everyone's surprise, the rebuilt car ran. It wasn't very long afterward that Chrysler accepted a job as a factory manager for Buick, where his supervisory skills helped increase production several times over. Soon he became vice president of manufacturing for all of General Motors. By the time he was in his mid-40s, he'd become wealthy on GM stock and was in a financial position to quit the company when he felt his authority was being undermined. Investors hired him to turn around two ailing automakers, first Willys-Overland and then Maxwell-Chalmers.

By 1925, he was ready to establish his own automobile manufacturing company. Like General Motors, Chrysler's company had an art department, but its role was limited to selecting colors and other minor details for cars designed by Chrysler's engineers.

Occasional design help came from coachbuilders such as LeBaron and Briggs, but Chrysler was a company with an emphasis on engineering, so its cars were designed by the automaker's technical and mechanical staff.

Oliver Clark was the chief body engineer, but the key players were the so-called Three Musketeers – Fred Zeder, Carl Breer and Owen Skelton – who helped establish Chrysler's reputation for engineering. In 1934, the trio was responsible for the stunning Chrysler Airflow, a car whose design was dramatic, taking wind-cheating cues from aerodynamic locomotives and honing them on clay models placed in a small wind tunnel.

The Airflow also had a revolutionary and roomy passenger compartment with a three-across front seat and a back seat placed ahead instead of on top of the rear axle.

This architecture allowed the roof to be lower and also provided a smoother ride for those seated ahead of instead of atop the rear axle. With a low floor, the Airflow's center of gravity was closer to the ground, enhancing the driver's dynamic control.

While the Airflow may have been an automotive milestone, it was a millstone for Chrysler. The car-buying public wasn't ready for such a radical-looking car, one that would be derided as "the magnificent turkey."

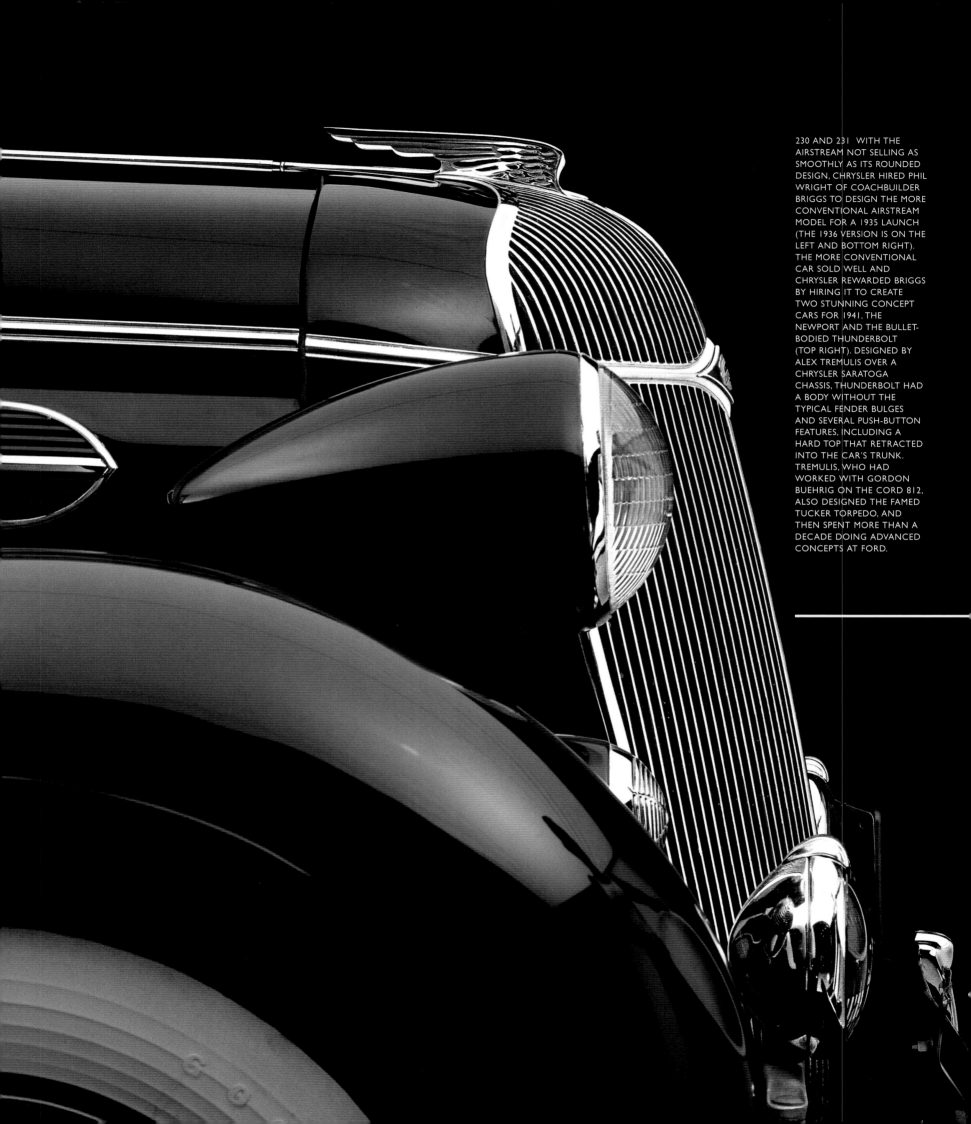

230 AND 231 WITH THE AIRSTREAM NOT SELLING AS SMOOTHLY AS ITS ROUNDED DESIGN, CHRYSLER HIRED PHIL WRIGHT OF COACHBUILDER BRIGGS TO DESIGN THE MORE CONVENTIONAL AIRSTREAM MODEL FOR A 1935 LAUNCH (THE 1936 VERSION IS ON THE LEFT AND BOTTOM RIGHT). THE MORE CONVENTIONAL CAR SOLD WELL AND CHRYSLER REWARDED BRIGGS BY HIRING IT TO CREATE TWO STUNNING CONCEPT CARS FOR 1941, THE NEWPORT AND THE BULLET-BODIED THUNDERBOLT (TOP RIGHT). DESIGNED BY ALEX TREMULIS OVER A CHRYSLER SARATOGA CHASSIS, THUNDERBOLT HAD A BODY WITHOUT THE TYPICAL FENDER BULGES AND SEVERAL PUSH-BUTTON FEATURES, INCLUDING A HARD TOP THAT RETRACTED INTO THE CAR'S TRUNK. TREMULIS, WHO HAD WORKED WITH GORDON BUEHRIG ON THE CORD 812, ALSO DESIGNED THE FAMED TUCKER TORPEDO, AND THEN SPENT MORE THAN A DECADE DOING ADVANCED CONCEPTS AT FORD.

BRIGGS

Phil Wright of coachbuilder Briggs was brought in to design a much more conventional Airstream model for 1935. While Chrysler's well-engineered production cars were ordinary-looking at best, the company showed its appreci- ation for good design in 1941 when it commis- sioned coachbuilder Briggs to create a pair of exceptionally beautiful concept cars on Chrysler platforms. They were the bullet-shaped Thun- derbolt, designed by Alex Tremulis, and the ele- gant dual-cowl Newport, designed by Ralph Roberts. By the late 1940s, Chrysler executives realized that to be strong in the post-war econ- omy, they'd need to add style to their vehicles, so they recruited Exner to show them the way.

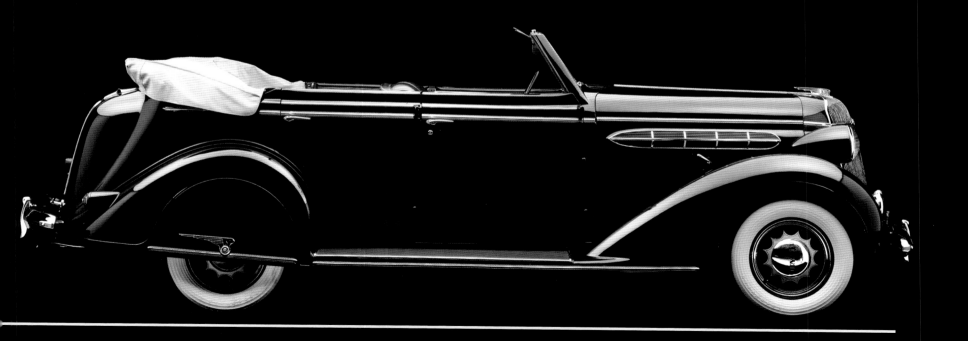

VIRGIL EXNER

Virgil Exner was born in 1909 in Ann Arbor, Michigan, where he was adopted by a couple from the rural southwestern part of the state. He knew at an early age that he wanted to design cars and enrolled at the nearby University of Notre Dame to study art. Like Notre Dame, the Studebaker car company was located in South Bend, Indiana. After two years at school, Exner took a job as an illustrator with the local agency that handled Studebaker's advertising. One of his bosses at the agency knew Harley Earl and suggested that Exner take his sketches and apply for a position in Earl's design department.

Exner started in the General Motors Art & Colour Section in 1934 and at age 27 was promoted to the head of the Pontiac studio, a job he held for two years before he and several other GM designers were recruited away to join Raymond Loewy's industrial design company in New York City. Before long, Exner found himself back in South Bend; Loewy's firm was handling the design of Studebaker's vehicles. Exner liked being back home, but became frustrated by Loewy's absentee management style. Friction became fire when Exner, encouraged by Studebaker's chief engineer Roy Cole, created an alternative design proposal for the 1947 Studebaker that was picked over the one Loewy submitted. Loewy fired Exner, who immediately was hired by Studebaker. But with Cole nearing retirement, Exner was about to lose his strongest ally, and Cole encouraged him to accept Chrysler's offer to move to Detroit to run an advanced styling studio where Exner could create what at the time were called "idea" cars.

Chrysler chairman K.T. Keller wanted a special vehicle to wrap around the company's new 310-horsepower Hemi V8 engine, and Exner did just that, designing the K-310 (K for Keller, 310 for the Hemi's horsepower rating), which he had built by the expert craftsmen at Ghia, the famed Italian coachbuilder. One of Exner's first designs after arriving at Chrysler had been the Crown Imperial, long and dual-cowl vehicles used for parades and other special events. But building such vehicles within Chrysler proved very expensive, and Exner discovered he could save money and take advantage of the Italian coachbuilding tradition by having his dream cars built by Ghia. Working together for a period of several years — Exner designing and Ghia building — the partnership would produce a succession of concept vehicles that rivaled GM's Motorama dream car fleet.

The K-310 was an elegant two-door hardtop that showed both the sculptural forms, marvelous proportions and exquisite details that would characterize Exner vehicles.

232 TOP VIRGIL EXNER POINTS OUT THE DETAILS OF A SCALE MODEL OF A PROPOSED CHRYSLER CONCEPT CAR, IN THE 1950S.

232 BOTTOM SHOWN ON THE STAND OF THE PARIS MOTOR SHOW IN 1961 IS THE CHRYSLER TURBOFLITE. THE CONCEPT CAR USED A PLYMOUTH CHASSIS, BUT MOUNTED ON IT WAS A TURBINE (JET) ENGINE. THE CAR WAS DESIGNED BY CHRYSLER AND BUILT BY GHIA.

233 THE CHRYSLER SPECIAL WAS A CONCEPT CAR OR DREAM MACHINE DESIGNED BY CHRYSLER, BUILT BY GHIA OF ITALY AND UNVEILED AT THE 1952 PARIS MOTOR SHOW. THE CAR WAS FOUR INCHES LOWER THAN THE CHRYSLER NEW YORKER ON WHICH IT WAS BASED AND HAD SUCH SPECIAL FEATURES AS A SPARE TIRE MOUNTED IN A TRAY THAT SLID OUT OF THE BACK OF THE CAR LIKE A DRAWER.

In 1953, Exner and Ghia created the Chrysler Special, De Soto Adventurer, Chrysler D'Elegance. A year later there were the even more radical Adventurer II, the Plymouth Explorer and the stunning quartet of Dodge Firearrows – two roadsters, a coupe and a convertible. Next came the Chrysler Falcon and Flight-Sweep concepts – a coupe and convertible. In 1956, they combined on the Chrysler Plainsman (wagon) and Norseman (lost at sea when the *Andrea Doria* sank) and the absolutely stunning and B.A.T.-like but American-sized Dodge Dart.

Yet others followed, such as the 1959 De Soto Cella with its electrochemical propulsion system, the 1960 Plymouth XNR (a proposed Corvette competitor with an amazing asymmetrical design) and the 1961 Chrysler Turboflite (a turbine-powered vehicle with a huge rear wing and a roof that opened via a rear hinge). Not that the team in Detroit wasn't busy while Ghia was building those concept cars.

In addition to designing the concepts, Exner, who in 1953 was promoted to Chrysler's director of styling, and his staff – led by Cliff Voss – were working on a new and modern version of the American sedan – the so-called *Forward Look,* introduced in the fall of 1954 on the

company's new 1955 models. These cars proved so popular that Chrysler doubled its sales over the previous year.

While the cars weren't quite as advanced as Exner might have wanted, they certainly were colorful – with 56 single-tone shades, 173 two-tone options offered in various patterns known as the Chrysler "color-sweep," and with three-color combinations on selected models.

234-235 THE 1953 CHRYSLER D'ELEGANCE WAS ANOTHER OF VIRGIL EXNER'S DREAM MACHINES THAT WAS DESIGNED AT CHRYSLER AND BUILT BY GHIA, WHICH LIKED THE DESIGN SO MUCH THAT IT SCALED IT DOWN INTO THE VOLKSWAGEN KARMANN GHIA. D'ELEGANCE FEATURED A THREE-ACROSS SEAT AND CUSTOM LUGGAGE THAT SAT IN THE CARPETED SHELF BEHIND THE SEAT. THE SPARE TIRE WAS MOUNTED ON THE REAR DECK LID AND HAD A HYDRAULIC MECHANISM THAT LIFTED IT UP AND OUT WITHIN EASY REACH BEHIND THE REAR BUMPER.

236 TOP CHRYSLER'S 1957 MODELS NOT ONLY HAD TALL REAR WINGS, BUT RODE ON A NEW SUSPENSION SYSTEM THAT LOWERED THEIR RIDE BY MORE THAN FIVE INCHES AND ENHANCED THEIR DYNAMIC CAPABILITIES AS WELL BY LOWERING THE CENTER OF GRAVITY. FLAGSHIP OF THE CHRYSLER FLEET WAS IMPERIAL, A LUXURY LINE LAUNCHED IN 1954. SHOWN HERE IS THE 1957 IMPERIAL CROWN COUPE.

236-237 AMONG THE IMPERIAL'S UNIQUE STYLING TOUCHES WAS A SECOND REAR ROOF SECTION THAT WRAPPED OVER THE STANDARD ROOF. THE D'ELEGANCE STYLE SPARE TIRE COVER WAS A COSMETIC OPTION, NOT A FUNCTIONAL FEATURE. ANOTHER NEW ELEMENT OF THE DESIGN FOR 1957 WAS TO INCORPORATE THE TAIL LAMPS INTO THE TAIL FINS; IN 1956 THE LIGHTS SAT AWKWARDLY ON TOP OF THE FINS.

But Exner was just getting warmed up. For 1956, every Chrysler was equipped with some form of rear fin, a form seen on only the most expensive of GM products, the Cadillac. Then, for the 1957 model year, Exner and the Chrysler engineers unleashed the cars that put GM designers into panic mode. Not only did the '57s have a long and high-winged design, but it was accentuated by a new suspension system from Chrysler engineers that allowed the company's cars to be 5 inches lower and to have much improved dynamic capabilities. However, to gain a competitive edge in the marketplace, the new bodies and suspension components were rushed into production a year early and thus the cars would suffer from broken suspension parts and premature rust within body panels. Still, there was no doubt that Exner's designs were beyond anything GM or Ford had in production, and in 1957 he was promoted to Chrysler vice president of styling. Exner showed his creativity again when Detroit started producing more compact vehicles. Exner didn't want just a scaled-down version of a full-size sedan for his compact, so for 1960 he created the Plymouth Valiant with its Ferrari-like grille, long hood and short rear deck absent of tail fins. Again, his design provided a new direction for American car design. Exner already was nearing the end of his Chrysler career as the Valiant was being developed. He had suffered a serious heart attack in the mid-1950s and in 1961 would leave Chrysler and establish a private design business with his son. However, before leaving Chrysler, Exner again showed his design skills with the Plymouth Super Sport proposal for the 1962 model year. The Super Sport would have been Plymouth's competitor for Chevrolet's sporty Impala, though Chrysler management never put the car into production.

CHRYSLER BRIDGES
DESIGN ERAS

Elwood Engel, who had designed the successful 1961 Lincoln Continental at Ford, was brought in as the new head of the Chrysler studios. He led styling efforts for the 1964 model year and for such subsequent vehicles as the Dodge Charger and Challenger and Plymouth Barracuda.

Former Packard designer Richard Macadam was in charge after Engel retired in 1972 and had to deal with the energy crisis and vehicle downsizing and the so-called K Car. In 1980, Don De-LaRossa, Ford's former designer, was lured out of retirement to lead Chrysler design in 1980 as the company, which had become financially distressed, was being bailed out by a federal government loan. Nonetheless, DeLaRossa was in charge when the minivan was being designed, and he also established a new Chrysler design facility – Pacifica – on the West Coast of the United States, where designers could be absorbed in a very different automotive culture from Detroit. In the coming years, this studio would become a spawning ground for new vehicle concepts.

238-239 IN THE 1960S, POLARA WAS DODGE'S LARGE OR FULL-SIZE CAR, AVAILABLE AS A COUPE, SEDAN OR CONVERTIBLE. THOUGH THE MUSCLE CAR ERA WOULDN'T OFFICIALLY BEGIN UNTIL 1963 WHEN PONTIAC OFFERED THE G.T.O. OPTION PACKAGE IN ITS MID-SIZE LE MANS, CARS SUCH AS THE POLARA WERE FORERUNNERS – FULL-SIZE VEHICLES POWERED BY VERY LARGE AND POWERFUL ENGINES SUCH AS THE RAMCHARGER AND HEMI V8S. SHOWN HERE WITH LARGE HOOD SCOOPS TO SUPPLY COOLING AIR TO ITS V8 ENGINE IS A 1964 POLARA 500.

239 TOP CHRYSLER WAS IN THE FOREFRONT OF THE MUSCLE CAR MOVEMENT. MUSCLE CARS WERE MID-SIZE FAMILY CARS INTO WHICH ENGINEERS CRAMMED THE LARGEST ENGINES AVAILABLE. THEY DIDN'T TURN OR STOP LIKE EUROPEAN SPORTS CARS, BUT THEY WERE BLISTERING FAST WHEN IT CAME TO ACCELERATING IN A STRAIGHT LINE FROM A TRAFFIC LIGHT. MUSCLE CARS OFTEN WERE PAINTED IN FLAMBOYANT COLORS, LIKE THIS 1970 DODGE CHALLENGER HEMI CONVERTIBLE.

Chrysler drives down costs for next century vehicles

Chrysler's newest technology concept, the Intrepid ESX2, combines unique lightweight body technology with a new diesel-electric hybrid powertrain. The ESX2 has potential to meet future emissions requirements and achieve 70 miles per gallon. While Chrysler estimates the ESX2 to be $15,000 more than a 1998 Dodge Intrepid, innovative technology and unconventional thinking helped Chrysler lower costs by $45,000 from its original hybrid concept shown two years ago. Chrysler is working to clear the remaining hurdles of cost, weight, emissions, durability and reliability.

Lightweight Body:

Nearly 100 percent recyclable, the new thermoplastic body invented by Chrysler and its suppliers is half the weight and investment cost of a traditional steel-bodied car. The thermoplastic body and light weight aluminum frame help offset the additional cost and weight of the two power sources in the hybrid powertrain

Efficient Powertrain:

Chrysler's strategy called a "mybrid," or mild hybrid, uses a small battery to power accessories and provide a boost to the engine during hard acceleration. Other hybrids require bigger, more expensive batteries to power an electric motor almost the entire time the vehicle is running — a battery that might cost up to $10,000 by itself

Source: Chrysler Corporation

240 TOP LEFT VIRGIL EXNER WAS KNOWN FOR THE "FORWARD LOOK" OF HIS CHRYSLER DESIGNS. TOM GALE AND HIS STUDIO DESIGNED THE "CAB FORWARD" ARCHITECTURE THAT PUSHED ENGINES FORWARD AND CREATED MORE ROOM FOR PEOPLE IN SEDANS THAT HAD LOW, COUPE-LIKE ROOFLINES. THE DODGE INTREPID ESX2 WAS A CONCEPT CAR THAT EXPANDED ON THIS THEME BY USING A SMALL GASOLINE ENGINE TO POWER ELECTRIC MOTORS THAT MOVED THE CAR DOWN THE ROAD.

240 TOP RIGHT THE P.T. CRUISER WAS A BREAKTHROUGH CAR FOR CHRYSLER AND CREATED A WHOLE NEW CATEGORY OF AMERICAN AUTOMOBILE. PART CAR, PART TRUCK, THE P.T. CRUISER HAD A RETRO DESIGN THAT RECALLED THE PANEL DELIVERY VEHICLES OF A BYGONE ERA.

TOM GALE

Chrysler finally would go through a design renaissance under Tom Gale, who became design director in 1935, nearly 20 years after joining the Chrysler design staff. Gale had grown up in Flint, Michigan, where his father was an engineer for General Motors. Gale wanted to design cars, but was encouraged to study engineering rather than art, and so he studied both — and also business — in college. When he joined Chrysler, it was as an engineer. He held positions in engineering, design and product planning before going back to design in 1981. Eventually, Gale not only would lead the entire Chrysler design department, but would eventually become the first design director to also oversee an automaker's international operations and all product development.

As the new head of design in 1985, Gale inherited the uninspiring and aging K Car-based fleet, but like Exner used a succession of stunning concept cars to show the way forward. "It takes a long time for something to come through the production pipeline and the only way we could really try to establish some credibility quickly was to get out there with concepts," Gale remembers of an era when Chrysler was still doing K Car derivatives while Ford was selling its futuristic-looking Taurus. In 1987, Chrysler unveiled its Portofino concept at the Frankfurt show. The car was badged as a Lamborghini, the Italian brand at the time owned by Chrysler, but once you got past the quartet of scissor-hinged doors, the design introduced the "cab-forward" front-wheel-drive architecture planned for a new generation of

Chrysler sedans. Two years later, at the Detroit show, Chrysler unleashed the Dodge Viper, an overly aggressive, almost cartoonish but hugely popular sports car concept with a huge V10 engine. In 1990, Chrysler showed an opposite extreme, Voyager III, a two-piece mini/maxivan with a smaller, three-seat forward section that could be driven independently or attached to a secondary section with room to carry as many as eight more people. Then there were the Plymouth Prowler, a modern hot-rod; Chronos, a V10-powered and modern tribute to Exner's D'Elegance concept; Atlantic, with its straight-eight engine and lush forms paying homage to such classic vehicles as the Talbot-Lago; the 300 Hemi C, a concept for a new generation of rear-drive and V8-powered American sedans; the Viper-inspired Copperhead; the Proto Cruizer, designed to showcase a new engine but actually a preview of the PT Cruiser; new forms of Jeeps and many, many others.

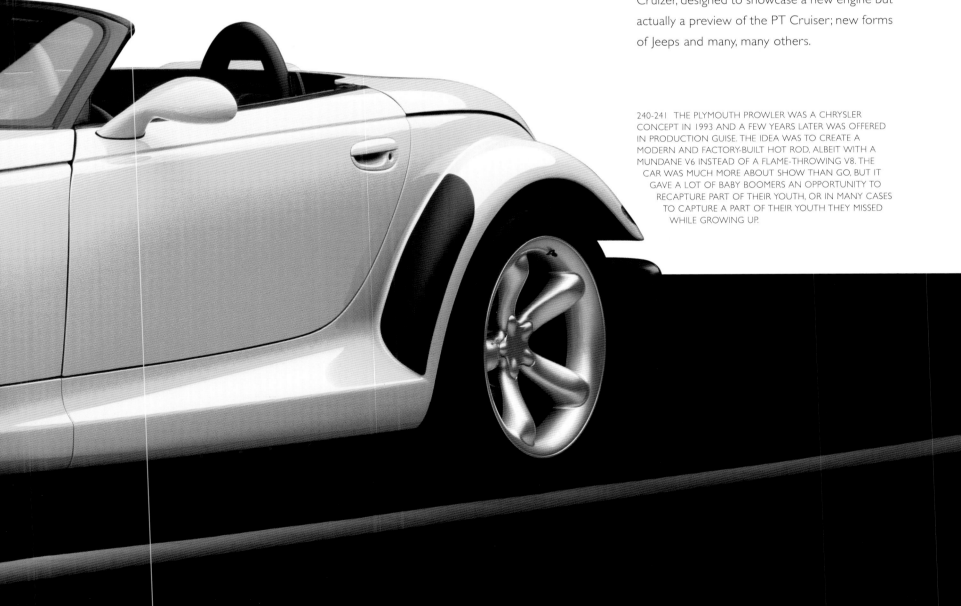

240-241 THE PLYMOUTH PROWLER WAS A CHRYSLER CONCEPT IN 1993 AND A FEW YEARS LATER WAS OFFERED IN PRODUCTION GUISE. THE IDEA WAS TO CREATE A MODERN AND FACTORY-BUILT HOT ROD, ALBEIT WITH A MUNDANE V6 INSTEAD OF A FLAME-THROWING V8. THE CAR WAS MUCH MORE ABOUT SHOW THAN GO, BUT IT GAVE A LOT OF BABY BOOMERS AN OPPORTUNITY TO RECAPTURE PART OF THEIR YOUTH, OR IN MANY CASES TO CAPTURE A PART OF THEIR YOUTH THEY MISSED WHILE GROWING UP.

242-243 AND 243 TOP THE LAMBORGHINI PORTOFINO WAS A CONCEPT CAR THAT CELEBRATED SEVERAL THINGS – CHRYSLER'S OWNERSHIP OF THE ITALIAN EXOTIC CAR BRAND, THE APPLICATION OF FOUR-WHEEL DRIVE TO A LARGE SEDAN AND THE FIRST PUBLIC GLIMPSE AT CHRYSLER'S NEW CAB-FORWARD DESIGN. THE CAB-FORWARD ARCHITECTURE FIRST SEEN ON THE PORTOFINO MOVED FROM THE AUTO SHOW STAND TO THE ROAD IN 1993 WITH THE LAUNCH OF THE DODGE INTREPID, EAGLE VISION AND CHRYSLER CONCORDE.

244 TOP THE DODGE VIPER WAS UNVEILED AT THE NORTH AMERICAN INTERNATIONAL AUTO SHOW IN DETROIT IN 1989. ITS FACE EMPHASIZED AN EMBOLDENED DODGE CROSSHAIR GRILLE. BEHIND THAT GRILLE WAS A V10 ENGINE THAT WAS DEVELOPED BY ADDING A COUPLE OF CYLINDERS TO A LAMBORGHINI V8.

244-245 PERHAPS THE MOST OUTRAGEOUS OF ALL THE MANY CHRYSLER CONCEPT CARS WAS THE VIPER R/T10, AN ALMOST CARTOONISH LOOKING SPORTS CAR WITH BIG, FAT TIRES AND WITH SIDE-MOUNTED EXHAUST PIPES YOU HAD TO BE CAREFUL NOT TO TOUCH WITH THE BACK OF YOUR LEGS AS YOU EXITED THE COCKPIT. THE VIPER WAS CHRYSLER'S IDEA FOR CREATING A CONTEMPORARY VERSION OF THE SHELBY COBRA, THE FERRARI-BEATING AMERICAN SPORTS CAR OF THE 1960S.

TREVOR CREED

While the concepts kept coming, so did new concept-based production vehicles, beginning in 1992 with the Dodge Viper and in 1993 with the introduction of the "LH" sedans inspired by the Portofino concept.

Unlike many design executives, Gale was quick to share credit, not only with his top lieutenants such as Trevor Creed, Neil Walling and John Herlitz, but with younger designers as well, some of whom would be recruited away from Chrysler, others who would be promoted within the company's studios.

Gale retired in 2000 with Creed becoming the new vice president of design.

Creed was a native of England who worked at Ford from 1966 until he joined Chrysler in 1985. Like Exner and Gale, he used wonderful concepts to explore new ideas for production vehicles and to excite both consumers and designers alike.

246 TOP CHRYSLER WAS ONE OF MANY AUTOMAKERS TO ESTABLISH ADVANCED DESIGN STUDIOS IN SOUTHERN CALIFORNIA, THE HOT BED OF AMERICAN CAR CULTURE. AT CHRYSLER'S PACIFICA STUDIO, YOUNG DESIGNERS COULD EXPLORE THEIR IDEAS FOR FUTURE VEHICLES AWAY FROM THE PRESSURES OF THE PRODUCTION STUDIOS BACK IN THE DETROIT AREA.

246 BOTTOM WHILE CONCEPT CARS ARE BUILT BY HAND, THOSE THAT ADVANCE TO PRODUCTION HAVE TO BE ABLE TO TRAVEL DOWN A REGULAR ASSEMBLY LINE. SHOWN HERE ARE WELDING ROBOTS IN A CHRYSLER PLANT IN BELVEDERE, ILLINOIS, WHERE CHRYSLER BUILT THE PRODUCTION VERSION OF THE NEON CONCEPT.

246-247 BRITISH-BORN AND EDUCATED TREVOR CREED LED CHRYSLER'S DESIGN STUDIOS IN THE EARLY YEARS OF THE 21ST CENTURY. LIKE VIRGIL EXNER AND TOM GALE, CREED USED A VARIETY OF INNOVATIVE CONCEPT CARS TO EXPLORE NEW IDEAS FOR FUTURE VEHICLES. HERE, AT THE DETROIT SHOW IN 2004, HE DISCUSSES THE TREO CONCEPT, AN "URBAN ACTIVITY" VEHICLE DESIGNED TO HOLD THREE PEOPLE OR TWO PEOPLE AND THEIR GEAR AND TO RUN ON A CLEAN, HYDROGEN FUEL CELL DRIVE SYSTEM.

248-249 AND 249 TOP AMONG THE CHRYSLER CONCEPTS UNVEILED IN 2007 WERE THE JEEP
TRAILHAWK (BELOW) AND CHRYSLER NASSAU (OPPOSITE PAGE). THE TRAILHAWK IS A LARGE
VEHICLE WITH REMOVABLE GLASS ROOF AND WINDOWS TO CREATE A CONVERTIBLE EFFECT.
THE PASSENGER COMPARTMENT IS SET BACK ON THE CHASSIS TO CREATE A LOOK LIKE AN
ARROW DRAWN BACK AND READY TO FLY. NASSAU IS A LARGE SEDAN THAT VISUALLY BELIES
ITS SIZE BECAUSE OF ITS ELEGANT, TAPERING AND ALMOST BOAT-TAIL REAR DESIGN.

AMERICAN STYLE:
EDSEL DID, INDEED, HAVE
A BETTER IDEA FOR FORD

FROM BASIC BLACK
TO BACK TO THE FUTURE

GENTLEMEM
OUR
COUNTRY

HENRY FORD. AND HIS FIRST CAR.

*T*hough the Ford Motor Company was the first, and for many years the largest, of Detroit's so-called Big Three automakers, it also was the last and the least to include styling in its vehicles. Henry Ford was a tinkering mechanic with a dream who found a wealthy partner and founded what would become the Ford Motor Company in 1903.

The Model Ts that company produced from 1908 to 1927 would represent more than half of the motorcars on the planet at that time, but it wasn't until 1931 that the Ford Motor Company employed its own designer – and six years later it had only four such employees on its payroll. Even years later, when Ford finally did build up its design staff, with only a few impressive exemptions, it would be decades until those designers exerted much influence over Ford's fleet of vehicles.

Henry Ford saw no need for artistic stylists when it came to building motorcars. His Model T was the horseless carriage that put America – and the world – on motor-powered wheels and that was enough for Henry Ford. In fact, because black paint dried faster, that was the only color available on his Model T until 1926, when he finally was persuaded to add some other shades.

That persuasion came from Ford's son, Edsel, who started drawing cars as a teenager and who would develop a deep appreciation for art and style. It also had been Edsel who had convinced his father to buy the Lincoln Motor Car Co. in 1922 and thus to add a larger, more luxurious and elegant model to the Ford vehicle lineup. Edsel worked with various American coachbuilders to create bodies for the Lincoln line.

He also pushed – pushed for many years before his father finally relented – for the Model T replacement, and then did everything he could to pattern the new 1928 Model A after the Lincoln.

250-251 THE FORD GT40 WAS A RACECAR THAT BEAT FERRARI AT LE MANS IN THE 1960S. THE FORD GT WAS A RACECAR-INSPIRED CONCEPT CAR UNVEILED AT THE NORTH AMERICAN INTERNATIONAL AUTO SHOW IN DETROIT IN 2002.

252 HENRY FORD DRIVES HIS FIRST CAR, THE 1896 QUADRICYCLE, POWERED BY AN ENGINE HE BUILT. HE SOLD THE CAR FOR $200 AND USED THE MONEY TO WORK ON A SECOND CAR. SOON HE BECAME CHIEF ENGINEER OF THE DETROIT AUTOMOBILE COMPANY, AND IN 1901 LAUNCHED THE HENRY FORD COMPANY.

253 TOP DATED JUNE 26, 1903 IS HENRY FORD'S STOCK CERTIFICATE, SHOWING THAT HE OWNS 255 SHARES IN THE AUTOMOBILE MANUFACTURING COMPANY THAT BEARS HIS LAST NAME.

253 CENTER HENRY FORD'S SON, EDSEL, DOES THE CEREMONIAL GROUND BREAKING FOR A FORD MOTOR COMPANY PLANT AT DAGENHAM, ESSEX, ENGLAND IN THE LATE 1920S.

253 BOTTOM LONG BEFORE THE VOLKSWAGEN BEETLE, CITROËN 2CV OR FIAT 500, HENRY FORD WANTED TO BUILD A PRACTICAL CAR THAT ANYONE COULD AFFORD TO OWN AND DRIVE. THAT CAR WAS THE FORD MODEL T.

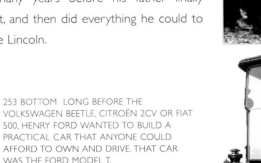

EUGENE T. GREGORIE

Finally, in 1931, Lincoln hired its own full-time designer, Eugene T. "Bob" Gregorie, a 23-year-old who had grown up in a wealthy family on Long Island, New York, where his family drove cars imported from Europe and where he designed boats but wanted to design cars like those his family owned.

Gregorie worked for New York automotive coachbuilder Brewster for a year, tried to catch on with various American luxury-car builders, even spent a little time in Harley Earl's design studios at

General Motors and was designing yachts until he landed at Lincoln.

As the only designer within the Ford Motor Company, Gregorie's first assignment wasn't a new Lincoln but what would become the 1932 Model Y for Ford's British division.

The same car, though enlarged to American scale, would become the 1933 U.S. Ford. Gregorie also did a two-seat sports car version of the car. Edsel Ford decided it didn't fit into the Ford line-up, but he offered it to Jensen Cars Ltd. of Britain,

254 TOP EUGENE T. "BOB" GREGORIE WAS A 23-YEAR-OLD WHO WAS DESIGNING BOATS AND AUTOMOTIVE BODIES FOR AN AMERICAN COACHBUILDER WHEN HE WAS HIRED TO DESIGN CARS FOR LINCOLN, FORD'S LUXURY MODEL.

254-255 BECAUSE THERE WERE FORD MODELS THAT NEEDED THE DESIGNER'S ATTENTION, IT WOULD BE FIVE YEARS BEFORE GREGORIE'S FIRST LINCOLN HIT THE ROAD. THE ZEPHYR WAS LAUNCHED IN 1936 AND HELPED BOOST LINCOLN SALES THROUGH THE DEPRESSION ERA.

255 THE LINCOLN ZEPHYR, THE 1937 MODEL IS SHOWN HERE IN THE DRIVEWAY OF A HOUSE THAT SHOWS THE INFLUENCE OF ART DECO IN ITS ARCHITECTURAL STYLE. THE CAR WAS POWERED BY A 12-CYLINDER ENGINE AND PROVIDED A ROOMY INTERIOR.

which produced it for several years. Finally, for 1936, Gregorie created his first Lincoln, the Zephyr. Edsel Ford needed a new and lower-priced car if the Lincoln brand was going to survive the Depression.

He had underwritten development on John Tjaarda's radically aerodynamic mid-engine design at Briggs, but that car's engine placement was deemed too radical, and after Chrysler's sales de-

bacle with its 1934 Airflow, Ford wasn't willing to take a risk on anything quite so rounded.

But Gregorie's Zephyr provided a handsome alternative that sold well and earned Gregorie a promotion to manage design at Lincoln and Ford. By 1938 the Zephyr needed better cooling for its engine, so the design was freshened to include a new, horizontal grille that would echo across Detroit and change the face of the American sedan.

About this same time, Edsel Ford was coming home from a European tour where he decided that he wanted to bring "continental" styling to the American automobile, and he wanted to do it in time for his annual winter vacation in Palm Beach, Florida. In less than an hour, Gregorie did preliminary sketches for such a car.

Edsel liked what he saw, a 20-inch scale model was built, full-size plans were drawn and the Zephyr chassis was stretched and lowered to carry the new sheetmetal.

Edsel drove the car back from Florida, talking about how impressed everyone was with it and that he could sell a thousand of them and thus the 1941 Lincoln Continental came to be, and would become the car of choice among Hollywood types and over three years more than 2000 of them were built and sold.

256-257 WHEN EDSEL FORD VISITED EUROPE AND CAME HOME WANTING A CAR OF HIS OWN WITH WHAT HE CALLED CONTINENTAL FLAIR. HE SET BOB GREGORIE TO WORK AND IN LESS THAN AN HOUR HE HAD DONE PRELIMINARY SKETCHES FOR THE LINCOLN CONTINENTAL. EDSEL DROVE THE PROTOTYPE TO FLORIDA AND CAME HOME WITH ENOUGH ORDERS FROM HIS FRIENDS AND OTHERS THAT THE CAR WENT INTO PRODUCTION IN 1941.

257 TOP THE LINCOLN CONTINENTAL WAS POPULAR WITH THE RICH AND FAMOUS, PEOPLE SUCH AS HOLLYWOOD STAR RITA HAYWORTH. ONLY SOME 2000 CONTINENTALS WERE BUILT, WITH PRODUCTION INTERRUPTED BY THE WAR.

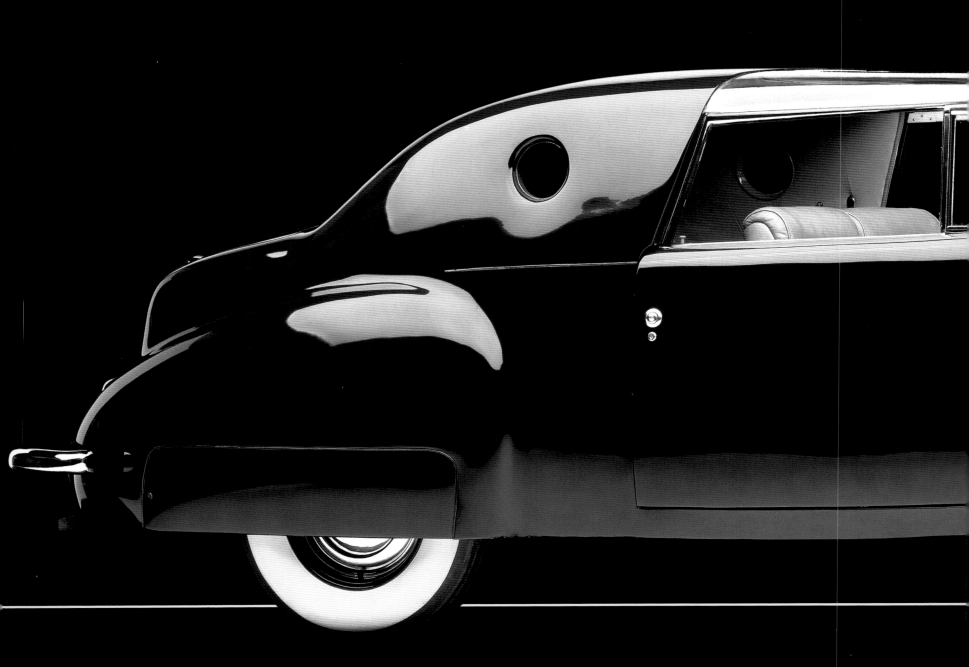

GEORGE WALKER

But then came the war, and automobile production ended and in 1943 Edsel Ford died after surgery for stomach ulcers and Bob Gregorie was out of work, though only for a few months. Tom Hibbard, the former coachbuilder, was brought in to work on possible post-war car designs.

Soon, however, Henry Ford II, Edsel's 25-year-old son who had strong support from his mother and grandmother, was taking over the family-owned automaker.

He offered Gregorie his old job, with Hibbard as Gregorie's assistant.

He also hired the so-called Whiz Kids, a group of former Air Force officers and management specialists, and brought in Ernest Breech, a former vice president at General Motors.

Ford pinned its future on its post-war, 1949 model, and the new managers set up a design competition between Gregorie's staff and an outside firm, George Walker Associates.

Gregorie lost, and although his proposal became the 1949 Mercury, a car that would become popular with hot-rodders, his authority was taken away and he soon left Ford.

Meanwhile, the '49 Ford sold in record numbers and Ford Motor Company enjoyed its first million-car year since 1930.

Ford's new management started recruiting designers from General Motors, among them Gene Bordinat and Don DeLaRossa.

Then, in 1948, Breech brought back Walker and his team, this time with Walker as Ford's official design director, with Joe Oros in charge of Ford cars and trucks and Elwood Engel overseeing Lincoln and Mercury. In addition, Alex Tremulis was given responsibility for an advanced design studio. Walker, who in 1955 would become Ford's first vice president for styling, had been a semi-pro football player and didn't study art until he was 27 years old.

In addition to his design firm, he was involved in other businesses; one of them did well by selling trim pieces to Detroit's automakers.

Although Ford's designs – concept and production vehicles – lagged behind those from the GM and Chrysler studios, there was the occasional exception, such as the 1955 Ford Thunderbird (created in GM alumnus Frank Hershey's studio) and the 1961 Lincoln Continental (by Engel).

Of course, there also was the 1958 Edsel, the automotive ugly duckling with its horse-collar grille.

258 ONE TRICK DESIGNERS EMPLOY IS TO BUILD HALF OF A SCALE MODEL, THEN TO SET IT AGAINST A MIRROR, WHICH CREATES THE ILLUSION OF A FULLY BODIED VEHICLE. THIS PHOTO SHOWS A FORD DESIGNER IN 1952 MAKING SOME VERY CAREFUL ADJUSTMENTS TO ONE SUCH HALF MODEL OF A CAR PROPOSAL THAT USES AN AIRPLANE ENGINE AND PROPELLER TO PULL IT DOWN THE ROAD.

259 TOP WHAT LOOKS TO BE A THREE-DIMENSIONAL VEHICLE IS ACTUALLY A RENDERING THAT A FORD ARTIST IS CAREFULLY AIRBRUSHING TO ENHANCE THE VISUAL IMPACT. THE PHOTO WAS TAKEN IN THE FORD DESIGN STUDIO IN THE SPRING OF 1957.

259 BOTTOM LEFT GEORGE WALKER BECAME THE FIRST PERSON TO EARN THE TITLE OF VICE PRESIDENT FOR STYLING AT THE FORD MOTOR COMPANY. WALKER HAD BEEN AN INDEPENDENT DESIGNER WHOSE TEAM CREATED THE VERY POPULAR 1949 FORD. WALKER BECAME FORD DESIGN DIRECTOR AND FROM 1955 TO 1961 HELD THE VICE PRESIDENT'S TITLE.

259 BOTTOM RIGHT NOT EVERY DESIGN IS A SUCCESS. IN 1958 FORD INTRODUCED THE EDSEL TO WHITE-COATED MEMBERS OF THE NEWS MEDIA. THE CAR'S HORSE-COLLAR FRONT GRILLE AND ITS EXPENSIVE PRICE TAG WERE FACTORS IN ONE OF DETROIT'S MOST HISTORIC FAILURES.

260 TOP FINS WERE IN IN AMERICAN CAR DESIGN IN THE 1950S. SOME CARS HAD HUGE
WINGS THAT SOARED FAR ABOVE THE ROAD. THE FORD THUNDERBIRD HAD MUCH SHORTER
FINS THAT GAVE ITS TAIL A NICELY FINISHED AND FRAMED APPEARANCE.

260-261 FOR THE 1955 MODEL YEAR, FORD LAUNCHED THE THUNDERBIRD. EVEN WITH A V8
ENGINE, THE T-BIRD, AS IT WAS KNOWN, WAS MORE OF A TWO-SEAT AMERICAN CRUISER
THAN A EUROPEAN SPORTS CAR. BUT THE CAR WAS NICELY PROPORTIONED AND VERY
POPULAR, FAR OUTSELLING THE CHEVROLET CORVETTE. THE THUNDERBIRD CAME
STANDARD WITH A REMOVABLE FIBERGLASS TOP THAT FEATURED PORTHOLE-STYLE
WINDOWS. A CONVERTIBLE TOP WAS AN OPTION.

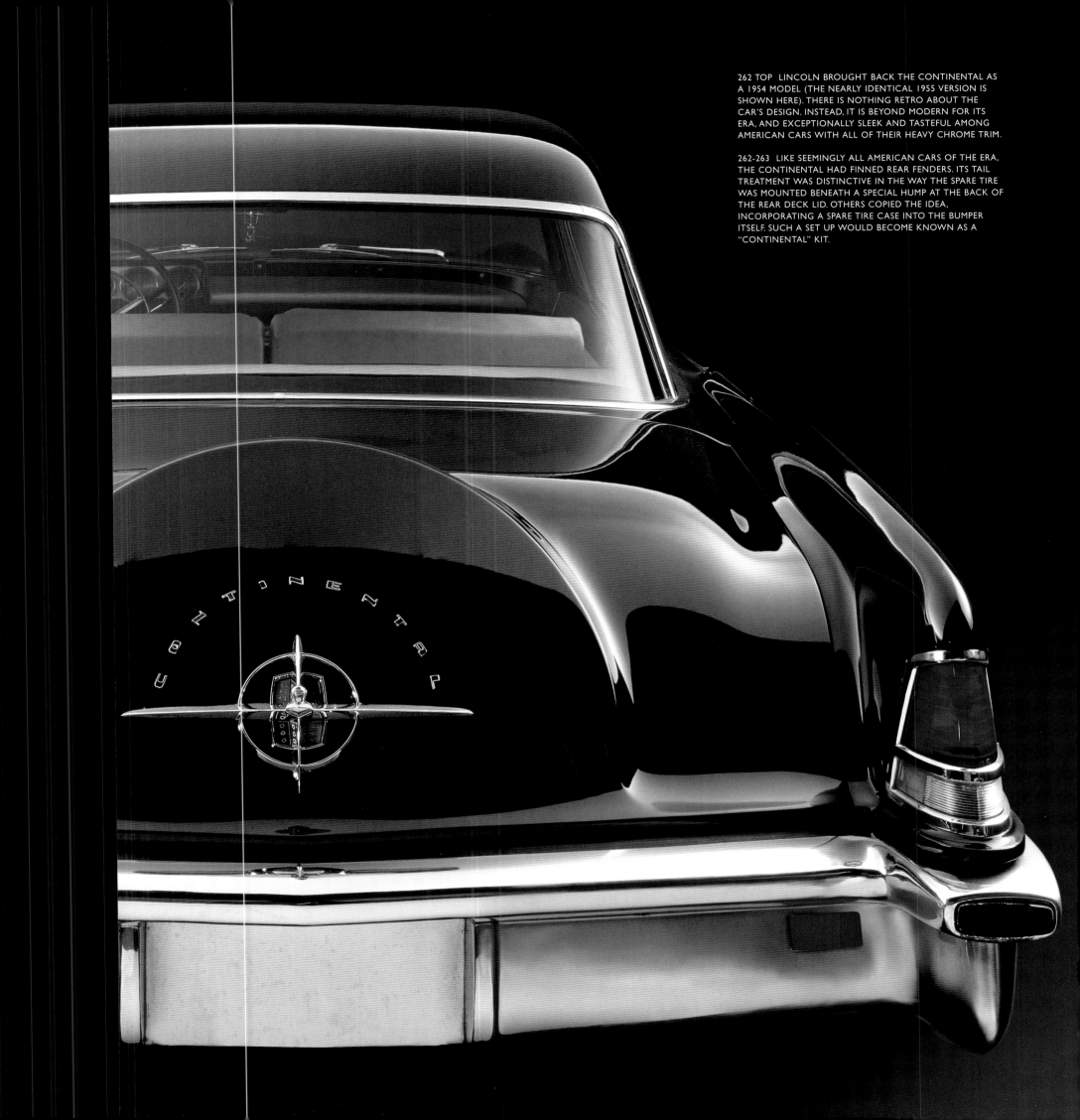

262 TOP LINCOLN BROUGHT BACK THE CONTINENTAL AS A 1954 MODEL (THE NEARLY IDENTICAL 1955 VERSION IS SHOWN HERE). THERE IS NOTHING RETRO ABOUT THE CAR'S DESIGN. INSTEAD, IT IS BEYOND MODERN FOR ITS ERA, AND EXCEPTIONALLY SLEEK AND TASTEFUL AMONG AMERICAN CARS WITH ALL OF THEIR HEAVY CHROME TRIM.

262-263 LIKE SEEMINGLY ALL AMERICAN CARS OF THE ERA, THE CONTINENTAL HAD FINNED REAR FENDERS. ITS TAIL TREATMENT WAS DISTINCTIVE IN THE WAY THE SPARE TIRE WAS MOUNTED BENEATH A SPECIAL HUMP AT THE BACK OF THE REAR DECK LID. OTHERS COPIED THE IDEA, INCORPORATING A SPARE TIRE CASE INTO THE BUMPER ITSELF. SUCH A SET UP WOULD BECOME KNOWN AS A "CONTINENTAL" KIT.

EUGÈNE BORDINAT

Walker retired in 1961 and was replaced by Bordinat (with Engel soon leaving Ford to go to Chrysler).

Bordinat was born in 1920 and went to school with Walker's children, and may have seen his first automotive sketches while riding in the Walkers' car. He studied art at the University of Michigan and automotive design at the school Harley Earl had established to prepare people to work in the Detroit automakers' studios (Joe Oros, Elwood Engle and future GM design vice president Irv Rybicki were among Bordinat's classmates).

Bordinat joined the GM staff in 1939 and returned there after military service, though he was among those recruited away by Ford in the late 1940s.

As vice president of styling at Ford, he was caught up in fierce internal corporate wrangling during the Lee Iacocca management era, but forever will be credited with being in charge when the Ford Mustang was designed and developed.

264 TOP THE CLAY MODEL OF THE ORIGINAL FORD MUSTANG CONCEPT CAR IS CAREFULLY CRAFTED IN 1962. THIS ORIGINAL MUSTANG CONCEPT WAS A MID-ENGINE SPORTS CAR AND WAS DESIGNED TO BE THE ROAD-GOING COMPANION TO THE FORD GT40 RACECAR.

264-265 THE FORD MUSTANG, LAUNCHED AS A 1964 MODEL, WAS DESIGNED IN A FORD STUDIO LED BY GENE BORDINAT. THE CAR WAS AN INSTANT AMERICAN CLASSIC AND HAS ACHIEVED ICONIC STATUS AS NOT JUST A PART OF AMERICAN CAR CULTURE, BUT OF AMERICAN CULTURE ITSELF. THE MUSTANG LAUNCHED AN ENTIRE NEW CATEGORY OF AMERICAN SPORTY CAR. THOUGH CHEVROLET, PONTIAC, CHRYSLER AND AMERICAN MOTORS ALL HAD THEIR OWN CAR IN THE CATEGORY, THE GENRE WILL FOREVER BE KNOWN AS PONY CAR IN HONOR OF THE GALLOPING HORSE ON THE MUSTANG'S GRILLE.

DON KOPKA

Like Bordinat, his successor – not the heir apparent DeLaRossa – but Don Kopka, grew up in a Detroit suburb bisected by the famed Woodward Avenue, where he could watch prototypes and the newest production models rolling down the street.

Kopka studied mechanical engineering and then industrial design and began his career at Chrysler in 1950, but moved with Virgil Exner's former top lieutenant, Cliff Voss, to Ford in 1964. Kopka was promoted after Bordinat retired in 1980 and oversaw a new era in Ford design.

Italy's Ghia studio had become part of Ford and Kopka used it to do a lot of work on using aerodynamic designs to enhance fuel economy. From 1979 to 1985, these studies took shape in the form of five Probe concept vehicles.

Ghia also would produce many other concepts for Ford in the coming years.

Building on the aero-shaped Probe studies, Ford also produced the Taurus during Kopka's tenure. Though some compared the sedan's styling to a jellybean, it became the best-selling car in the world's largest automotive market.

266 DON KOPKA SHARES HIS IDEAS WITH THE DESIGN STAFF. KOPKA HAD WORKED UNDER VIRGIL EXNER AT CHRYSLER AND, LIKE EXNER, USED THE GHIA STUDIO IN ITALY TO CREATE A SUCCESSION OF STUNNING CONCEPT CARS FOR FORD.

267 TOP FORD DESIGNERS ARE SHOWN AT WORK IN 1968.

267 BOTTOM LEFT A FORD DESIGNER WORKS ON THE DASHBOARD DETAILS IN 1968.

267 BOTTOM CENTER A MODEL MAKER MAKES FINE ADJUSTMENTS TO A FULL-SIZE CLAY MODEL OF WHAT APPEARS TO BE THE 1968 MERCURY COUGAR.

267 BOTTOM RIGHT NOT ONLY ARE FULL-SIZE CLAY MODELS PRODUCED IN THE DESIGN DEPARTMENT, BUT SO ARE SEATS, DASHBOARDS AND OTHER INTERIOR COMPONENTS THAT NEED TO BE VIEWED IN FULL SCALE AND WITH PROPER SURFACE TREATMENTS BEFORE THEY ARE APPROVED FOR PRODUCTION.

JACK TELNACK

Kopka retired in 1987 and was succeeded by Jack Telnack, who had led the Taurus design team but who later would turn Ford — at least its concept vehicles — to what was termed the New Edge style with creases replacing curves as a key element. Telnack was born in Dearborn, home of the Ford Motor Company, had studied at the famed Art Center College in California and had learned about fluid dynamics and flow over surfaces through sailing. He'd started at Ford in the Lincoln-Mercury studio in 1958. Bordinat recognized Telnack's talent and in 1966 sent him to Ford's Australian operation.

After three years back in Dearborn, Telnack was overseas again, this time as head of design for Ford of Europe. He returned to the U.S. as director of North American design in 1976.

268 TOP JACK TELNACK INTRODUCED AERO-ORIENTED DESIGN AT FORD WHEN HE CREATED THE EUROPEAN FIESTA IN THE EARLY 1970S. HE NOT ONLY STREAMLINED THE STYLING OF FORD VEHICLES, BUT BROUGHT FORD DESIGN INTO THE DIGITAL AGE BY LINKING ITS STUDIOS AROUND THE WORLD WITH MODERN ELECTRONIC COMMUNICATION TECHNOLOGY.

268-269 BOTTOM SOME SAID THE FORD TAURUS HAD A "JELLY BEAN" SHAPE, BUT JELLY BEANS WERE POPULAR AND THE TAURUS WAS THE BEST-SELLING CAR IN THE UNITED STATES FOR MANY YEARS.

268-269 TOP JUST LIKE HIS GRANDFATHER DID WHEN HE SHOWED THE FORD RIVER ROUGE PLANT TO EUROPEAN LEADERS A HALF CENTURY EARLIER, HENRY FORD II SHOWS CHINESE VICE PREMIER TENG HSIAO-PING THROUGH A FORD ASSEMBLY PLANT IN 1979. THREE DECADES LATER, CHINA WOULD EMERGE AS A MAJOR AUTOMOTIVE MANUFACTURER AND MARKET.

J MAYS

J Mays grew up in rural Oklahoma, where his father farmed and owned an auto parts store. Mays grew up wanting to design cars and after studying journalism in Oklahoma he enrolled at the Art Center College of Design in Pasadena, California. His first job was in Germany, with Audi, in 1980. Three years later he joined BMW in Munich, but after a year went back to Volkswagen/Audi and for the 1991 Tokyo auto show created the AVUS concept car, a stunning and polished aluminum homage to the great German racing cars of the 1930s.

By 1989, Mays was back in the United States, as head of Volkswagen's American design center, where he and Freeman Thomas began work on the Concept 1, a modern interpretation of the classic Volkswagen Beetle.

Volkswagen was struggling in the American market and many expected the German au-

tomaker to simply withdraw, as had other European marques (Fiat, Alfa Romeo, Renault, Peugeot, Rover).

Instead, Concept 1 was unveiled at the Detroit show in 1994 and was so popular that Volkswagen put the New Beetle into production and carried the entire brand back to prominence.

Mays did another stint in Germany with Audi, then went to a private branding and design company to help guide the launch of the New Beetle. In 1997, he was hired by Ford as Telnack's successor, and was in charge of the design direction not only of Ford but of Volvo, Mazda, Land Rover, Jaguar and Aston Martin, which were automakers Ford either owned outright or at least held a controlling financial interest.

With Peter Horbury at Volvo, Ian Callum at Aston Martin and then Jaguar, with Callum's brother Moray at Mazda and with other star

In addition to vehicles such as the Taurus, Telnack moved Ford design into the digital age with electronically linked studios around the world. His successor took Ford to the forefront of international automotive design, and in the process became the best known American automotive designer since Harley Earl, and perhaps the most controversial ever.

270 TOP J MAYS DESIGNED THE STUNNING AVUS CONCEPT AT AUDI, GUIDED THE DESIGN AND LAUNCH OF THE NEW BEETLE AT VOLKSWAGEN AND IN 1997 BECAME HEAD OF DESIGN AT FORD, WHERE HE GUIDES THE STYLING NOT ONLY OF FORD VEHICLES AROUND THE WORLD, BUT ALSO FOR VOLVO, MAZDA, LAND ROVER, JAGUAR AND ASTON MARTIN, MAKING HIM ONE OF THE MOST INFLUENTIAL AUTO DESIGNERS EVER.

designers in the Ford system, Mays and his crew turned out stunning concept vehicles on a regular basis, vehicles the equal of Harley Earl's at GM or Virgil Exner and Tom Gale's at Chrysler.

Indeed, Mays was honored by Harvard University and his designs were showcased at the Museum of Contemporary Art in Los Angeles.

But there also was criticism of Mays. "Retro-futurism" was his term for his design style, and many thought he spent too much of his effort on the retro part of the equation.

While the 2005 Ford Mustang and 2005 Ford GT captured the spirit of two Ford classics, too few of Ford's new production vehicles fulfilled on the promises made by the studios' stunning concept vehicles.

270-271 MAYS HAS INCREASED FORD'S USE OF CONCEPT CARS NOT ONLY TO PREVIEW UPCOMING PRODUCTION CARS, BUT ESPECIALLY TO EXPLORE IDEAS FOR POSSIBLE NEW VEHICLES. THUS IN 2007 FORD UNVEILED THE AIRSTREAM CONCEPT, A JOINT VENTURE WITH ICONIC RECREATION VEHICLE MAKER AIRSTREAM FOR A NEW TYPE OF CROSSOVER.

271 RIGHT AIRSTREAM IS KNOWN FOR BUILDING MOBILE CAMPING TRAILERS SHEATHED IN AIRCRAFT-STYLE ALUMINUM SKIN. WITH PEOPLE SPENDING MORE TIME IN THEIR VEHICLES, AND WITH MORE OF THOSE VEHICLES BEING SO-CALLED "CROSSOVERS," THE FORD/AIRSTREAM CONCEPT EXPLORES THE NEW GENRE WITH A CAR THAT HAS DESIGN CUES FROM THE AIRSTREAM TRAILERS AS WELL AS SUCH FUTURE AUTOMOTIVE TECHNOLOGIES AS REAR-VIEW CAMERAS AND A HYBRID HYDROGEN FUEL CELL POWERPLANT THAT EMITS WATER RATHER THAN GREENHOUSE GASES AS ITS BYPRODUCT. INSIDE, THE AIRSTREAM CONCEPT IS A LIVING ROOM-STYLE ENVIRONMENT WITH VARIOUS ENTERTAINMENT FEATURES. ACCESS TO THE VEHICLE IS WIDE OPEN THANKS TO A CURBSIDE CANOPY-STYLE DOOR.

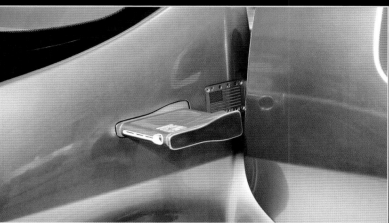

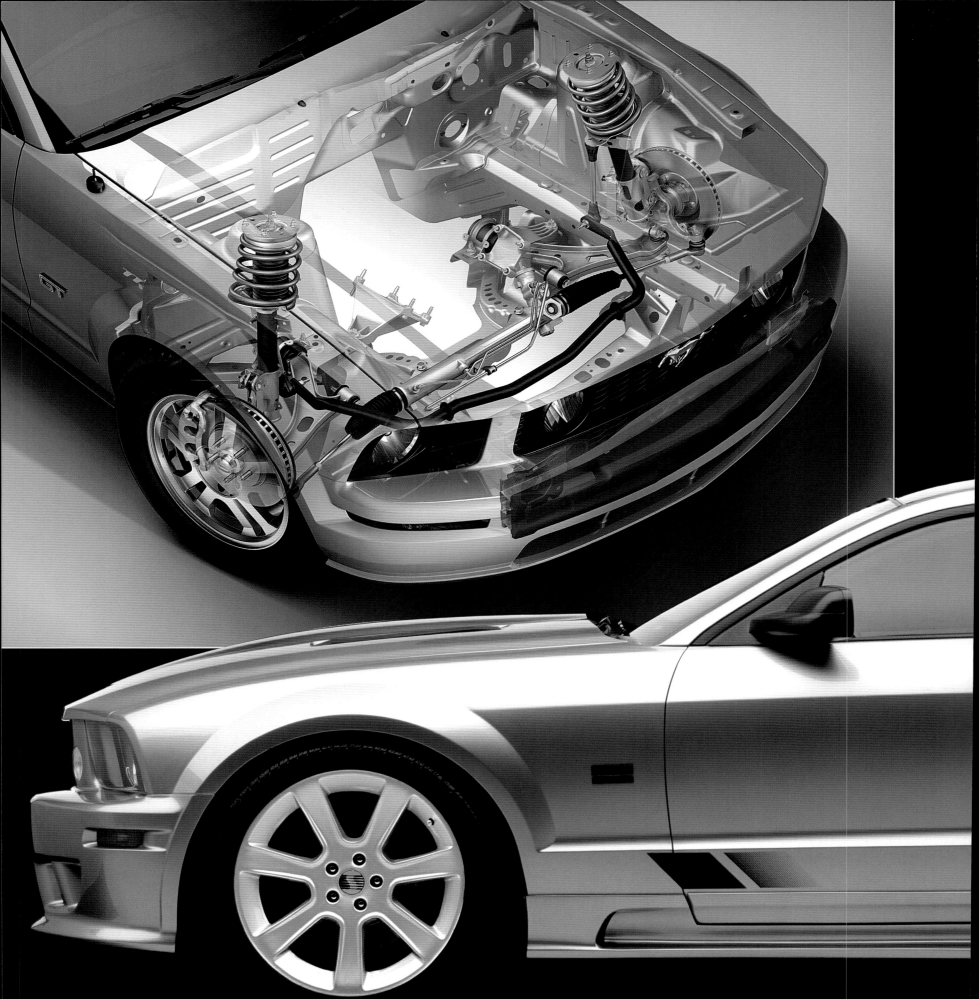

272 TOP AND 272-273 UNDER J. MAYS, FORD "REINTRODUCED" SOME OF ITS MOST FAMOUS NAMEPLATES WITH CONTEMPORARY CARS THAT SHOWED VERY STRONG, EVEN RETROSPECTIVE STYLING. THIS INCLUDED CARS SUCH AS THE THUNDERBIRD OR THE 2005 MUSTANG SHOWN HERE. THIS VERSION OF THE MUSTANG HAS BEEN MODIFIED BY SALEEN, A CALIFORNIA COMPANY THAT ADDS BOTH MECHANICAL COMPONENTS (OPPOSITE PAGE) AND BODY TRIM PANELS (BELOW) TO CARS TO ENHANCE THEIR DYNAMIC PERFORMANCE. THE BODY PANELS SUCH AS THE EXTREME ROCKER PANELS AND FRONT AND REAR BUMPERS ON THIS CAR ARE DESIGNED TO IMPROVE HIGH-SPEED AERODYANMICS, SUCH AS THOSE FOUND ON THE RACETRACK.

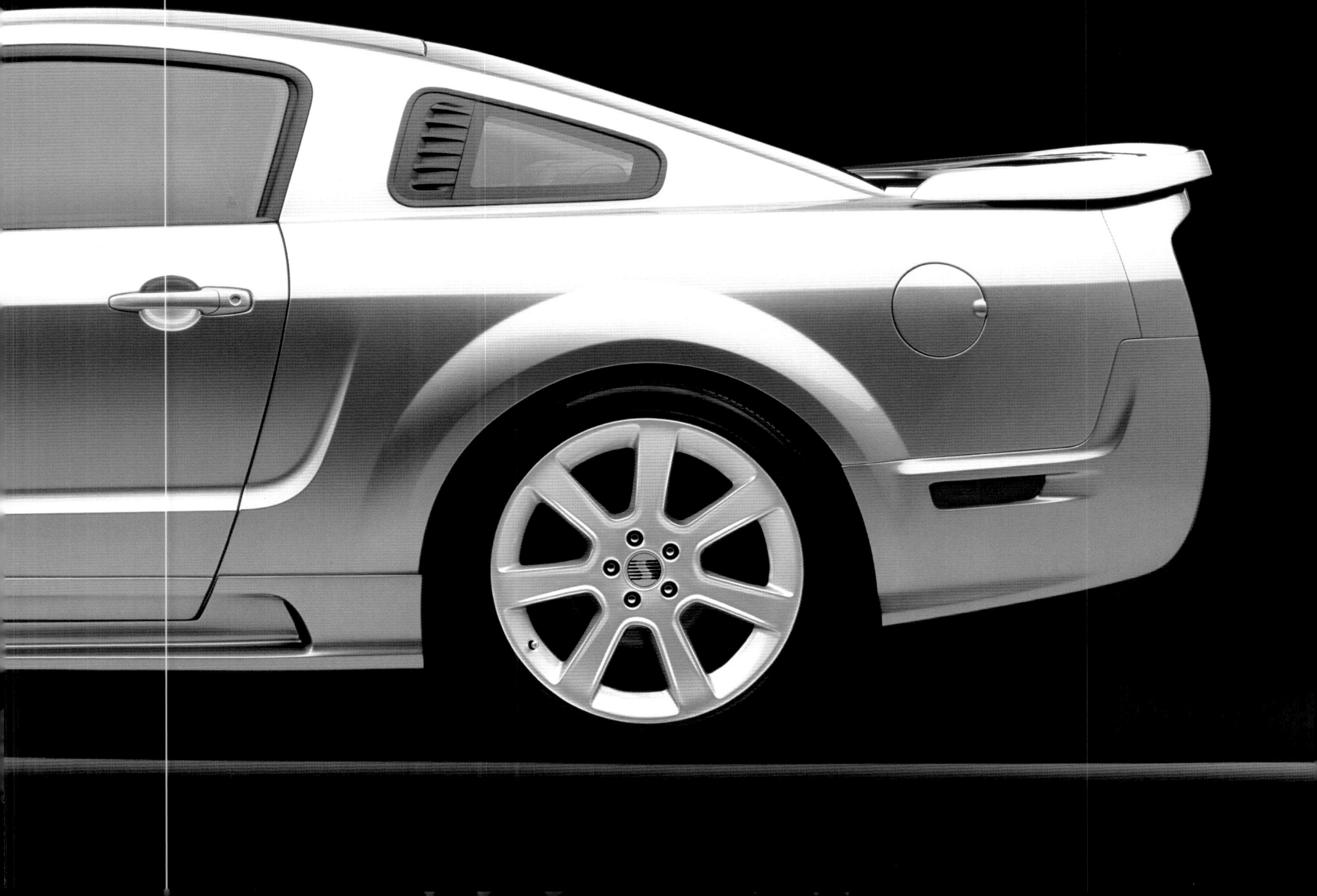

THE COMING OF ASIA: A NEW DESIGN CENTURY

LAWRENCE KIYOSHI "LARRY" SHINODA

"Coming of age" is a phrase used to describe someone who is reaching maturity, who has gone from childhood through adolescence and achieved adulthood, and not just in terms of age but of ability and independence. Dictionaries offer words such as "development" and "responsibility" and "prominence" in giving definition to the phrase.

As the 21st century nears the completion of its first decade, a "coming of age" is taking place within automotive design.

In this instance, this coming of age could be termed the "coming of Asia." Certainly, there have been automotive designers of Asian heritage for many decades: Bud Sugano was a Japanese-American who worked in Harley Earl's studio at General Motors and was credited for the so-called flying-wing or cantilevered roof that marked not only the company's 1959 models but the Chevrolet Corvair as well.

Lawrence Kiyoshi "Larry" Shinoda was another Japanese-American.

Along with the rest of his family, he spent time in an internment camp during World War II. Later, he studied at California's famed Art Center and went from California hot-rodder to Detroit automotive designer. At General Motors, Shinoda designed the Mako Shark concept car as well as the famous 1963 "split-window" Chevrolet Corvette.

Recruited to Ford, he styled the Boss version of the 1969 Mustang, as well as the full herd of 1970–73 pony cars.

His impact on Ford was so strong that he was considered a leading candidate to succeed Gene Bordinat as head of Ford design.

That job, however, would go Don Kopka, who originally had been recommended for promotion within the Ford studio by Shinoda himself.

274-275 WHEN NISSAN DECIDED TO BRING ITS FAMED Z CAR BACK INTO PRODUCTION, THE DESIGN OF THE NEW NISSAN 350Z WAS CREATED BY AJAY PANCHAL, THE SON OF PARENTS FROM INDIA BUT WHO WAS BORN AND EDUCATED IN ENGLAND. HE WENT TO WORK FOR NISSAN, WHICH WAS HEADED BY A FRENCH-SPEAKING BRAZILIAN, CARLOS GHOSN, AND WAS ASSIGNED TO WORK NOT IN JAPAN BUT IN THE NISSAN DESIGN STUDIO LOCATED IN SOUTHERN CALIFORNIA.

BRONCO OFF THE ROAD

276-277 LARRY SHINODA GREW UP IN CALIFORNIA IN THE POST-WAR YEARS AND HE ENJOYED DRIVING HOT RODS, CARS MODIFIED FOR POWER AND SPEED. HE ALSO STUDIED AUTOMOTIVE DESIGN AND HIS CREDITS INCLUDE THE HIGH-PERFORMANCE "BOSS" VERSION OF THE 1970 FORD MUSTANG.

277 TOP LARRY SHINODA CHECKS DRAWINGS FOR A FORD BRONCO CONCEPT VEHICLE, AND LOOKS OVER ANOTHER DESIGNER'S DRAWINGS IN THE FORD STUDIO.

TATEO UCHIDA, JOJI NAGASHIMA, HIDEO KODAMA, SATOSHI WADA

Tateo Uchida, son of a former director of Hino, a Japanese diesel engine and commercial vehicle maker, grew up in Japan but became so fascinated by Italian automotive design that he taught himself the language and moved to Italy, where he became a trainee in 1964 at Michelotti, the coachbuilding firm founded by Giovanni Michelotti, whose work included vehicles such as the Cunningham C3, Ghia-Aigle, BMW 1500 and several Triumph sports cars. Michelotti also did a lot of design consulting for Japanese automakers. Uchida became chief designer at Studio Tecnico Carrozzeria Design Michelotti after the founder's death and earned credit for the styling of the Scimitar SS1, the Meera S and the Pura, a glass-topped roadster, among others.

Joji Nagashima was born in Japan, studied design in the United States and worked at Opel and Renault before joining BMW, where, according to design director Chris Bangle, Nagashima has become the only person ever to have designed three complete and distinct BMW models – the 1996 Z3 roadster, the 1997 5 Series sedan and the 2007 3 Series sedan.

Hideo Kodama studied design at Tama University of the Arts in Tokyo and was a leading designer for Opel for many years. Another Japanese native,

Satoshi Wada, also found success in automotive styling in Europe. Wada, who earlier had worked at Nissan, created the Pikes Peak and Avantissimo concept cars at Audi before styling the latest version of the A6 sedan and the all-new Q7 sport utility production vehicles.

278 AND 279 JOJI NAGASHIMA WORKED AT OPEL IN GERMANY AND RENAULT IN FRANCE BEFORE JOINING BMW, WHERE HE IS CREDITED AS THE ONLY PERSON TO HAVE DESIGNED THREE COMPLETE AND DISTINCT VEHICLES, THE LATEST 3 SERIES SEDAN (THAT'S NAGASHIMA WITH THE 2007 335I ABOVE), THE 5 SERIES SEDAN GENERATION INTRODUCED IN 1997 (BELOW) AND THE Z3 ROADSTER INTRODUCED IN 1996 (AND SHOWN ON THE OPPOSITE PAGE).

280 AND 281 CENTER THE Q7 IS ONE OF SEVERAL VEHICLES THAT SATOSHI WADA, A NATIVE OF JAPAN, HAS DESIGNED FOR AUDI, THE GERMAN LUXURY CAR PRODUCER. LIKE MOST DESIGNERS, WADA DRAWS A SUCCESSION OF SKETCHES (BOTTOM) AS HE DEVELOPS A VEHICLE'S DESIGN. SOME ARE SIMPLE LINE DRAWINGS (OPPOSITE PAGE) WHILE OTHERS HAVE MORE DRAMATIC DETAILING (BELOW).

280-281 AND 281 TOP THE "CAVE" (ABOVE) IS A VIRTUAL REALITY ROOM WHERE DESIGNERS AND ENGINEERS CAN VIEW A VEHICLE IN THREE DIMENSIONS TO VERIFY THEIR DESIGNS BEFORE EXPENSIVE PRODUCTION HARDWARE IS CREATED. SATOSHI WADA AND Q7 DESIGN PROJECT MANAGER DANY GARAND CONFIRM DETAILS (ABOVE RIGHT) OF THE AUDI Q7, A SPORT UTILITY VEHICLE PREVIEWED WITH THE UNVEILING AT THE DETROIT AUTO SHOW IN 2003 OF THE WADA-DESIGNED AUDI PIKES PEAK CONCEPT VEHICLE (BELOW).

TSUTOMU "TOM" MATANO, KIYOYUI "KEN" OKUYAMA, BENJAMIN DIMSON, JOE NJOO, ERWIN LUI, JIN WON KIM

282 AND 283 TSUTOMU "TOM" MATANO WAS BORN IN JAPAN AND STUDIED AUTOMOTIVE ART IN CALIFORNIA. HE WORKED FOR SEVERAL MAJOR AUTOMAKERS, BUT IS BEST KNOWN FOR HIS DESIGN OF THE MAZDA MX-5, KNOWN IN JAPAN AS THE EUNOS ROADSTER AND IN THE UNITED STATES AND ELSEWHERE AS THE MIATA. SHOWN HERE ARE TWO OF MATANO'S MANY SKETCHES AS HE EXPLORED VARIOUS LINES FOR THE CAR THAT COMBINED THE SPIRIT AND DEXTERITY OF THE CLASSIC BRITISH ROADSTER WITH THE BUILD QUALITY AND MECHANICAL RELIABILITY OF A JAPANESE PASSENGER CAR. NEITHER OF THE IMAGES SHOWN REPRESENTS THE ACTUAL MIATA, BUT THEY ILLUSTRATE HOW DESIGNERS CONSIDER A WIDE RANGE OF IDEAS AS THEY HONE IN ON THE FINAL PRODUCT.

Tsutomu "Tom" Matano worked in design studios at GM, Volvo, BMW and Mazda.

At Mazda, he designed the Miata/Eunos roadster. Kiyoyui "Ken" Okuyama worked at Porsche, GM and Pininfarina, where he created the Ferrari Enzo and later became design director.

Matano and Okuyama, both Japanese natives, also served as heads of automotive design schools in the United States – Matano at the Academy of Art College in San Francisco, Okuyama at the famed Art Center College of Design in Pasadena.

But Japan isn't the only Asian country that produced talented automotive designers.

Benjamin Dimson, a native of the Philippines, worked at Porsche and served as chief designer at Mercedes-Benz' advanced styling studio in southern California. Joe Njoo, an Indonesian, did several vehicles for Opel.

More recently, Ajay Panchal, born in England of parents who had moved there from India, created the Nissan 350Z sports car.

Likewise, Erwin Lui, born in the United States after his parents moved from China, designed the 1992 Lexus SC 300 and the 2004 Toyota Prius and Toyota FT-HS hybrid concept.

Korean-born and American-educated Jin Won Kim designed the 2006 Toyota FJ Cruiser.

284 AT A TIME WHEN MOST SPORT UTILITY VEHICLES HAD THE AESTHETIC APPEAL OF A BOX WITH WHEELS, NISSAN LAUNCHED THE MURANO, NAMED FOR THE FAMED ITALIAN GLASS AND SHAPED MORE LIKE AN EXOTIC WAGON THAN ANYTHING THAT RESEMBLED A TRUCK. THE MURANO EVEN DREW INSPIRATION FOR ITS INTERIOR NOT FROM A WORKHORSE UTILITY VEHICLE BUT FROM THE NISSAN 350Z SPORTS CAR.

MURANO

285 SKETCHES SHOW HOW DESIGNERS PUSH FOR EVEN MORE DRAMATIC STYLING. OFTEN, HOWEVER, THEIR MOST DRAMATIC DESIGNS CANNOT SURVIVE THE REALITY OF THE AUTOMOTIVE DEVELOPMENT AND MANUFACTURING PROCESSES. STILL, AS THESE ILLUSTRATIONS SHOW, NISSAN WAS ABLE TO STAY TRUE TO THE DESIGNER'S DESIRES WHEN IT BUILT THE MURANO.

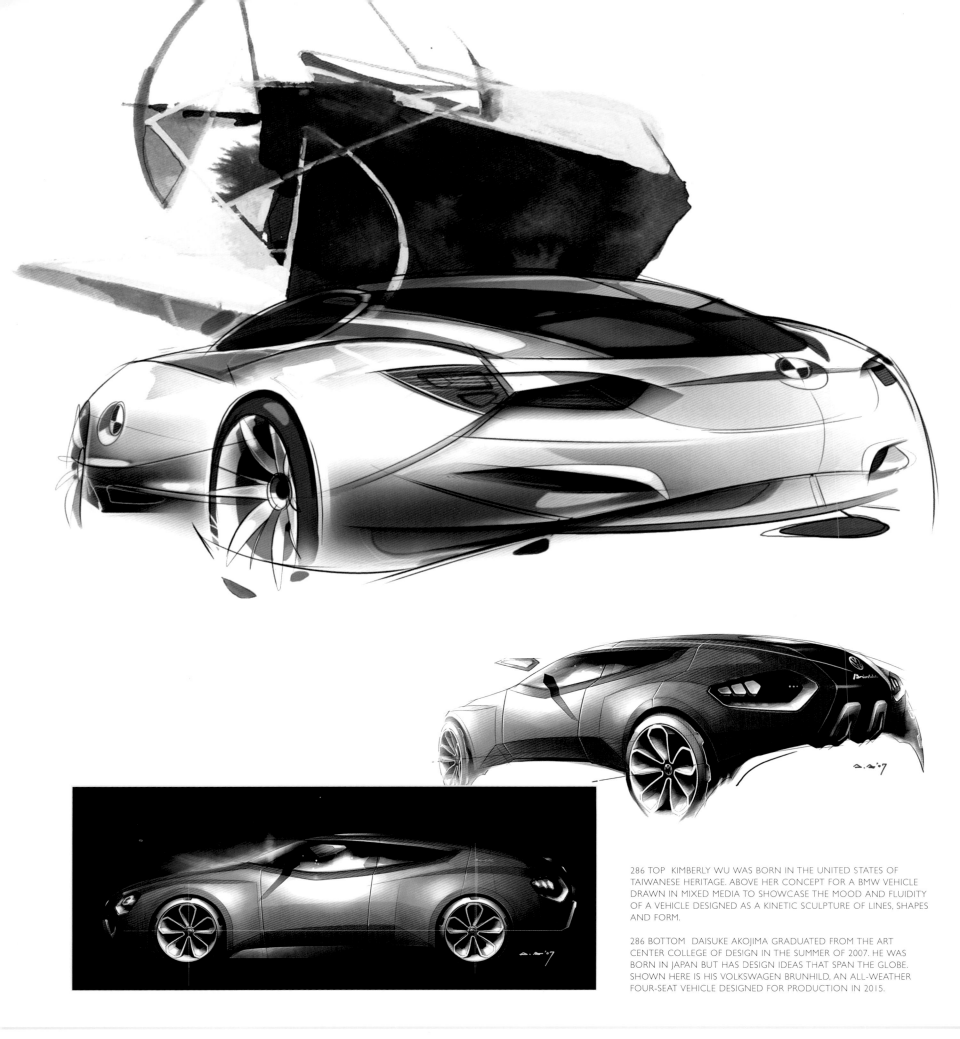

286 TOP KIMBERLY WU WAS BORN IN THE UNITED STATES OF TAIWANESE HERITAGE. ABOVE HER CONCEPT FOR A BMW VEHICLE DRAWN IN MIXED MEDIA TO SHOWCASE THE MOOD AND FLUIDITY OF A VEHICLE DESIGNED AS A KINETIC SCULPTURE OF LINES, SHAPES AND FORM.

286 BOTTOM DAISUKE AKOJIMA GRADUATED FROM THE ART CENTER COLLEGE OF DESIGN IN THE SUMMER OF 2007. HE WAS BORN IN JAPAN BUT HAS DESIGN IDEAS THAT SPAN THE GLOBE. SHOWN HERE IS HIS VOLKSWAGEN BRUNHILD, AN ALL-WEATHER FOUR-SEAT VEHICLE DESIGNED FOR PRODUCTION IN 2015.

ART CENTER COLLEGE

Many more Asian designers could have been included in the last section. Indeed, if automotive design has a face, the likelihood of that face having Asian characteristics in the future seems certain, if for no other reason than if one looks around the classrooms at such leading automotive design schools as the Art Center College in Pasadena, California, perhaps half of the faces are those of Asian ancestry.

There are also excellent design schools in Asia, such as Hong-ik University in South Korea, and other newly created institutions in places such as Shanghai, China that are, or soon will be, producing designers not only for the growing Asian automotive industry but for automakers' studios around the world.

This growing Asian influence seems inevitable as the magnetic center of the world appears ready to make another westward shift, this time not across the Atlantic Ocean – from Europe to the United States – but across the Pacific, where China and India are poised to join Japan and South Korea in becoming powerhouse economies of the 21st and future centuries.

Until recently, the history of Asian automotive design has had its roots as much in Europe and the United States as it has on home soil. As in much of the world, the first cars in Asia were largely Ford Model T's. Henry Ford set up factories in many countries, including Japan, to build his cars.

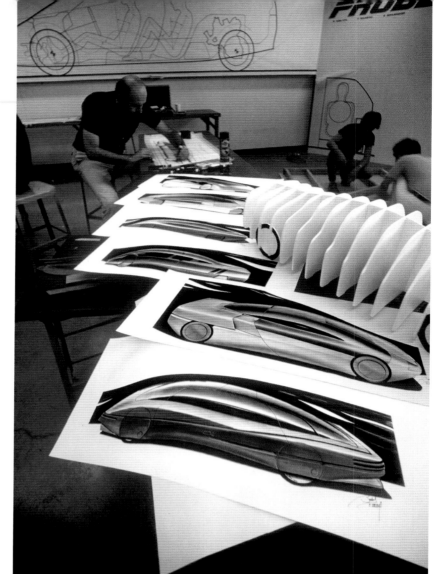

287 STUDENTS FROM AROUND THE WORLD STUDY TRANSPORTATION DESIGN AT THE ART CENTER COLLEGE OF DESIGN IN PASADENA, CALIFORNIA, WHERE THEY LEARN TO WORK IN A VARIETY OF MEDIA AND MODELING TECHNIQUES. JOO JIN WAS BORN IN KOREA AND GRADUATED FROM THE ART CENTER COLLEGE OF DESIGN IN THE SPRING OF 2007. HIS WORK AS A STUDENT INCLUDED THIS BUGATTI, A CONTEMPORARY VEHICLE INSPIRED BY THE FAMED BUGATTI TANK RACE, A CAR FULLY ENVELOPED WITHIN A TEAR DROP BODY.

288-289 THREE ANGLES OF THE ACURA BABY MUSCLE, A TWO-SEAT SPORTS CAR DESIGNED BY DAISUKE AKOJIMA FOR THE YEAR 2015 AS A FUSION OF AMERICAN MUSCLE AND JAPANESE SOPHISTICATION.

Japan's own auto industry was born in the 1920s and '30s, though the cars produced by Mitsubishi, Nissan and Toyota looked much like those being built in Europe and the United States, they were smaller to better fit the confines of the island nation.

Much of Japan's automotive production immediately after World War II was restricted to commercial vehicles needed for the nation's reconstruction.

Production of cars for the public would follow, though again, the significant difference was not in style or even engineering architecture, but in their smaller size, which also tended to make them more fuel efficient and thus attractive for export as other nations suffered through fuel crises.

"Although cars from the Far East were linked with advanced manufacturing techniques and affordability, their reputation, where their appearance was concerned, was for being derivative, unimaginative, and aesthetically unsophisticated," wrote British design professor Penny Sparke. "Whereas Japan managed to call on its unique craft and design traditions in the areas of contemporary architecture and product design, its car designers seemed unable to translate a similar level of sensitivity into that complex object, the automobile."

Some would say the Japanese simply copied Western vehicle designs. Others would add that it wasn't just a rip-off, but rather a desire to learn by emulating what was considered the state of the automotive art.

Yet others would say that the Japanese national culture does not encourage the sort of individualism of expression evident in Western design. and, in fact, duplicating Western designs was the ultimate form of Oriental flattery and respect. And, in fact, many of the Japanese cars were being designed by Westerners, especially by the various Italian design houses, which were being hired as consultants.

For example, paging through the portfolio of Giorgetto Giugiaro and Italdesign, you see vehi-

cles for Isuzu, Hyundai, Subaru, Toyota, Lexus and Daewoo alongside his many cars for various Italian, German, Swedish and British automakers. Likewise, Pininfarina did projects with Honda, Bertone with Mazda.

And those are the ones that have been made public.

Increasingly, the role of outside consultants has been downplayed as automakers — and not just Asian automakers but European and American automakers as well — have built their own

design studios and are rallying around brand identity as their marketing mantra.

"In terms of design consultancy, it has not changed significantly," said Andrea Pininfarina, grandson of the founder of the famed Italian design studio.

"It is true that every original equipment manufacturer is giving more and more importance to design as a key factor for the choice of the customer and therefore is making more and more significant investment in creating their own

design identity, their own brand identity, with their own design centers. But they continue to use design consultancies as a window to open to get fresh air, and to understand what an external view could provide to a new project. That's not significantly changing the amount of activities we are performing, though it is true that OEMs [original equipment manufacturers] in general terms like less than in the past talking about this consultancy."

And thus only close observers may have noticed at the 2005 North American International Auto Show in Detroit when designers from Toyota invited Leonardo Fioravanti up onto the stand to share the limelight at the unveiling of the Lexus LF-A sports car concept. Fioravanti had worked for many years at Pininfarina, then was hired as Ferrari's design director before opening his own design consulting business near Turin, Italy.

"Mr. [Wahei] Hirai [Toyota's managing director for design] asked us to work with him," Fioravanti explained months after the car was unveiled.

"It was an extremely simple design brief between professionals, to study with Toyota something representing the value of Lexus, the best quality in the world, and to design not a supercar but a sports car, rich in value."

The brief, Fioravanti said, was indeed brief: "First: Originality. Second: Simplicity. Third: Aesthetically speaking, something that you see one time and you never forget it. This is, by chance, exactly our company philosophy." The result of the collaboration speaks for itself.

290-291 DESIGNERS AND MODEL MAKERS AT WORK IN CALTY, THE TOYOTA DESIGN STUDIO IN SOUTHERN CALIFORNIA. IN ADDITION TO THEIR PRIMARY DESIGN STUDIOS, WHICH ARE PART OF THEIR HEADQUARTERS IN THEIR HOME COUNTRY, MOST AUTOMAKERS HAVE SATELLITE STUDIOS IN OTHER LOCATIONS, WHERE THEY CAN TAKE ADVANTAGE OF BOTH DESIGN AND MARKET TRENDS AS WELL AS OF CREATIVE TALENT FROM OVERSEAS NATIONS AND DESIGN SCHOOLS.

291 BOTTOM THE LEXUS LF-A WAS A STUNNING AND VERY ADVANCED CONCEPT CAR ON THE TOYOTA STAND AT THE 2005 NORTH AMERICAN INTERNATIONAL AUTO SHOW. THE CAR WAS A TOYOTA DESIGN PROJECT BUT THE JAPANESE AUTOMAKER INVITED LEGENDARY ITALIAN DESIGNER LEONARDO FIORAVANTI TO COOPERATE ON THE PROJECT.

SHIRO NAKAMURA

While still using outside consultants, albeit quietly, the Japanese and other Asian automakers are working hard to establish their own design departments, and not just on their home turf but around the world. For example, seemingly every major automaker has an advanced design center in southern California, which not only is the heart of the American automotive culture, but the largest single automotive market area within the world's largest national automotive market. But even before General Motors or Ford or Chrysler established design bases in southern California to tap into this well-spring of American cultural momentum, Toyota was there, with its CALIfornia ToYota (Calty) design and research center, in 1973.

The California design studios not only tap into California car culture, but into the supply of young designers coming out of the Art Center College for Design, which for many years was producing at least half of the world's new automotive designers. Through their sports car designs and their roles as leaders in design education, Tom Matano and Ken Okuyama brought newfound prominence to Asian designers, but the most prominent of those Asian designers and the leader of the new Asian auto-

motive design force is Shiro Nakamura, who leads the design department at Nissan. Ask contemporary auto designers whose work they admire and Nakamura's name is among the first mentioned.

Nakamura was born in 1950 in Osaka. His family loved music and art, and his uncle was a classical violinist. Young Shiro studied music, and became an accomplished bass player in both classical and jazz genres, but his passion was drawing cars. By the time he was 12, he knew he wanted to be a car designer, even though he had no real idea of how he might make his dream come true. All he knew was that someone was designing the cars he saw on the streets – and even more so those he so admired on the pages of car magazines. "My knowledge was very limited," he recalls. "In 1962, the car industry in Japan was not what it is today. There were not many imported cars." It was through the pages of the car magazines that Nakamura became "much fascinated" by racy Italian sports cars and by the chromed American cars of the 1960s. Through the Japanese magazine *Car Graphic*, Nakamura also discovered Hideo Kodama, one of the top Japanese car designers who was in the midst of a long and successful career

with German automaker Opel. Nakamura read that Kodama had attended art school. "O.K.," he told himself, "this is how I can be a car designer."

Nakamura enrolled at the Musashino Art University in Tokyo. At graduation, he had to decide between pursuing a career in music or in design. He accepted a position at Isuzu, which had just entered a financial partnership with General Motors. Nakamura's first assignment was to join a team developing a new car that would be sold around the world by various GM brands.

293 THE TOKYO MOTOR SHOW IS THE SITE OF THE UNVEILING OF SOME OF THE MOST ARTISTICALLY AND TECHNOLOGICALLY INNOVATIVE DESIGNS. AT TOKYO IN 2005, NISSAN UNVEILED THE PIVO, A SMALL URBAN ELECTRIC VEHICLE WITH AN EGG-SHAPED PASSENGER COMPARTMENT THAT CAN SPIN WITHIN THE CHASSIS SO THE DRIVER IS ALWAYS FACING FORWARD, EVEN WHEN THE CAR IS "BACKING" INTO A PARKING PLACE OR OUT OF A DRIVEWAY.

292 THE "STAR" AMONG ASIAN DESIGNERS AT THE TURN OF THE 21ST CENTURY WAS SHIRO NAKAMURA, HEAD OF DESIGN FOR NISSAN. WHILE MOST JAPANESE AUTOMAKERS HAVE KEPT THEIR DESIGNERS OUT OF THE SPOTLIGHT, NISSAN HAS ALLOWED AND ENCOURAGED NAKAMURA TO BE VERY PUBLIC, MAKING HIM PERHAPS THE COUNTRY'S FIRST WESTERN-STYLE DESIGN DIRECTOR, MORE IN THE TRADITION OF HARLEY EARL, BRUNO SACCO, TOM GALE OR J MAYS.

"Isuzu had a lot of good designers and their skills were very high," Nakamura remembers, "and Isuzu was using the same process as GM, so technically, at that time, Isuzu design was the highest in Japan." However, much of the world had no idea of the caliber of Isuzu's studio because Isuzu's most interesting designs were on vehicles sold only in the home market, not for export. Meanwhile, Nakamura was learning a lot, and in 1980 Isuzu offered him the opportunity to accelerate his design education with a year of study at the Art Center design school in California, where his classmates would include people such as Chris Bangle, now head of design at BMW. Not wanting to miss anything, Nakamura swept through the usual three-year Art Center program in a single year.

His student projects included potential models for Toyota and GM, including a possible new direction for the Corvette sports car. In 1985, GM invited him to spend a year in its advanced design studio in Detroit, and in 1990 he went overseas again, this time to Belgium, to establish Isuzu's new European design center, where his work included the Vehicross, a new and dramatic looking Isuzu sport utility vehicle.

Nakamura returned to Japan in 1993 as Isuzu design manager. Four years later, the company sent him to the United States as its vice president for North American product planning.

He returned to Japan in the spring of 1999 as general manager of Isuzu's worldwide design efforts, with the specific assignment of reorganizing the global design department.

He quickly showcased the company's new design direction with a concept vehicle, the Kai, but within just a few months of his return to Japan he received a telephone call that presented an opportunity that would propel him into a staring role on a stage much larger than Isuzu could ever provide. In August 1999, Shiro Nakamura started his new job – as the head of design for Nissan, Japan's second largest automaker, where he would become the person responsible for giving shape in sheetmetal to the vehicles that would fulfill Carlos Ghosn's aggressive Nissan Revival Plan.

Not only would Nakamura and his design staff create some 20 new concept vehicles to point the way, but also two dozen new production models, and all in a very sport time span.

In the process, Nakamura would break several long-standing Japanese design molds, would establish a new Nissan design direction built emphatically around Japanese culture and heritage, and would himself become the new face of Asian automotive design to the rest of the world.

"Moving from one company to another at that level in Japan is never done," Nakamura acknowledges. "Nobody had done it before."

But Nakamura did, because the opportunity was so great. "Nissan was moving ahead," Nakamura explains. "Carlos Ghosn had come from France [at the behest of Nissan's financial partner, Renault] and he put design as a very high priority and he wanted to make it clear that Nakamura is going to be the head of design."

No longer would the head of the design department of a Japanese automaker be merely a manager. Ghosn brought a new level of responsibility and accountability.

"It used to be very vague," Nakamura says. "If you made a mistake, there was no clear responsible person. The *company* made a mistake." But under Nissan's new setup, "we have clear responsibility and accountability and I think it's good for design, for the company."

Nissan's new design direction would be Nakamura's vision – and his responsibility.

But that also meant that any mistakes would be his as well. "This is the breaking of Japanese

traditional management style," Nakamura says, adding that he knew such an opportunity would be a once in a lifetime event. A good designer has to be confident, and Nakamura was confident, and not only in his own design skills, but in his leadership ability, and in a design staff scattered in studios around the world. "I have some confidence," he says with a wry smile. Such self-confidence has been the key to the recent emergence of Asian automotive design.

Nakamura acknowledges that Japanese, and later other Asian automakers as well, leaned heavily on outside designers, especially the Italian design houses. Then they began looking toward America, sending students to Art Center to learn about creating with clay models and what Nakamura calls "nice rendering." Like those students, the Asian automakers were learning about design and its importance.

"The heads of the companies wanted to have a wide range of ideas. They were not confident enough in their own in-house design," Nakamura explains.

295 SHIRO NAKAMURA WAS A REMARKABLE STUDENT WHO COMPLETED THE FULL TRANSPORTATION DESIGN CURRICULUM AT THE FAMED ART CENTER COLLEGE OF DESIGN IN CALIFORNIA IN A SINGLE YEAR. ONE OF HIS STUDENT PROJECTS WAS TO CREATE A POTENTIAL NEW LOOK FOR THE CHEVROLET CORVETTE. THESE ARE HIS FINAL DRAWINGS FOR HIS IDEAS FOR A FUTURE CORVETTE. AFTER SCHOOL, GENERAL MOTORS INVITED NAKAMURA TO DO ADDITIONAL WORK IN ITS ADVANCED DESIGN STUDIO, THEN TO ESTABLISH GM PARTNER ISUZU'S NEW EUROPEAN STYLING CENTER.

But they also knew that to be successful, both at home and abroad, they would need their own well-staffed and well-equipped design departments that could interpret unique brand characteristics into sheetmetal shapes and interior environments.

Nakamura oversees two studios in Japan, two in the United States, one in Europe and another in Taipei. His staff of some 300 designers represents more than 15 nationalities, including Koreans and Chinese.

"Even though the Korean and Chinese and Japanese people look quite the same, they are different, and the major characteristics of their design is quite different," he says.

"China and Korea are part of the continent. There's the space, much more of it.

"You can see that the Chinese architecture is not the same as Japanese architecture.

"Ours is much more delicate, but in China they make houses, even for the ordinary people, from rock or stone. Even the land itself, if I look from an airplane, you can see how the houses are arranged [much differently than in Japan]."

Nakamura said he has had good success in get-

ting Korean and Japanese designers to work together, to blend their cultural styles and talents on behalf of the brand.

And perhaps that's the true sign that Asian designers have come of age, that their work is about their brand, not their nationality. "Certainly you cannot deny the influence of Asian designers, they're in all companies," says Chris Bangle, an American who was Nakamura's classmate at Art Center and who heads design at BMW, a German automaker.

"Just the other day we had a series of projects up on the board," Bangle continues. "We go through our project reviews and they always have the designer's name listed.

"I said, 'Stop for a minute, guys. Look through this roster of names up there.' It was the most international roster of names I've ever seen in BMW Group's history.

"We had names up there which were Arab names, Asian names, European classic names, names which could have been American, although almost every name could be American.

"We had the complete gamut of internationalism. It made me feel really good because nobody

noticed it. It was like this was natural. These people are integrated in a team. Nobody says, 'Oh, that's the car being done by so-and-so because he's of some particular origin.' It doesn't come across that way.

"It comes across as *designers*. That's a wonderful thing. That means there's no sense of national barriers to the idea of car design. Car design is an open frontier."

At the close of the 20th century, an international panel of automotive journalists honored Italy's Giorgetto Giugiaro as the century's leading car designer.

When another such panel meets at the close of the 21st century, might it be honoring a designer of Asian heritage?

Bangle has doubts, not about Asian designers. "You can't deny the impact of a huge amount of Asian wealth, huge number of Asians in design schools, a pool of available designers which have Asian origins," he says.

His doubts are whether there will ever be another designer with Giugiaro's degree of influence.

"The question is," he says, "can any one person in the future have the type of influence over car

design that Giugiaro had in his heyday? Can anyone have that type of influence in the era of team structure, in the era of industrial commitments like we have? It is very difficult to imagine.

"You might have an individual designer with a string of successes, but the idea that hundreds of cars could be coming from one guy's pen because dozens of car companies repeatedly went to him is becoming less and less a viable scenario." But having said that, Bangle reiterates that car design is an open frontier.

"There's also no sexual barriers," he says, noting that when BMW did its product design review, "some of the names were women's names and this is a wonderful thing to see happen."

Nakamura notes that in one recent year, Nissan hired six new designers, and five of them were women. One aspect of Asian automotive design that may differ from that in the West is more equality between the sexes, says Patrick Le Quément, head of design at Renault, which employs Japanese, Korean, Indian, Malaysian and Mongolianborn designers as well as Asian-Americans in its various studios around the world.

296-297 AND 297 ONE OF THE WORLD'S MOST EXCITING CARS, DYNAMICALLY IF NOT AESTHETICALLY, HAS BEEN THE NISSAN SKYLINE GT-R (SHOWN HERE – LOWER RIGHT – IN ITS 1999 MODEL YEAR GUISE). AT THE TOKYO MOTOR SHOW IN 2005, NISSAN UNVEILED ITS CONCEPT FOR THE NEXT GENERATION SKYLINE. THE CONCEPT WAS DESIGNED UNDER THE DIRECTION OF SHIRO NAKAMURA AND SHOWS A SUPER SPORTS CAR MUCH MORE IN KEEPING WITH NISSAN'S CONTEMPORARY DESIGN LANGUAGE.

AKINO TSUCHIYA

"We're observing in these countries which came late to the automotive industry that the male/female roles are not as ingrained as they are in Western society," says Le Quément, noting that boys don't necessarily grow up playing with cars and girls with dolls. Thus, he adds, that in a place such as Korea, "we are amazed by the number of very good female car designers." To the point, he adds, that not only might a future Giugiaro be of Asian heritage, but "she could be a she."

Although she works for Chrysler, Akino Tsuchiya is an example of this new breed of Asian-born female auto designers. Born in Japan, the daughter, niece and granddaughter of architects and with a mother and sister who both taught music, Tsuchiya says that instead of playing with a dollhouse as a child, she used cardboard, rope and her stuffed animals to construct her own miniature amusement park. As an exchange student, she studied sociology at Washington and Lee University in the United States, finished her degree back at Rikkyo University in Tokyo. She enrolled in art classes "for fun" and discovered a passion for design. After graduating in 1996 with a degree in transportation design from Art Center in Pasadena, California, she joined Chrysler's Pacifica advanced concepts studio, designed the interiors for the Chrysler Citadel and Dodge Kahuna concept cars as well as the exterior of the Dodge Razor concept.

Then, in the fall of 2005, she went to the Tokyo Motor Show with the Chrysler Akino concept vehicle. Not only was she the designer of both the interior and exterior, but in an honor rare even for the most accomplished of automotive designers, the vehicle bore her name – in Japanese, Akino means "autumn field."

Autumn field brings pleasant visual images, but in regard to the coming of age of Asian automotive design, it's not autumn, but spring, and the buds are just starting to burst into flower.

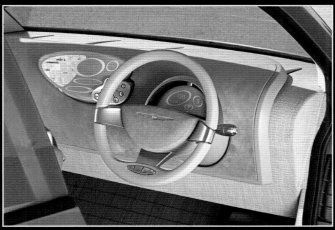

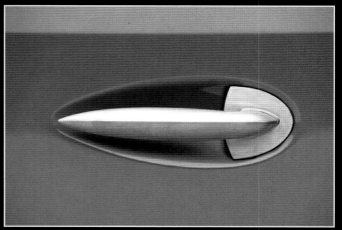

298 TOP AKINO TSUCHIYA SITS INSIDE THE CHRYSLER AKINO, A CONCEPT CAR THAT BEARS HER NAME, WHICH IS JAPANESE FOR "AUTUMN FIELD." THE AKINO CAR CONCEPT WAS UNVEILED AT THE 2005 TOKYO MOTOR SHOW. THOUGH VERY COMPACT IN ITS FOOTPRINT, THE CAR PROVIDES COMFORTABLE SPACE FOR FIVE OCCUPANTS.

298 BOTTOM AND 299 THESE ILLUSTRATIONS SHOW DETAILS OF THE CHRYSLER AKINO CONCEPT VEHICLE, WHICH WAS DESIGNED TO PROVIDE "THE SOOTHING, COMFORTING FEELING OF A LIVING ROOM ON THE INTERIOR ALL SURROUNDED BY AN ELEGANT FORM THAT REFLECTS THE CHRYSLER BRAND," SAID AKINO TSUCHIYA,

THE 37-YEAR-OLD DESIGNER. "WE VERY MUCH WANTED A FEELING OF BEING AT HOME ON THE ROAD." TSUCHIYA ADDED THAT FOR THOSE IN JAPAN, DRIVING ON A WEEKEND OR FREE TIME IS AN EXPERIENCE OF BEING TOGETHER SUCH AS THROUGH FAMILY OUTINGS OR TRAVELING WITH FRIENDS.

THE NEW COACHBUILDERS:
THE WHEEL TURNS
FULL CIRCLE

PININFARINA

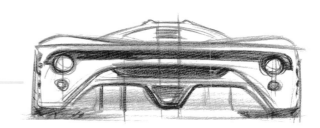

300-301 HENRIK FISKER
DESIGNED CARS SUCH AS
THIS 2005 ASTON MARTIN DB9
WHEN HE WORKED IN AN
AUTOMAKER'S DESIGN STUDIOS.
AFTER TWO OF HIS CARS
EARNED STARRING ROLES IN
JAMES BOND MOVIES, FISKER
LAUNCHED HIS OWN BUSINESS,
THAT OF A CONTEMPORARY
COACHBUILDER.

302 DESIGN SKETCHES EXPLORE
POSSIBLE ELEMENTS THAT
TRANSFORM THE ENZO FERRARI
INTO THE FERRARI P4/5.
AMERICAN FILM MAKER JAMES
GLICKENHAUS WAS CLOSELY
INVOLVED WITH PININFARINA
AND ITS DESIGNERS IN THE
DEVELOPMENT OF THE
COACHBUILT CAR.

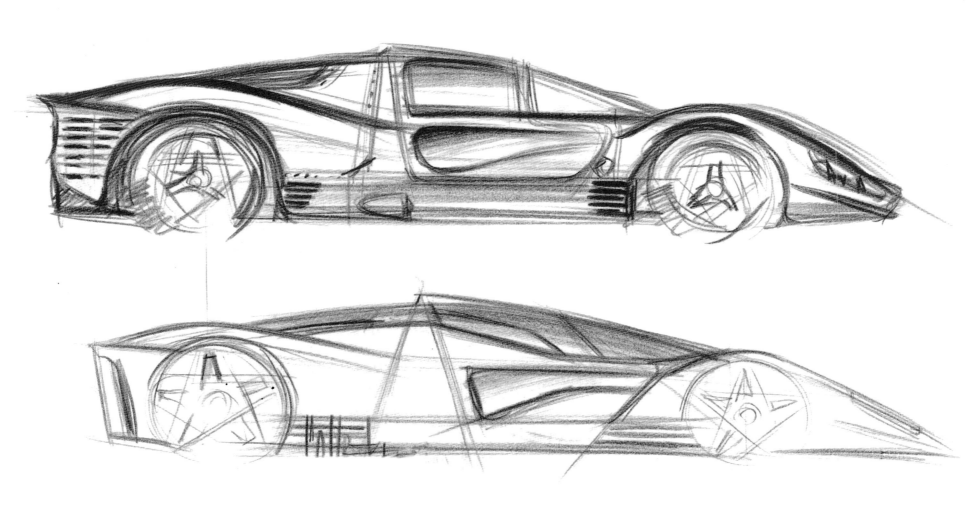

You might think it would be enough for anyone to own and drive a Ferrari Enzo, the $670,000, turn-of-the-21st-century supercar. Designed as the ultimate example of the proud breed of the Prancing Horse, this stallion looks like the offspring from a mating between a Grand Prix racecar and a Stealth jet fighter. But the beauty is much more than skin deep. The car was developed in conjunction with Ferrari's championship-winning Formula One team and its superstar driver, Michael Schumacher. The 12-cylinder engine pumps out 660 horsepower. Top speed reaches 350 k/hr (a nice round number equivalent to 217 mph). With such character and capability, the car was named not with a mere number or even for a geographic location significant to Ferrari history, but in honor of *Il Commendatore* himself. And yet, at least one customer wanted something more, something, well, unique — as if the fact that only 399 Enzos would ever be built didn't make the car exclusive enough. Thus American film writer and producer James Glickenhaus would commission a truly unique version of the Enzo, the P4/5, a car bearing the looks and name in homage to

one of Ferrari's famed LeMans racecars of a bygone era. Like the Enzo itself, the P4/5 was designed by — and then coachbuilt at — Pininfarina. "In the last few years," says Andrea Pininfarina, chairman and chief executive of the family-owned automotive design, engineering and production supplier that had been born in his grandfather's garage and studio, "there is an interest from a few selective customers to go back to the idea of the one-off. This is, from a technology and certification standpoint, much more difficult than it was seventy or eighty years ago and we are, of course, responding to this challenge."

303 TOP AMERICAN FILM MAKER JAMES GLICKENHAUS WANTED HIS ENZO FERRARI TO BE UNIQUE, SO HE TURNED TO PININFARINA TO CREATE THE P4/5 WITH A COACHBUILT BODY THAT RECALLS FAMOUS FERRARI LE MANS RACERS OF THE 1960S.

303 BOTTOM ANDREA PININFARINA'S GRANDFATHER STARTED THE FAMILY BUSINESS AS A COACHBUILDING COMPANY, OR *CARROZZERIA* AS THE ITALIANS SAY IT. PININFARINA HAS BECOME FAMOUS AROUND THE WORLD FOR ITS AUTOMOTIVE DESIGN WORK, ESPECIALLY FOR FERRARI, BUT ALSO FOR MANY OTHER AUTOMAKERS.
NOW, WITH RECENT PROJECTS SUCH AS THE P4/5 AND SCAGLIETTI "K," THE COMPANY AGAIN IS CREATING COACHBUILT BODIES AND INTERIORS FOR WEALTHY CLIENTS.

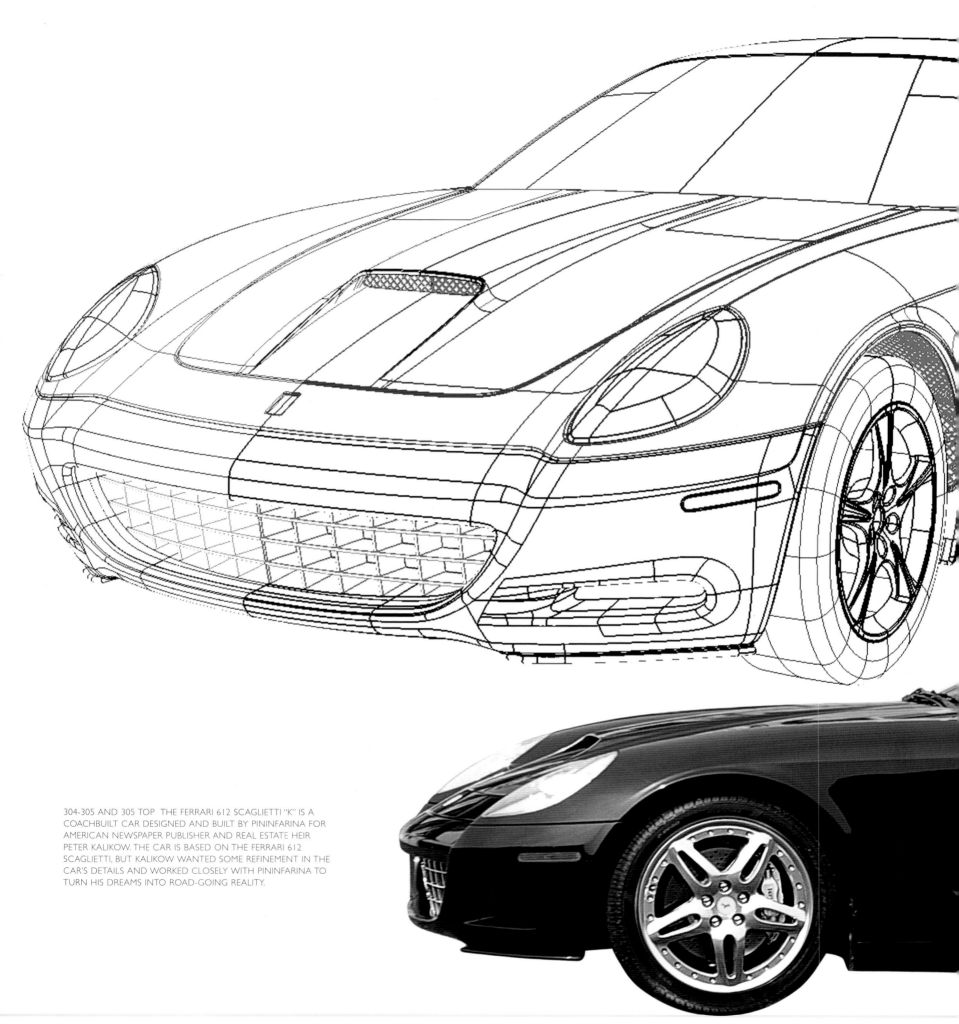

304-305 AND 305 TOP THE FERRARI 612 SCAGLIETTI "K" IS A COACHBUILT CAR DESIGNED AND BUILT BY PININFARINA FOR AMERICAN NEWSPAPER PUBLISHER AND REAL ESTATE HEIR PETER KALIKOW. THE CAR IS BASED ON THE FERRARI 612 SCAGLIETTI, BUT KALIKOW WANTED SOME REFINEMENT IN THE CAR'S DETAILS AND WORKED CLOSELY WITH PININFARINA TO TURN HIS DREAMS INTO ROAD-GOING REALITY.

HENRIK FISKER

Pininfarina isn't the only firm firmly back into the coachbuilding business. Former BMW and Aston Martin designer Henrik Fisker, American hot-rod and custom car designer Chip Foose and several others are reviving the coachbuilding tradition as they seek to become contemporary counterparts to Hibbard and Darrin, Saoutchik and Figoni et Falaschi.

Just as in the 1920s and '30s, a clientele has emerged that wants very special vehicles to drive. Fisker met many of these people while he was chief designer for Aston Martin.

"I was seeing how Aston Martin [sales volume] exploded and how Bentley really exploded and how cars that I saw as a kid and maybe I would see one every six months and I would go 'wow,' and sometimes I wasn't even sure what it was, but now three of your neighbors have one and it becomes almost a commodity," says the Danish-born designer who resides in southern California. "Brands like Bentley and Lamborghini and Ferrari to a certain extent and Porsche for sure are not exclusive any more."

Part of the exclusivity that those customers want has to do with the sheetmetal, but another part, Fisker insists, has to do with the people behind the sheetmetal.

Cities and businesses seek out famous architects to create what become new civic and corporate landmarks. It's not enough to build a multi-million-dollar house, you need the right interior designer to make that house into a home. On the red carpet, celebrities are asked "Who are you wearing?" as if it was the designer not the dress that wraps around their torso.

"People are looking for the human aspect," Fisker continues as he explains the comeback of custom built. "There's actually a guy who did this. It's not just some marketing department that created a project and a product and sent it to China and it was made and now I'm buying it.

"It's almost like how people want to know who the cook is in the kitchen at a famous restaurant, or like [French designer Philippe] Starck and his hotels. Why are they using him and his name? They wouldn't have done that twenty years ago, but they are now because, wow, it's personal."

"This is not just the case of selling a product," says Andrea Pininfarina. "It's the case of selling an experience, of making the product together [with the customer]."

Glickenhaus' P4/5 project was one of two such coachbuilt vehicles that Pininfarina unveiled in 2006. The other was the Ferrari 612 Scaglietti "K"

FISKER COACHBUILD, LLC

2007 FISKER LATIGO CS

for New York real estate scion and newspaper publisher Peter Kalikow. While long-time Ferrari owner Kalikow considered the 612 to be the finest of Ferrari's road cars, he thought some styling details could be enhanced. Though the entire body of his "K" version is new, the changes are subtle, unlike the significant visual modifications to Glickenhaus' car.

Both men participated with Pininfarina in every phase of their car's design and development, or as Andrea Pininfarina puts it, "the process of creating their own car."

Pininfarina said both men wanted not just one-off cars, but cars they could drive on a daily basis. That meant not just a mere reskinning, but also enough engineering to assure the cars were certifiable regarding licensing issues such as crashworthiness and emissions and built with the quality and reliability required for daily use.

"We saw at the end that both customers are very happy, not just with the product they received but with the experience they made with us," he adds. While Pininfarina can accommodate such extensive and expensive one-off projects,

Fisker Coachbuild is doing its vehicles as limited editions of 150.

"A one-off coachbuilt car in the 1930s went for around $25,000," Fisker says. "That would be like $2 million today. Our cars are starting at around $250,000. That's what other luxury mass-manufactured cars like Bentley and Aston Martin cost, but we offer something extremely unique and exclusive, with only 150 worldwide for the same price you would buy a mass-produced luxury car."

Fisker and partner Bernhard Koehler launched their company early in 2005, announcing plans to turn BMW's 6 Series coupe and convertible into the Fisker Latigo CS and the Mercedes-Benz SL into the Fisker Tramonto. Fisker also has announced plans to build a bespoke premium and hybrid-powered four-door sedan.

Rather than a one-off vehicle in which each piece may be unique — for example, Pininfarina designed and developed some 200 new parts and panels for Glickenhaus' P4/5 — Fisker says that producing 150 of each model not only makes the vehicle more affordable, but makes it feasible to create tooling to produce a supply of spare parts

for making repairs easier after a mishap in traffic. Mechanical maintenance on the vehicles can be done at any BMW or Mercedes-Benz dealership.

Unlike Pininfarina, which in many ways is returning to its roots with its coachbuilding efforts, Fisker entered the business because he reached a point in his corporate career where he had exceeded his personal goals about the same time that he discovered a clientele that wanted something special, something he could offer.

306 HENRIK FISKER WORKS IN A VARIETY OF SCALES AS HE WORKS UP THE DESIGN OF HIS MODERN COACHBUILT VEHICLES. HIS SKETCH (BELOW) SHOWS SOME OF THE DESIGN DETAILS THAT TURN THE BMW 6 SERIES COUPE INTO THE FISKER LATIGO CS.

307 THE FISKER TRAMONTO CAME OUT OF THE MERCEDES-BENZ FACTORY AS AN SL-CLASS LUXURY SPORTS CAR. FISKER COACHBUILD MODIFIES NOT ONLY MUCH OF THE CAR'S EXTERIOR BUT, JUST LIKE THE FRENCH AND ITALIAN COACHBUILDERS OF A BYGONE ERA, OFFERS ITS CUSTOMERS A VARIETY OF PERSONAL OPTIONS FOR THE CAR'S INTERIOR DESIGN AND DETAILS.

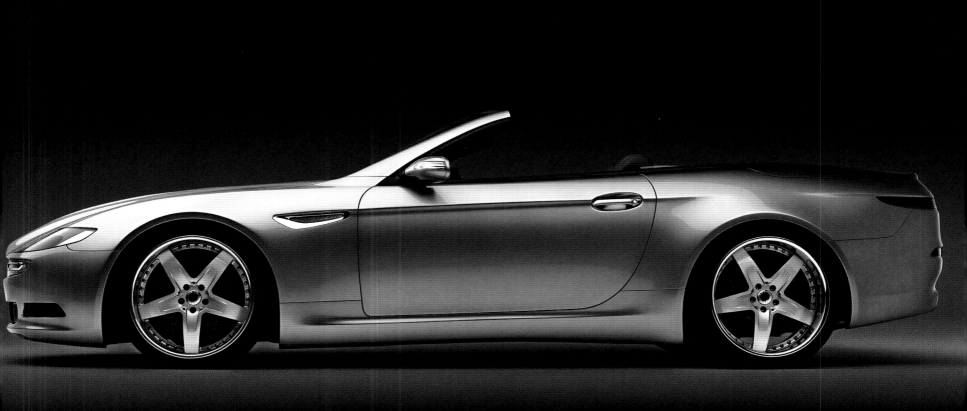

At BMW, Fisker designed the Z8, a turn-of-the-century sports car that carried forward the spirit of the famed 507 of the 1950s. Then, at Aston Martin, he did concept and production cars including the DB9 and V8 Vantage. Ironically, it was his BMW that got the role – and then got sliced in half – in a James Bond movie, *The World Is Not Enough.*

"I always believe that when you reach a goal, you have to set a new goal immediately to keep yourself moving," Fisker says. For Fisker, that new goal became the design and production of coach-built cars.

Fisker knew that in a corporate environment,

it takes several years to complete the design and development of any new vehicle. But he also knew that once that vehicle is finished, designing what is called a "facelift" can be done fairly quickly. He also was hearing from Aston Martin owners that they were eager for cars with even more exclusivity than seemingly any automaker might provide.

Fisker talked to Koehler, who began his career as a designer but gravitated to project planning and management aspects of the industry, "and he said it would be possible." So they put together a business plan and raised the money they needed to get started, much of it coming from people who would become their customers. "The only people who believed us were our investors, and they hadn't worked in the car industry," Fisker says, "because if they had, they wouldn't have believed us either."

By January 2005, not only did Fisker and Koehler figure they could have a car on the stand at a major international auto show later that year, they decided to go a step further: If they were actually going to convince people in and out of the auto industry that they were credible, they'd launch not with one car but with two models, and they did, at the Frankfurt motor show in 2005.

Less than a year later, they were delivering vehicles to customers, and contemplating that their next coachbuilt project could be a four-door sedan, and that at some point they might like to do a project in conjunction with an automaker. For example, Fisker says, it is both time-consuming and very expensive for a major automaker to produce a very limited run of ultra-luxury vehicles. But, he adds, something such as the Cadillac 16 concept car that met with such widespread acclaim when it was unveiled at the North American International Auto Show in Detroit might be much more readily produced in a joint venture between a major automaker and a coachbuilding specialist.

"We are still too small. We have to prove ourselves, have several cars on the road," Fisker knows.

But he can see the day coming when, for example, a major automaker delivers a running chassis with its powertrain and electrical and safety systems to a coachbuilder that adds the custom bodywork and personalized interior accoutrements sought by a particular clientele.

308 TOP AND 308-309 ACTOR PIERCE BROSNAN POSES NEXT TO THE BMW Z8 THAT HIS CHARACTER, JAMES BOND, DROVE IN THE 1999 MOVIE *THE WORLD IS NOT ENOUGH.* AUTOMOTIVE DESIGNER HENRIK FISKER SAID ONE REASON HE CONSIDERED VENTURING OUT INTO CONTEMPORARY COACHBUILDING WAS THAT HE HAD ALREADY DOUBLED ONE OF HIS CAREER GOALS – DESIGNING A CAR THAT WOULD APPEAR IN A JAMES BOND MOVIE. FISKER ALSO DESIGNED THE ASTON MARTIN DB9 THAT BOND, NOW PLAYED BY DANIEL CRAIG, DROVE IN THE 2006 BOND FILM, *CASINO ROYALE.*

CHIP FOOSE

That's also the goal for Chip Foose, an American hot-rod designer who has become an iconic figure in the American custom car culture. Foose grew up working in his father's hot-rod shop, honed his skills at the prestigious Art Center College of Design, and was responsible for the design of a series of spectacular hot-rod and custom cars built by Boyd Coddington and sheetmetal specialist Marcel De Ley.

"I always told Boyd, why don't we build ten of these?" Foose says. "Boyd said, 'no, I only want to build one'." Later, Foose went to Jerry Kugel with some of his drawings and they produced a series of Muroc hot-rods, 10 roadsters and 10 more with fenders.

While in college, Foose sketched out a hot-rod roadster that Chrysler liked enough that it inspired the Plymouth Prowler. More than a decade later, Foose updated his sketches into a car unveiled late in 2006 as the Hemisfear, with plans to build 50 of them with Metalcrafters, a family-owned, southern California firm that had earned an international reputation for advancing the art of concept-car building on behalf of a long list of original equipment au-

tomakers. Built of state-of-the-art carbon fiber and with a big V8 engine mounted behind the passenger compartment, the renamed Foose Coupes sell for $319,000, and Foose Design and Metalcrafters already are making plans for another vehicle to produce after the Foose Coupe production ends. Still, Foose notes, such vehicles are what are known as "component" cars. What Foose wants to do is true coachbuilding, creating custom bodies for chassis

from an automaker, just like in the 1930s when Duesenberg and Delahaye would sell chassis to coachbuilders.

Foose has worked with automakers such as Ford on several concept car programs and thus he went to Ford design chief J Mays, among others from the car companies, "and told them I thought it would be really cool to build and develop a chassis that has fenders, has a hood and a cowl, has a dash and has seats in it, and with this chassis would be a very, very expensive, I'm figuring the chassis would be two-hundred and fifty to five-hundred thousand dollars, and with this chassis you get a book and the book has designers and coachbuilders in it and as long as you use a combination of people in that book, that Pebble Beach [site of the annual and world-famous Concours d'Elegance] would have a slot where you could debut your car, and wouldn't that be a great marque, the pinnacle for say Lincoln or Cadillac or Chrysler?," Foose adds with his patriotism showing.

But any major automaker could supply such a chassis, providing a powertrain and a vehicle identification number (VIN) that brings added legitimacy, value and validation to such a project.

Like "Joseph" Figoni or "Jacques" Saoutchik, Franco Scaglione or Giorgetto Giugiaro, Harley Earl or

310 AND 311 CHIP FOOSE SKETCHED A HOT ROD WHILE STUDYING AT THE ART CENTER COLLEGE OF DESIGN IN PASADENA AND CHRYSLER DESIGNERS WERE SO IMPRESSED

THEY TOOK THE IDEA IN ONE DIRECTION AND CREATED THE PLYMOUTH PROWLER, A FACTORY-BUILT HOT ROD. FOOSE TOOK THE SKETCHES IN ANOTHER DIRECTION AND CREATED

THE HEMISFEAR HOT ROD. WITH HELP FROM FAMED CONCEPT CAR BUILDER METALCRAFTERS, THE CAR BECAME THE FOOSE COUPE, WITH 50 COPIES TO BE COACHBUILT FOR SALE.

312 TOP AND 312-313 RON WHITESIDE BOUGHT A THREE-WINDOW 1934 MERCURY COUPE AS A TEENAGER AND HE AND HIS BROTHER USED THE CAR UP DRAG RACING IT. BUT WHITESIDE KEPT THE CAR AND TOOK IT TO CHIP FOOSE FOR A TRANSFORMATION THAT TURNED IT INTO THE STALLION, WHICH WON THE PRESTIGIOUS RIDDLER AWARD AT THE DETROIT AUTORAMA IN 2003. ANOTHER FOOSE CREATION, BOB AND WES RYDELL'S 1935 CHEVROLET "GRAND MASTER," WON THE RIDDLER THE PREVIOUS YEAR, MAKING FOOSE THE FIRST DESIGNER TO TAKE THE AWARD TWO YEARS IN A ROW.

Virgil Exner, or like so many other masters of the automotive design arts, what Chip Foose and the modern coachbuilders do is to make dreams come true. "What we're doing is we're designing what I term automotive dreams that are becoming reality," Foose explains. "We work with a client and they come in and they tell you what their dream car is and, as a designer, my goal is to build that dream. But my personal goal is to make it 10 times better than what they ever thought it would be. "They may have thought they wanted a '36 Ford [hot rod], but what I want to do is to take the essence of a '36 Ford and start from scratch. I start designing without using any current body panels or body panels that were built in that era,

start using photos of that car as the theme and mix and blend it with different themes that I think will work together." As an example, he offers Impression, a hot-rod roadster he created with and for Ken Reister. "When we were building that car, my goal was to make it look as if this is what a '36 Ford show car would be if Ford were building it today," says Foose. "Everything about that car uses the '36 flavor, including the engine [a modern V8 but designed to look as though it were a Flathead Ford]. Even the wheels were designed to bring forward the look of the late 1930s. "Everything on it had that essence, that same feeling of what was on the '36 Ford, but done today," Foose adds. "Ken had no idea what we were going to end up with.

The best compliment that he paid me was when he said that there's not enough money in the world to get this car away from him, that he'll never sell it, that it was beyond anything he ever thought it would be." The car was named "America's Most Beautiful Roadster" for 2006. "He said he can't imagine ever building anything better than this," Foose remembers Reiser telling him. Maybe he can't, but Foose can. "I have lots of ideas," says the automotive artist, a modern master of his work, his words echoing those of his predecessors, and paving the way for those who will design tomorrow's works of automotive art. No doubt, they'll be cars that even Foose and his fellow modern masters can hardly imagine.

BIBLIOGRAPHY

Books

A Century of Automotive Style: 100 Years of American Car Design, Michael Lamm and Dave Holls. Stockton, California, 1996

A Century of Car Design, Penny Sparke. London, 2002

American Cars: Past to Present, Matt DeLorenzo. New York, 2004

Bertone, Decio Giulio Riccardo Carugati. Milan, 2002

Bertone: 90 Years (two volumes), Luciano Greggio. Milan, 2001

Car Men 5 / Giorgetto Giugiaro & Fabrizio; Italdesign, Giuliano Molineri. Milan, 1999

Car Men 6 / Patrick Le Quément Renault Design, George Mason. Milan, 2000

Car Men 10 / Harmut Warkuss, Volkswagen Design; Marco Degl'Innocenti, Milan, 2002

Car Men 15 / Shiro Nakamura, Nissan Design, Marzia Gandini. Milan, 2003

Cars Detroit Never Built: Fifty Years of American Experimental Cars, Edward Janicki. New York, 1990

Concept Cars, Larry Edsall. Vercelli, Italy, 2003

Ferrari: Design of a Legend; The Official History and Catalogue, Gianni Rogliatti, Sergio Pininfarina, Valerio Morelli. New York, 1990

Harley Earl, Stephen Bayley. New York, 1990

Legendary Cars; Larry Edsall. Vercelli, Italy, 2005

Mercedes-Benz: Portrait of a Legend; Ingo Seiff, London, 1989

Pininfarina: Art and Industry 1930-2000, Antoine Prunet. Milan, 2000

Pininfarina Cinquantanni. Turin, 1980

The Art of American Car Design: The Profession and Personalities, C. Edson Armi. University Park, Pennsylvania, 1988

The Beaulieu Encyclopedia of the Automobile: Volume 1, 2 & 3, Nick Georgano (editor). London and Chicago, 2000

The Beaulieu Encyclopedia of the Automobile: Coachbuilding, Nick Georgano (editor). London and Chicago, 2001

The Designers, L.J.K. Setright. Edinburgh and London, 1976

The GM Motorama: Dream Cars of the Fifties, Bruce Berghoff. Osceola, Wisconsin, 1995

The Standard Catalog of American Cars, 4th edition. Iola, Wisconsin, 1997

Magazine articles

AutoWeek.
- Exhausted Empire, Kevin A. Wilson, March 8, 1993

Automobile Quarterly: The Connoisseur's Magazine of Motoring Today, Yesterday and Tomorrow
- A Shark Is Not a Grouper: A personal profile of Bill Mitchell; Strother MacMinn, Vol. XXVI, No. 2
- Aerodynamics and Style: Bertone's B.A.T.s; Strother MacMinn, Vol. XXXIII, No. 3
- Ahrens von Sindelfingen: Crating the classic Mercedes, Griffith Borgeson, Vol. XXV8, No. 4
- Aston Martin Bertone; Stanley Nowak, Vol. XXVI, No. 4
- Bella Macchina! A Portfolio of Ghia Fords; Vol. XXVI, No. 4
- Bodies by Saoutchik; Ferdinand Hediger, Vol. XLII, No. 2
- Carrosserie Nonpareil J. Saoutchik, Vol. IX, No. 3
- Disaster Is My Business: Howard "Dutch" Darrin, Vol.VII, No. 1
- Everybody's Favorite Designer: Giorgetto Giugiaro; Don Vorderman, Vol. 11, No. 3
- Form, Function and Fantasy: Seventy Years of Chrysler Design, Jeffrey Godshall, Vol. XXXII, No. 4
- Franco Scaglione: Forgotten Genius; Patrick O'Brien, Vol. XXXIII, No. 3
- Ghia: Ford's Italian Connection; David Burgess-Wise, Vol. XXVI, No. 4
- Harley Earl's California Years: 1893-1927; Michael Lamm, Vol. XX, No. 1
- John Tjaarda: Imagineer Extraordinaire; Karl Ludvigsen, Vol. XXXVIII, No. 4
- LaSalle: Companion Car to Cadillac; James D. Bell, Vol. V, No. 3
- Microphone Taillights and Doughnut Decks: Chrysler Cars of the Exner Era, Jeffrey Godshall, Vol. XXIX, No. 1
- My American Safari: Futher Adventures in the Automotive Jungle; Howard "Dutch" Darrin, Vol. X, No. 1
- The Coachbuilder as Sculptor; Griffith Borgeson, Vol. XX, No. 1
Tom Tjaarda: An American in Turin; Winston Goodfellow, Vol. XXXVIII, No. 4

Newspaper articles

Car of the century? Ford's Model T, of course; Richard A. Wright, *Detroit News*, December 20, 1999

Other sources

Christie's Dearborn auction catalog; 2002

Collection (catalog of vehicles in the Pininfarina museum)

The History of French Car Design; Serge Bellu (article for 2003 Michelin Challenge Design competition)

Museum of Modern Art (New York) catalog for auto design exhibit in 1951

Websites:
bbc.co.uk
infoplease.com
kolumbus.fi
panteraclub.com
Olympics.com.au
Wikipedia.com

INDEX

PHOTO CREDITS

Page 195 bottom Renault Communication/Dominique Dumas
Pages 196-197 www.carphoto.co.uk
Page 198 Bettmann/Corbis
Page 199 Rykoff Collection/Corbis
Page 200 top Fotostudio Zumbrunn
Page 200 bottom Fotostudio · Zumbrunn
Page 201 Archivio Scala.Firenze
Pages 202-203 Michael Furman Photography
Page 203 top Bettmann/Corbis
Page 203 bottom Bettmann/Corbis
Page 204 top, center and bottom General Motors Media Archive
Pages 204-205 General Motors Media Archive
Page 205 General Motors Media Archive
Page 206 General Motors Media Archive
Page 207 top Bettmann/Corbis
Page 207 bottom General Motors Media Archive
Pages 208-209 Ron Kimball Photography
Page 209 Ron Kimball Photography
Page 210 Ron Kimball Photography
Pages 210-211 Ron Kimball Photography
Page 212 General Motors Media Archive
Page 213 top Richard Kalvar/Magnum Photos/Contrasto
Page 213 bottom left JP Laffont/Sygma/ Corbis
Page 213 bottom right JP Laffont/Sygma/ Corbis
Page 214 General Motors Media Archive
Pages 214-215 www.carphoto.co.uk
Page 215 General Motors Media Archive
Page 216 General Motors Media Archive
Pages 216-217 General Motors Media Archive
Page 217 General Motors Media Archive

Page 218 top General Motors Media Archive
Page 218 bottom Ron Kimball Photography
Page 219 Getty Images
Page 220 top and bottom General Motors Media Archive
Page 221 top and bottom General Motors Media Archive
Page 222 top General Motors Media Archive
Page 222 bottom General Motors Media Archive
Pages 222-223 General Motors Media Archive
Page 224 Tom Pidgeon/Epa/Corbis
Pages 224-225 Ron Kimball Photography
Pages 226-227 Ron Kimball Photography
Page 228 top and bottom Mary Evans Picture Library
Pages 228-229 Fotostudio Zumbrunn
Page 229 Courtesy of the Daimler Chrysler Corporation
Pages 230-231 Peter Harholdt/Corbis
Page 231 top Car and Bike Photo Libraries
Page 231 bottom Peter Harholdt/Corbis
Page 232 top General Motors Media Archive
Page 232 bottom Farabolafoto
Page 233 Getty Images
Pages 234-235 Ron Kimball Photography
Page 236 Ron Kimball Photography
Pages 236-237 Ron Kimball Photography
Pages 238-239 Ron Kimball Photography
Page 239 Ron Kimball Photography
Page 240 top left Photo12.com
Page 240 top right Ron Kimball Photography
Pages 240-241 Ron Kimball Photography
Pages 242-243 Ron Kimball Photography
Page 243 Ron Kimball Photography
Page 244 Ron Kimball Photography

Pages 244-245 Ron Kimball Photography
Page 246 top Getty Images
Page 246 bottom Getty Images
Pages 246-247 Courtesy of the Daimler Chrysler Corporation
Pages 248-249 Car Culture/Corbis
Page 249 Car Culture/Corbis
Pages 250-251 Ron Kimball Photography
Page 252 Bettmann/Corbis
Page 253 top Bettmann/Corbis
Page 253 center Archivio Scala, Firenze
Page 253 bottom www.carphoto.co.uk
Page 254 Ford Motor Company Archives
Pages 254-255 www.carphoto.co.uk
Page 255 Bettmann/Corbis
Pages 256-257 Ron Kimball Photography
Page 257 Underwood & Underwood/Corbis
Page 258 Ford Motor Company Archives
Page 259 top Ford Motor Company Archives
Page 259 bottom left and right Ford Motor Company Archives
Page 260 Car Culture/Corbis
Pages 260-261 Fotostudio Zumbrunn
Page 262 Fotostudio Zumbrunn
Page 262-263 Fotostudio Zumbrunn
Page 264 Ford Motor Company Archives
Pages 264-265 Ron Kimball Photography
Page 266 Ford Motor Company Archives
Page 267 top Ford Motor Company Archives
Page 267 bottom left, center and right Ford Motor Company Archives
Page 268 Ford Motor Company Archives
Pages 268-269 top Bettmann/Corbis
Pages 268-269 bottom Car Culture/Corbis
Page 270 Ford Motor Company Archives
Pages 270-271 Car Culture/Corbis
Page 271 top Car Culture/Corbis

Page 271 center top Car Culture/Corbis
Page 271 center bottom Car Culture/Corbis
Page 271 bottom Car Culture/Corbis
Page 272 Ford Motor Company Archives
Pages 272-273 Ron Kimball Photography
Pages 274-275 Ron Kimball Photography
Pages 276-277 Ron Kimball Photography
Page 277 top left and right Ford Motor Company Archives
Page 278 top Courtesy of the BMW of North America, LLC
Page 278 bottom Courtesy of the BMW of North America, LLC
Page 279 top Historic Media Archives/BMW Group
Page 279 bottom Ron Kimball Photography
Page 280 top e bottom Courtesy of the Audi AG/Audi Media Services
Page 281 top left and right bottom Courtesy of the Audi AG/Audi Media Services
Page 281 center Courtesy of the Audi AG/Audi Media Services
Page 281 bottom Courtesy of the Audi AG/Audi Media Services
Page 282 Courtesy of the Mazda Motor Corporation
Pages 282-283 Courtesy of the Mazda Motor Corporation
Page 283 Courtesy of the Mazda Motor Corporation
Page 284 top and bottom Courtesy of the Nissan Design America, Inc.
Page 285 top and bottom Courtesy of the Nissan Design America, Inc.
Page 286 top and bottom Courtesy of the Art Center College of Design
Page 287 top Lowell Georgia/Corbis
Page 287 bottom Courtesy of the Art Center College of Design
Pages 288-289 Courtesy of the Art Center College of Design
Pages 290-291 David Butow/Corbis
Page 291 Mark Scheuern/

Alamy Images
Page 292 Reuters/Contrasto
Page 293 Tayama Tatsuyuki/Gamma/Contrasto
Page 294 Courtesy of the Nissan Design America, Inc.
Page 295 top and bottom Courtesy of the Nissan Design America, Inc.
Pages 296-297 Courtesy of the Nissan Design America, Inc.
Page 297 top Courtesy of the Nissan Design America, Inc.
Page 297 bottom Ron Kimball Photography
Page 298 top Courtesy of the Daimler Chrysler Corporation
Page 298 bottom left and right Courtesy of the Daimler Chrysler Corporation
Page 299 top Courtesy of the Daimler Chrysler Corporation
Page 299 bottom left, center and right Courtesy of the Daimler Chrysler Corporation
Pages 300-301 Ron Kimball Photography
Page 302 top, center and bottom Pininfarina S.p.A.
Page 303 top Pininfarina S.p.A.
Page 303 bottom Pininfarina S.p.A.
Page 304 top Fisker Coachbuild, LLC
Page 304 bottom Fisker Coachbuild, LLC
Page 305 Fisker Coachbuild, LLC
Pages 306-307 top Pininfarina S.p.A.
Pages 306-307 bottom Pininfarina S.p.A.
Page 307 Pininfarina S.p.A.
Page 308 The Kobal Collection
Pages 308-309 Ron Kimball Photography
Page 310 Courtesy of the JMPR Public Relations
Pages 310-311 Courtesy of the JMPR Public Relations
Page 311 Courtesy of the JMPR Public Relations
Page 312 Courtesy of the JMPR Public Relations
Pages 312-313 Courtesy of the JMPR Public Relations